THE ARDEN SHAKESPEARE

GENERAL EDITOR: RICHARD PROUDFOOT

ALL'S WELL THAT ENDS WELL

THE ARDEN SHAKESPEARE

All's Well That Ends Well: edited by G. K. Hunter
Antony and Cleopatra: edited by M. R. Ridley
As You Like It: edited by Agnes Latham
The Comedy of Errors: edited by R. A. Foakes
Coriolanus: edited by Philip Brockbank
Cymbeline: edited by J. M. Nosworthy
Hamlet: edited by Harold Jenkins
Julius Caesar: edited by T. S. Dorsch
King Henry IV, Parts 1 & 2: edited by A. R. Humphreys
King Henry V: edited by John H. Walter
King Henry VI, Parts 1, 2 & 3: edited by Andrew S. Cairncross
King Henry VIII: edited by R. A. Foakes
King John: edited by E. A. J. Honigmann
King Lear: edited by Kenneth Muir
King Richard II: edited by Peter Ure
King Richard III: edited by Antony Hammond
Love's Labour's Lost: edited by Richard David
Macbeth: edited by Kenneth Muir
Measure for Measure: edited by J. W. Lever
The Merchant of Venice: edited by John Russell Brown
The Merry Wives of Windsor: edited by H. J. Oliver
A Midsummer Night's Dream: edited by Harold F. Brooks
Much Ado About Nothing: edited by A. R. Humphreys
Othello: edited by M. R. Ridley
Pericles: edited by F. D. Hoeniger
The Poems: edited by F. T. Prince
Romeo and Juliet: edited by Brian Gibbons
The Taming of the Shrew: edited by Brian Morris
The Tempest: edited by Frank Kermode
Timon of Athens: edited by H. J. Oliver
Titus Andronicus: edited by J. C. Maxwell
Troilus and Cressida: edited by Kenneth Palmer
Twelfth Night: edited by J. M. Lothian and T. W. Craik
The Two Gentlemen of Verona: edited by Clifford Leech
The Winter's Tale: edited by J. H. P. Pafford

THE ARDEN EDITION OF THE
WORKS OF WILLIAM SHAKESPEARE

ALL'S WELL THAT
ENDS WELL

Edited by
G. K. HUNTER

METHUEN
LONDON and NEW YORK

The general editors of the Arden Shakespeare have been
W. J. Craig (1899–1906), R. H. Case (1909–44),
Una Ellis-Fermor (1946–58), Harold F. Brooks (1952–82),
Harold Jenkins (1958–82) and Brian Morris (1975–82)

Present general editor: Richard Proudfoot

This edition of *All's Well That Ends Well*, by G. K. Hunter,
first published in 1959 by
Methuen & Co. Ltd
11 New Fetter Lane, London EC4P 4EE
Reprinted with minor corrections 1962
Reprinted 1966

First published as a University Paperback 1967
Reprinted three times
Reprinted 1983

Published in the USA by
Methuen & Co.
in association with Methuen, Inc.
733 Third Avenue, New York, NY 10017

ISBN 0 416 47560 4 (hardback edition)
ISBN 0 416 49610 5 (paperback edition)

Printed and bound in Great Britain by
Richard Clay (The Chaucer Press) Ltd,
Bungay, Suffolk

CONTENTS

PREFACE

THIS edition is not based on the earlier "Arden" edition of W. Osborne Brigstocke, though Brigstocke's judicious notes have been consulted, and sometimes reproduced. The work done depends at every turn on the labours of predecessors, both editors and critics; I should like to record especially the names of Charles and Mary Cowden Clarke (so often underrated), E. M. W. Tillyard, and J. Dover Wilson. Many of the notes, often beyond acknowledgement, are the product of a free interchange of knowledge and experience at the University of Hull; I am indebted to all my colleagues there, in particular to Mrs Margaret 'Espinasse who read and enriched the commentary. The anonymous reader for the Broadwater Press has generously supplied interpretations which I have embodied in the commentary.

To Mr John Wilbur Lowes and Harvard University Archives I am grateful for permission to see and use unpublished material by the late John Livingston Lowes.

Mr John Crow, Mr J. C. Maxwell, and the General Editor have helped generously; Dr H. F. Brooks has commented at large and has improved every section of the book; my wife has read everything, many times, with sympathy and uncommitedness—for which I am grateful.

The errors and omissions are my own fault.

G. K. HUNTER

The University, Reading
January 1957

ABBREVIATIONS

Abbott	E. A. Abbott, *A Shakespearian Grammar* (edn of 1886).
Brigstocke	edn of *All's W.*, ed. W. Osborne Brigstocke (1904) in The Arden Shakespeare.
The Clarkes	edn of *All's W.* in *Works*, ed. Charles and Mary Cowden Clarke [1864–8].
Dekker	*Dramatic Works*, ed. Fredson Bowers (1953 ff.).
E.E.T.S.	Early English Text Society.
Franz	Wilhelm Franz, *Die Sprache Shakespeares* (4th edn, 1939).
Herford	edn of *All's W.* in *Works*, ed. C. H. Herford (1899).
Jonson	*Works*, ed. Herford and Simpson (1925–52).
King	A. H. King, *The Language of the Satirised Characters in Poetaster* (1941).
Kökeritz	Helge Kökeritz, *Shakespeare's Pronunciation* (1953).
M.L.R.	*Modern Language Review.*
M.S.R.	Malone Society Reprint.
N.S.	edn of *All's W.* (1929) in *Works*, ed. Sir Arthur Quiller-Couch and John Dover Wilson.
Noble	Richmond Noble, *Shakespeare's Biblical Knowledge* (1935).
O.E.D.	*A New English Dictionary on Historical Principles*, ed. Murray, Bradley, Craigie, Onions (1884–1928).
On.	*A Shakespeare Glossary*, ed. C. T. Onions (edn of 1946).
Partridge	Eric Partridge, *Shakespeare's Bawdy* (1947).
R.E.S.	*Review of English Studies.*
Sh. Q.	*Shakespeare Quarterly.*
Shak. Eng.	*Shakespeare's England* (1916).
Thiselton	A. E. Thiselton, *Some Textual Notes on All's Well* (1900).
Tilley	*A Dictionary of the proverbs in England in the sixteenth and seventeenth centuries*, ed. M. P. Tilley (1950).

In the collations, editions of *All's Well* subsequent to those in the four Folios (F, F2, F3, F4) are referred to by the name of the editor, with the exception of the "Variorum" editions 1773–1821 which are referred to by date, of the Cambridge and Globe editions of W. G. Clark and W. A. Wright ("Camb." and "Globe") and of N.S. (see above). For a full, dated list of major Shakespeare editions see "The Plan of the Work" set before any recent volume of the "New Variorum" Shakespeare (e.g. *2 H 4*, ed. Shaaber or *R 2*, ed. Black).

The abbreviations of the titles of Shakespeare's plays and poems are those of C. T. Onions, *A Shakespeare Glossary*, p. x.

All quotations from Shakespeare (except those from *All's Well*) use the text and lineation of *Works*, ed. Peter Alexander (1951).

INTRODUCTION

I. THE TEXT

All's Well That Ends Well was first published in the Shakespeare First Folio (1623) and the text we find there is our only authority. The text has been much complained of, but though it contains many irregularities there is no need for wholesale emendation; indeed one of the main concerns of the present editor has been to rid the text of superfluous emendations. The "copy" that the Folio compositor had before him must have been confused in places, but this very confusion is in some ways a guarantee of authenticity, and we should be thankful that no sustained effort to "clean up" the text seems to have been attempted.

There is no evidence that the printing was particularly careless; though the use of two skeleton formes may have made the composition speedy[1] it does not seem to have overstrained the compositors. The play seems to be set, in the main, by "B", the more careless of the two identified Folio compositors, but the pages probably set by "A" are not notably more accurate.[2]

The nature of the copy was at one time thought to be indicated by "a mixture of consistency with inconsistency which clearly marks it out as prompt-copy".[3] The more modern view is that the inconsistencies point away from prompt-copy towards the author's "foul papers"—the author's latest draft of the play, before

1. See Charlton Hinman, 'New uses for headlines as bibliographical evidence', *English Institute Annual 1941*, 207–22.
2. The composition of gathering V seems to have been divided between "A" and "B". "A" set the innermost formes, V3v, V4 and (probably) V3, V4v, and "B" set the rest. Using the evidence Hinman has provided ("Cast-off copy for the First Folio of Shakespeare", *Sh. Q.*, VI (1955), 259–73) two explanations of this seem possible. We may suppose that "A" began to set in one order common when the compositor was working alone (working from the middle to the outsides and that "B" took over and finished the job, or we may suppose that "B" began alone using the other common order (working from the outsides to the middle) and that "A" finished. The latter hypothesis is perhaps more probable, since "B" went on to set gathering X; "B" also set those pages of gathering Y on which *All's Well* appears.
3. "New Shakespeare" edn of *All's Well* (1929), p. 116.

it was regularized for use in the theatre. This point was first made clearly in 1935 when R. B. McKerrow[1] pointed out that inconsistency in speech-prefixes would be intolerable in a prompt-book, though an author might well change his mind about the best designation for his characters. This inconsistency is a clear feature of our text, most obvious in the cases of Bertram (who appears as *Ber.*, *Count.*, and *Ros.*) the Countess (*Mo.*, *Cou.*, *Old Cou.*, *La.*) and Lafew (*Laf.*, *Ol. Laf.*, and (once) *Ol. Lord*). In many cases it is perfectly obvious that the name given is that of the role which is uppermost in the scene in which it occurs. Thus the Countess is *Mo.* while she is saying farewell to her son, but *Cou.* when conversing with Helena. The first soldier (1. *Sol.*) is appointed interpreter at IV. i. 21, and thereafter he appears as *Inter.* There can be no doubt that this is the author's nomenclature[2] which has not been regularized or corrected by the book-keeper.[3]

1. *R.E.S.*, XI (1935), 459–65.

2. W. W. Greg (*The Shakespeare First Folio*, p. 352) suspects the hand of the book-keeper in S.D. like "Flourish Cornets" (I. ii and II. i) and "A Short Alarum Within" (IV. i).

3. Another factor appears to be involved in the F text of *All's Well* which does not seem to be present in any of the other Shakespeare texts normally suspected to be from "foul papers"—a certain correspondence between differences of speech-prefix and the bibliographical divisions of the book in which they first appear. The F text of *All's Well* spreads over three gatherings, bearing the signatures V, X, and Y. The break between X and Y corresponds to a sudden change in speech-prefixes: *Old La.* becomes *Coun.* and *Ber.* becomes *Ros.* (in X Bertram is called *Ber.* fifty times and *Count.* once; in Y he is always *Ros.*). Up to this point the trend has been towards greater consistency. In V there is a great deal of variation, and some evidence of uncertainty at the beginnings of new pages. In V5, for example, Lafew is called *Ol[.d] Laf.* but at the top of V5v he is called (uniquely) *Ol. Lord*; presumably both forms derive from *Ol. L.* in the copy. At the same point, at the beginning of V5v, Helena is called (again, uniquely) *La.* The appearance of these two unique forms at this one point is not likely to be due to chance, nor does the change from V5 to V5v correspond to a change of compositor; there seems no reason to blame author or copyist. The simplest explanation would seem to be that we have a failure at this point to remember the normalization of vague authorial speech-prefixes that the compositor (for only one, "B", is involved here) had used (or was to use) in V5. It is worth noting that the break between V5 and V5v also involves a switch from *Ros.* to *Ber.*

If we derive from this a hypothesis that the compositor may impose some consistency on a text with variations in speech-prefixes (cf. Walton, *The Copy for the F text of Richard III* (1955), pp. 74 ff.), the greater consistency of quire X in this respect is suspicious. This might be due to the compositor now having normal forms for most of the names fixed in his head. I believe that J. W. Schroeder (in *The Great Folio* (1956) which I have not seen) has suggested that *Twelfth Night* (which occupies the remainder of gathering Y) was not printed straight away after *All's Well*, but only after some hold-up. If the last two pages of *All's Well* were involved in this (and certainly the headlines show discontinuity) we might

Other features of the text also point to foul-papers copy:

(1) Vague or permissive S.D.: *"Enter one of the Frenchmen, with fiue or sixe other souldiers in ambush."* (IV. i); *"Enter . . . and some two or three Souldiours."* (IV. iii); *"Enter 3 or 4 Lords."* (II. iii. 51).

(2) Entry of mutes: Parolles' entry at III. iii.

(3) Ghost characters: Violenta in III. v.

(4) Songs printed as part of the context, as at I. iii. 58–61.

The evidence would seem to leave little doubt that the copy for the Folio text was Shakespeare's foul papers (or a transcript of these). To know this is not, however, to know anything very definite, since papers remain technically "foul" at all stages from the first to the last draft. A comparison with other texts derived from foul-papers copy suggests that the copy for *All's Well* was, comparatively speaking, of the "fouler" variety, i.e. comparatively unpolished and discontinuous.

Dr H. F. Brooks points out further that several of the characters begin with type-names and acquire personal names in the course of the play: "Widow" is discovered to have the name "Capilet" in v. iii; "Clown" acquires that of "Lavatch" in v. ii; the "French Lords" become the brothers Dumaine; the "Steward" becomes Rynaldo. It looks as if Shakespeare was finding out, in the course of composition, what to call these characters; if this inference is correct then the MS. behind F must represent a stage at which the play was still being composed.

Some scholars have argued from such textual irregularities for the view that *All's Well* is a revision of an earlier play,[1] or for the presence of an "editor", "botcher", or "finisher"; but if we view the text as deriving from comparatively "foul" foul papers we would seem to have sufficient explanation of them. Some of the curious stage-directions—*"Enter . . . the Frenchmen, as at first."* (III. vi), *"Enter . . . the Maide called Diana"* (IV. ii)—suggest the author reminding himself of his intentions, and the same explanation may be used to cover *"Enter a gentle Astringer."* (v. i. 6) if the present editor's view of this[2] is accepted. Greg has remarked that *"Parolles and Lafew stay behind, commenting of this wedding* [II. iii. 183] might . . . well be a note for his [Shakespeare's] own future guidance. But it has more the appearance of a phrase from an author's plot or scenario that has been accidentally preserved."[3] If the latter suggestion were accepted it might tie up with the view that the foul

---

have an explanation why the speech-prefixes change again when we get to Y: the compositor had forgotten, in the interval, his old normalizations.

1. See also under "Date", pp. xix ff.   2. See commentary on v. i. 6.

3. Greg, *Shakespeare First Folio*, p. 352.

papers for *All's Well* were in a comparatively primitive state,[1] but since nothing is known of the process by which a scenario was turned into a play there is not sufficient evidence to develop this idea. The former suggestion[2] conforms to the general air of tentativeness in the play, noted above in connection with other stage-directions. It is tempting to extend this view of "tentativeness" in the play to something more like "unfinishedness", and it may be worth noting that stage-directions like some in *All's Well* appear in *Timon of Athens*—generally allowed to be an unfinished play.[3] There is an absence, however, of the suspicious shortness of *Timon* and of the actual structural incoherence found there—the excellence of its plotting is one of the virtues of *All's Well*—nor is there any hint of irregularity about its appearance in the Folio. The incoherences found in *All's Well* do not argue an unfinished state in any serious or any ordinary sense; they are most simply (and satisfactorily) explained as the breaks, corrections, and additions one must expect in an author's (especially a perplexed author's) working draft.

The text of *All's Well* does not contain any significant number of obviously Shakespearian spellings or mis-spellings and the natural assumption from this would be that the compositor used a transcript of Shakespeare's foul papers, and not the autograph. On the other hand it is difficult to see what purpose such a transcript might ever have served, since little or no regularization seems to have been achieved (except, perhaps, the division into Acts) and such a manuscript would have satisfied neither a literary collector nor a stage-manager.[4] That it did not fully satisfy even printing-house requirements would seem to be indicated by the occasional "space-losing" at the foot of the Folio pages of *All's Well*—a feature now said to be due to "bad casting-off", or failure to estimate the correct amount of manuscript space required to fill one page of type. This failure seems normally to derive from difficult or confused copy.[5]

1. Cf. Greg's comment on S.D. in *Timon*: "It is not surprising that some of these directions are reminiscent of what may have been jottings in the author's original plot; where the drama has only half disengaged itself from the matrix of thought, it is natural that the directions should not have been fully adapted to the needs of the stage" (*op. cit.*, p. 410).

2. The two suggestions are not necessarily incompatible. If, as seems possible, the scenario formed the skeleton of the earliest drafts, S.D. of this kind would be "accidentally" preserved more easily in plays about which the author continued to feel uncertain. There is evident throughout *All's Well* a certain discontinuity between S.D. and speech-prefixes, the former, on the whole, seeming to belong to a more primitive level of the play (see for example the comments on IV. i below). This again may reflect a difficult and uncertain course of composition.

3. Greg, *op. cit.*, p. 408, and Una Ellis-Fermor in *R.E.S.*, XVIII (1942), 270–83.

4. Cf. however Fredson Bowers, *On Editing Shakespeare*, pp. 20 f.

5. Charlton Hinman, "Cast-off copy", pp. 262 f.

E. K. Chambers[1] has seen the hand of the book-keeper in the letters "E" and "G" by which the two lords are designated throughout the Folio text. Since the most obvious purpose these letters would serve would be to indicate the actors by whom the parts were to be played ("Ecclestone" and "Gough" are the expansions normally accepted), and since we find the book-keeper adding names (or initials) of actors to the speech-prefixes of the author in several surviving MSS., the theory seems plausible. But other factors tell against it. The cases[2] in which we know that the book-keeper has added names or initials all refer to characters already distinguished by the author's speech-prefixes; there is certainly no warrant for believing in wholesale substitution. It is inconceivable that the author should have written his play without distinguishing two characters who have different (and incompatible) roles to play, and have left the book-keeper to decide who should speak what speech; yet throughout the greater part of *All's Well* "E" and "G" are the only means of distinction in the text. W. T. Hastings (following Chambers) has suggested[3] that the book-keeper (or another) when he added "E" or "G" deleted Shakespeare's (originally consistent) "1" and "2". This has the appearance of an argument designed specifically to fit the case, and has too little support from anything outside the play.

The introduction of the book-keeper to explain "E" and "G" leaves, in fact, as many difficulties as it answers. No other instance is known in which an actor is indicated by an (ambiguous[4]) single letter. Such ambiguity is more likely to belong to the author's draft than to the book-keeper's annotation, and we know from Shakespeare's foul-papers copy in other plays[5] that he sometimes composed with particular actors in mind, whose names in consequence sometimes crept into his text. The assumption that Shakespeare was responsible for "E" and "G" does not, of course, remove all difficulties. The entry in IV. i gives a permissive form "*one of the Frenchmen*", but the first speech-prefix gives us "*1. Lord E.*" and thereafter "*Lo(r). E.*". The problem here is equally difficult whether it takes the form, "Why did the book-keeper not rationalize the entry when he added 'E' to the speech-prefixes?" or "Why was Shakespeare tentative in the entry and certain in the prefixes?" It is conceivable that both theories have an element of truth: that the "E" and "G" are additions, but additions made by Shakespeare

1. *William Shakespeare*, I. 450.   2. See Greg, *op. cit.*, pp. 117–21.

3. *Shakespeare Association Bulletin* x (1935), 232–44.

4. In the years to which the play is normally assigned, Gilburne as well as Gough seems to have been a member of the company.

5. E.g. *Ado*, IV. ii; *Rom.*, IV. v; *2 H 4*, V. iv.

at a later stage of composition than that to which the entry belongs.

This idea finds some support in the inconsistency with which "E" and "G" are used. At III. vi. 113 "E" leaves with Bertram to visit Diana, but in IV. i he appears, directing the ambush against Parolles. In IV. iii, however, it emerges that "G" directed the ambush. This is the kind of error which it is easy to pass by in a book but which production would soon make obvious. Moreover, if we examine the use of these names up to the point at which the muddle begins, it is possible to see a reason for it. The first scene in which they appear (I. ii) consistently uses "1" and "2" as well as "G" and "E" so that it is clear that "G" plays *First Lord* and "E" *Second Lord*. On their second appearance (II. i) the lords are not distinguished so consistently: when "G" speaks alone he is not given any numeral, but when the two speak antiphonally the numerals are given, as in I. ii. The next appearance (III. i) shows minor inconsistency— "1. *Lord*" for the first speech, but "*French E.*" and "*French G*" thereafter—nothing, however, to disturb the identification of "G" with the first Lord and "E" with the second. It is in III. ii that this difficulty first appears; the stage-direction reads: "*Enter Hellen and two Gentlemen*"; these "Gentlemen" are clearly derived from the source and might be considered different from the "Lords" of previous scenes. That Shakespeare at one time thought of them as different may be indicated by the stage-direction governing their next entrance (III. vi): "*Enter Count Rossillion and the Frenchmen, as at first*", that is, the "Lords" and not the "Gentlemen". Against this must be set the fact that the speech-prefixes in III. ii—"French E" and "French G"—are the same as those used in III. i for the "Lords".[1] Moreover there is continuity in the narrative between the "Gentlemen" here and the "Lords" elsewhere: the Gentlemen have come from Florence and "thither . . . bend again", are suspicious of Parolles—all points of alignment with the Lords; in IV. iii the Lords have delivered a letter which sounds suspiciously like that which the Countess sends by the Gentlemen. At any rate, it is in III. ii, in which there is some evidence of new roles for these actors, that "E" starts speaking before "G" in a way which would normally indicate that he now played the "first" role (as W. T. Hastings has pointed out). "E" continues to speak first till IV. iii. Before the restoration of "G" to his proper primacy, however, and perhaps connected with it, comes the convulsive tangle at the end of III. vi: "E" promises to go and catch Parolles, but "G" is given the

1. One exception must be considered—the prefix 1. *G.* at III. ii. 62. If this means "Gough playing First Gent." my argument falls to the ground. Editors, however, have normally taken this as a unique example of "G" = "Gentleman", and I accept their opinion gratefully.

exit for this purpose, and "E"'s exit is made in order to visit Diana. It may be that we have here a partial correction, due to Shakespeare's having noticed that E/G and 1/2 had got out of alignment, but if so he did not get beyond a correction of the actual exits. This correction (if correction there was) not only failed to go back beyond the exits in III. iv, but failed also to substitute "G" for "E" in IV. i; yet the fact that First Lord is intended in IV. i is clear from the first speech-prefix ("1. *Lord E.*"). I am suggesting, in short, that Shakespeare began by conceiving of the "Gentlemen" in III. ii as a separate group in which "E" = 1 and "G" = 2 and inadvertently maintained these equivalences when he returned to "the Frenchmen, as at first" in which "G" = 1 and "E" = 2. This confusion continued till at some point he realized that he had gone wrong. Then he corrected the III. vi exits and the distribution of roles in IV. iii, but failed to correct throughout the play. If this theory is tenable, the modern editor clearly must complete the work of correction; whether he must also maintain the distinction between "Gentlemen" in III. ii and "Lords" elsewhere is more dubious; I have given reasons above which suggest that the distinction later vanished and the two groups coalesced in the author's mind; I would add here that the difficulty of using the same actors (especially in a repertory company, without elaborate make-up) to play different but easily confused roles would be obvious to any practical man of the theatre; the distinction would be invisible to the audience.[1]

The modernization of the present text has presented throughout problems of compromise between faithfulness to the original and consistency and clarity for the modern reader; it cannot be pretended that the balance of compromise will satisfy readers who have strong feelings on either side; it can only be hoped that genuine reasons stand behind every individual choice. Some older forms of words are retained, where these imply a genuine (and notable) difference of pronunciation. Thus "Imposture" for "imposter" is not retained at II. i. 154 since both spellings seem to imply the same (usual) pronunciation, but vilde for vile, Rossillion for Rousillon, Marcellus for Marseilles, fadom for fathom are retained; there seems no reason why these should not be as acceptable as deboshed for debauched.

The punctuation follows that of the Folio wherever possible, but

1. It is true (as H. F. Brooks points out) that there was a strong tradition of doubling roles handed down from the Tudor interludes (eight actors play thirty-eight parts in *Cambyses*) but note that "objection seems to have been felt to using the same pair in a different connection" (Greg, M.S.R. *Alcazar and Orlando*, p. 57).

the aim throughout has been to render as nearly as could be done in modern pointing the structures indicated by the Folio pointing rather than to reproduce the actual points used in the Folio. In accordance with this aim a lighter punctuation than is usual in modern editions has been adopted, in an attempt to preserve something of the characteristic flexibility of syntax. The original punctuation is not recorded in the apparatus except where it would give a different sense.

The principal aim of the apparatus is to record variations of the present text from the Folio; but nothing has been recorded when the F reading is what the present editor considers an obvious misprint, or where the change is a simple modernization. The variants in the subsequent Folios are treated as emendations and are recorded only where they have intrinsic merit. The apparatus also seeks to convey incidentally something of the nature and quality of the original, to carry some indications of the nature of the editorial tradition, and, in the case of certain cruces, to provide a survey of plausible or influential emendations. It cannot do any of these things thoroughly, and I have aimed only at an outline of evidence, suitable for the beginner in textual study. A special effort has been made to collate the interesting readings of recent editions of the play (subsequent to the second Cambridge edn), since these are not recorded elsewhere. The obelus (†) has been used to mark one passage as hopelessly corrupt. Editorial *additions* to the text are placed in square brackets; in the collations these square brackets are not recorded. A plus sign (+) has been used in the apparatus to mean "most editors".

2. THE DATE

There is no known mention of this play before the entry in the Stationers' Register for the printing of the First Folio. At one time Malone thought that it was the same as *A Bad Beginning makes a Good Ending* which was acted at court by John Heminge's company in 1613, but this has not found general acceptance. The play has also been thought to have borne, at one time, the title *Loves labours wonne*, and this identification has both a long history and an important bearing on our view of the date and structure of the play.

When Francis Meres published in 1598 his *Palladis Tamia* he referred to Shakespeare as a writer of comedies thus: "for Comedy, witnes his *Gentlemen of Verona*, his *Errors*, his *Loue labors lost*, his *Loue labours wonne*, his *Midsummers night dreame*, & his *Merchant of Venice*." All the works referred to here are extant except *Loue labours wonne* and various attempts have been made to identify this title with some work of Shakespeare's which has survived under another name. The theory that *All's Well* is the play referred to by Meres was first put forward by Bishop Percy in a letter to Dr Farmer dated 28 February 1764[1]:

> I observe that *Meres* quotes a play of Shakespear's (under the Title of *Love's Labors wonne*) which does not at present appear. Perhaps it is some play that we have now under another title: It might have been given very aptly to *All's Well that ends well*: and indeed to other plays.

This suggestion was taken over by Farmer and printed in his *Essay on the learning of Shakespeare* (1767): "... *All's well that ends well*, or, as I suppose it to have been sometimes called, *Love's labour wonne*".[2]

Malone at first accepted this and accordingly dated the play 1598,[3] but later changed his mind, ignored Farmer's equation, and dated the play 1606.[4] The earlier date is not, indeed, acceptable to modern scholarship as a date for the complete work. The play's affinities with *Hamlet* and with *Measure for Measure*, its sombre tone, the maturity of the character-drawing and of much of the verse place it clearly in the later part of Shakespeare's output.

A second line of thought, however, has carried the theory that *All's Well* was once called *Loves labours wonne* down to modern times. This seems to have been given expression by Coleridge first (though printed first by Tieck[5]). Collier reports that Coleridge in his lectures of 1813 and 1818 pointed out that the play contains two very different kinds of thought and expression; Coleridge assumed from this that the play "as it has come down to us, was written at two different, and rather distinct periods of the poet's life."[6] This interpretation allowed that the present play might be later than 1598 and yet originally have been the *Loue labours wonne* of Meres' list; Collier took over and expanded this interpretation, supposing the original play to have been revised by Shakespeare about 1605. The theory that the play is a revision of an earlier *Loves labours wonne* became thereafter the standard view, and

1. Printed in *The Percy Letters*, ed. D. Nichol Smith and Cleanth Brooks, Percy-Farmer volume (1946), p. 68. I owe this reference to Mr J. C. Maxwell.

2. Reprinted in *Eighteenth Century Essays on Shakespeare*, ed. D. Nichol Smith (1903), p. 178.

3. See the 1778 Variorum edn of the works of Shakespeare.

4. See the 1821 Variorum edn.

5. In the introduction to his notes on the play in the Schlegel-Tieck translation (1832). Tieck indeed goes further than Coleridge: "Vielleicht ist dieses Schauspiel dreimal vom Dichter bearbeitet worden."

6. Quoted by J. P. Collier in the introduction to the play in his 1842–4 edn. Cf. Raysor, I, 237.

Gollancz could remark in 1894 that it was "very probable, almost certain".[1]

Of late, however, the idea has become less compelling. Certainly the whole assumption that incoherencies in the text point necessarily to revision or re-writing is no longer tenable.[2] The other assumption, that variation in stylistic level precludes unified construction, or is best explained as due to different layers of composition, also requires re-examination.

It is generally agreed that many passages in *All's Well* are written in the "supple, sinewy, dramatic verse of the *Hamlet* period"[3] and with this view no one presumably would quarrel. Critics since Coleridge, however, find also in the play "speeches full of the lyrical sweetness and the dainty artifice of the earliest comedies",[4] instancing ii. i. 129–209, ii. iii. 125–44, and the two rhymed letters, iii. iv. 4–17 and iv. iii. 215–23. They point out that Shakespeare's letters in his mature plays are always written in prose. Such a statement reveals, however, the general weakness of the position. A letter in a play cannot be isolated as an entity; it serves a particular function in a particular context and the form of expression will be determined primarily by these factors. The letter from Parolles to Diana is plainly a parody of the love-sonnet which a gallant was supposed to send to his mistress and to this extent is parallel to another verse-letter of Shakespeare's maturity—that which Hamlet sends to Ophelia (*Ham.*, ii. ii. 115 ff.). The letter from Helena which the Steward reads in iii. iv is not only in form a sonnet, but by its various inversions and alliterations produces an effect more archaic and formal than anything in *The Sonnets* or the early plays. It is hard to believe that Shakespeare at any stage of his career known to us wrote like this simply because he had no command of a better lyric style. On the other hand it is easy to find dramatic reasons for the stiffness and remoteness of the sonnet: the style is in keeping with the sense of dedication which the letter is meant to convey; the letter brings a voice from another world, and as such contrasts effectively with the business-like blank verse which surrounds it.

The view of the couplets, at the other two points cited, as "early" has no better justification. The metrical technique is not "early" but "late" as both Hertzberg[5] and Fripp[6] have pointed out. Neither imagery nor rhythm are "dainty" or "lyrical" in any

---

1. "Temple" edn (1894), p. v.   2. See under "Text".

3. "Eversley" edn (1899), p. 111.   4. *Ibid.*

5. In his introduction to the German Shakespeare Society edn of Schlegel and Tieck (ed. Ulrici) (1871).

6. *Shakespeare, Man and Artist* (1938), ii, 600.

ordinary sense—such as might be applied (for example) to *Love's Labour's Lost*, IV. iii. 314–50. The rhetoric is, in fact, contorted and gnarled by the pressure of thought[1] in a way which is totally un-lyrical. There is, moreover, a complete dramatic justification for the couplets in both II. i. 129–209 and II. iii. 125–44. In II. i the verse begins at the point at which a higher note of exaltation is required, just where Helena begins to enforce the claim to divine sanction and encouragement. The dialogue assumes an incantatory, litur-gical[2] tone, which may not please those in search of anthology "beauties", but which is eminently appropriate to the dramatic context; it is difficult indeed to see how this content could have been expressed otherwise. At II. iii. 125 the rhymed verse begins abruptly at the point at which particular advice to Bertram changes to gnomic generality and ceases again when particular dialogue returns. The association of gnomic sentiments with formal couplets is a constant factor in Shakespearian and indeed Eliza-bethan dramatic art (cf. *Othello*, I. iii. 199–209, *Cymbeline*, IV. ii. 26–9, 33–6) and should require no further defence.

That there is an unusual amount of variation in the verse-levels of *All's Well* (as of *Measure for Measure*) no one can deny, but both these plays may be seen as efforts to reconcile a sense of divine pur-pose with a salty practical wisdom[3] and this mixture may be held responsible for the mixture of styles, and for a genuine stratification deriving from the divergent interests of the play, rather than from different dates of composition.

If the play as we have it was composed at one time, the problem of dating is simplified, though anything but simple. There is no exact evidence which enables us to establish the date, but there are a number of pointers, which narrow down the possibilities.

The part of the clown is obviously designed for Robert Armin, who probably replaced Kempe as chief clown of Shakespeare's company in 1599, so that the play (if all of one piece) must be later than this.[4]

1. See under "Verse".

2. Cf. Tillyard: "He is deliberately evading drama and substituting ritual and cloudy incantation" (*Problem Plays*, p. 101). I am throughout indebted to Tillyard's excellent treatment of "stratification".

3. See critical introduction.

4. Leslie Hotson (*Shakespeare's Motley* (1952), p. 88) draws on the well-known distinction between Shakespeare's earlier boorish clowns (Launce, Dogberry, etc.) and his later courtly "wise fools" (Touchstone, Feste, etc.) to make a point about the dating of Lavatch. If, as is usually supposed, the change from clown to fool is connected with the replacement of Kempe by Armin, about 1599, as the company's leading comedian, then we ought to be able to date the role of Lavatch in relation to this. Hotson sees Lavatch as more rustic and boorish (i.e.

E. K. Chambers,[1] supposing that Lafew's "*Lustique, as the Dutchman says* [II. iii. 41] must clearly come from" *The Weakest Goeth to the Wall* which he does not regard as "much older than ... 1600", tries to date *All's Well* by reference to this. But "the Dutchman" may be interpreted quite satisfactorily as "any Dutchman" or "Dutchmen in general"; "lustique" seems to have been a stock piece of Dutchness; there is no good reason to suppose that it was especially associated with *The Weakest Goeth to the Wall*—where it occurs only thrice and even then without emphasis.

The "New Shakespeare" sees allusions to the Gunpowder Plot in I. i. 118 f. and IV. iii. 20 ff., but I cannot regard these as substantial, for the contexts provide sufficient justification for the words used in both cases; it also sees in I. iii. 90–2 a reference to the enforcement of the surplice in 1604: the vestment controversy certainly flared up at this time, but it should be pointed out that at no time in the preceding fifty-odd years was the controversy dormant.

These are the most probable pieces of external evidence that have been brought forward, and it can be seen that they do not add up to much. They concur in pointing to a date somewhere in the first decade of the seventeenth century, but have not enough force, even in combination, to constitute definite evidence.

The evidence of metrical tests applied to this play is also complex and indefinite. The late Professor John Livingston Lowes made a thorough metrical analysis of the play (which, unfortunately, he never published[2]); this gives a more exact form to the view that the play is deeply divided in its manner, but also makes it clear that the division is not between an early manner and a later one, but that the metrical characteristics are those of Shakespeare's middle and latest manners—Professor Lowes supposes that the play was finally revised about 1606–8. It also makes it clear that the division is not simply one between rhyme and blank-verse, some of the rhyme (II. iii. 125–44) having close affinities with the metric of the last plays. Moreover the detailed distinctions of style that Professor Lowes makes do not point inevitably to revision; they are

more like a Kempe clown) than Touchstone or Feste and presumes in consequence that the play must precede *As You Like It* and *Twelfth Night*. But Lavatch's "boorishness" is quite different from Dogberry's; it is only the stalking-horse behind which he shoots the arrows of his percipient and courtly wit. As a "shrewd and unhappy" fool he resembles the Fool in *Lear*, Apemantus, and Thersites more than he does Touchstone and Feste.

1. *William Shakespeare* (1930), I. 450 f.

2. I have been able to examine this through the courtesy of Mr John Wilbur Lowes and the Harvard University Archives.

perfectly explicable in the terms outlined above of an author oscillating between a more remote, impersonal, and hieratic presentation of his subject, and a more immediate and human treatment of it—between, in short, the manner of the middle plays and that of the last plays. If the internal evidence is interpreted in this way, it follows that it can only give a broad indication of dates within which such an oscillation is probable—i.e. 1601–8.

One last approach to the problem of date is possible through an attempt to relate this play to other plays of Shakespeare's in terms of themes, characters, handling. The two plays to which *All's Well* seems most closely related are *Hamlet* and *Measure for Measure*. The resemblances with *Hamlet* are restricted, and concentrated in Act I. Both plays begin with sorrow for fathers, with the departure of a young man for Paris and training in gentility: indeed Laertes is in many ways a parallel figure to Bertram. In both the same topics, "advice for a son" and "consolation for loss" (not elsewhere touched by Shakespeare),[1] are drawn on; in both we are presented with an ambiguous grief, explained subsequently in a soliloquy; in both there is much discussion of the substitution of step-parents for natural parents. When we compare *Hamlet* with *All's Well* in these respects we notice that the fuller, more expanded treatment occurs in *Hamlet*, and the more cryptic and compressed version in *All's Well*. J. L. Lowes refers to "lines which compress into half the space and embody in maturer phrase and rhythm Polonius' advice to Laertes", and the impression of the present writer is the same— that we find in *All's Well* versions of these ideas which are likely to be later than those in *Hamlet*.

How much later than the 1601–2 usually assigned to *Hamlet* is not indicated, of course, in such a comparison; though it is not probable that these formulae would continue to hang together in such detail over a wide period of time. G. B. Harrison has recently suggested (without explanation) a date as late as "after 1608"[2]; this is attractive, in view of the play's general relationship to the last plays but certain factors argue against it. Of these the most impostant is the relationship with *Measure for Measure*.

Measure for Measure and *All's Well* are obvious twins. The affinities they share might, of course, be due to nothing more than the chance similarity of their sources; but it is not probable that plot, characterization, themes, vocabulary,[3] even the tangles, per-

1. Though there is opportunity for the second in *Twelfth Night* and *Love's Labour's Lost* and for the first in *Richard II*. See my article in *Sh. Q.*, VIII (1957), 501–6.

2. "Penguin Shakespeare" edn (1955), p. 16.

3. See the articles by Alfred Hart in *R.E.S.*, XIX (1943).

plexities, and perversities of treatment should be shared, unless the mind and technique of the author were still at the same stage. What difference there is, points to a slight development and clarification of the material when it is handled in *Measure for Measure*.[1]

Thus (1) the woman with clear intelligence and a sense of divine mission, who starts out of her sphere and entangles a nobleman, is more powerfully realized in Isabella than in Helena; with Isabella, purity of mind and transparent singleness of purpose lie at the centre of the action (being the principal causes of Angelo's infatuation), but in Helena they appear rather as incidental by-products of the plot.

(2) The process of development out of frigid immaturity through active evil into humbled wisdom and acceptance of life has to be read into Bertram's career to account for many of its features; in the case of Angelo this intention is more obvious (though the source gives less excuse for it): Angelo's development is consistently credible where Bertram's is a series of poses, strung loosely along the thread of narrative. The discovery of "seeming" at the end of *Measure for Measure* is given depth and reality because it coincides with the emergence of the true Angelo; Bertram has never really deceived anyone, and thus the central deceiver cannot be used to drive home this central interest of the play; the secondary character of Parolles has to bear the principal weight in this respect.

(3) The legalistic handling of the dénouement is similar in both plays, but again we find that *Measure for Measure* expresses more easily and effectively what *All's Well* seems to be aiming at. The major difference in structure is that in *All's Well* Shakespeare centres everything on Helena—all the strings lead to her, and nothing is resolved until she appears, so that a top-heavy effect is produced—too much complication leading to too little resolution. In *Measure for Measure* the reconciliation receives greater emphasis by being twofold: a first reconciliation in terms of Justice points forward to a second in terms of Mercy.

In all these respects it is obvious that *Measure for Measure* is the less uncertain achievement; this in itself would not, of course, make it later, since achievements disintegrate as well as build up. What for the present editor clinches the argument is that in its added emphasis on reconciliation, on female purity, and on the achievement of humbled wisdom, *Measure for Measure* is a stage nearer the last plays, towards which, I take it, *All's Well* itself is pointing.

1. The "bed-trick" is inherent in the plot material of *All's Well*, but added to the plot of *Measure for Measure*; we might assume that it would appear first in a source-story and be added to another source only subsequently.

If *All's Well* is earlier than *Measure for Measure* it cannot be later than 1604—the date normally assigned to *Measure for Measure*, and from which I see no reason to dissent. The close interconnection of the two plays also implies that it is not much earlier. A tentative dating of *All's Well* 1603-4 is therefore the outcome of this inquiry.

3. THE SOURCE

The ultimate source of the main plot of *All's Well* is without doubt the ninth novel of the third day in Boccaccio's *Decameron*, which is not known to be based on any other extant piece of literature. We cannot be certain how Shakespeare came to know Boccaccio's tale; it does not seem probable that he went directly to the Italian, and certain names—Senois for Sanesi, Gerard de Narbon for Gerardo di Nerbona—suggest a French intermediary. Until recently it has always been assumed that the only possible intermediary was William Painter, who, in his *Palace of Pleasure* (1566, 1569, and 1575) translates (fairly closely) Decameron III. ix as his thirty-eighth novel. Professor H. G. Wright, however, showed in 1951[1] that Painter used not only the Italian Decameron, but also a French version by Antoine le Maçon; since le Maçon, no less than Painter, has "Senois", which has always been assumed to prove the link between Painter and Shakespeare, and also "Gerard de Narbonne" where Painter has "Gerardo of Narbone", the question arises whether le Maçon rather than Painter is not the intermediary. Shakespeare had some knowledge of French,[2] and the atmosphere of the play is decidedly French; the names Parolles, Lavatch, and Lafew seem to indicate a mind at work strongly imbued with a consciousness of French meanings. In a second article[3] Professor Wright has argued the case for le Maçon at some length, and is able to show that many of the apparent pointers to Painter are unsafe as evidence. At the end of his argument, however, the case remains open, and, other things being equal, it seems unlikely that Shakespeare would use a French rather than an English version.[4] In addition one should notice a likelihood that Painter's next novel ("Tancred of Salerne") influenced Shakespeare's handling of the preceding story. "Tancred"

1. *M.L.R.*, XLVI (1951), 431-5.
2. Professor Wright summarizes the evidence for this in *M.L.R.*, L (1955), 45 f.
3. *M.L.R.*, L (1955), 45-8.
4. He may, of course, have used both. Medieval and Elizabethan translators often used several versions of the work they were translating (Painter himself is a case in point) and Shakespeare is supposed to have drawn on several parallel source-books for some of his plays.

contains the same[1] opposition of virtue and gentility as Shakespeare imports into *All's Well*, and the great speech of Gismunda on this topic resembles the King's speech in *All's Well*, II. iii. I have found only one verbal echo between Painter's "Tancred" and *All's Well* (see note on I. i. 90); in the absence of sustained verbal parallels this evidence against le Maçon cannot weigh heavily; Shakespeare could anyway have read the Tancred story in le Maçon's version of the Decameron, or in other Elizabethan adaptations—though these tend to conceal the democratic implications.

From whatever version Shakespeare derived the story, he was not content to present it exactly as he found it. He has made a number of changes in emphasis and effect, and we may see something of the author's attitude to his plot by considering the changes, arranged under the effects they seem designed to produce.

(*A*) Dramatic compression.

As usual, when dealing with narrative sources, Shakespeare drastically reduces the time involved in the action.

(i) In Painter, Bertram's father dies; then "a little while after" Giletta's father dies, and she desires to go to Paris but she is hindered for what must be quite some time, for "she hearde tell, that hee was growen to the state of a goodly yong gentleman." In Shakespeare, the two fathers' deaths are presented simultaneously, and the departure of Bertram begins the train of thought which carries Helena to Paris without a break.

(ii) Shakespeare reduces the time within which Helena promises to cure the king from eight days to two.

(iii) In Painter, Beltramo lies with his wife "not onelye . . . at that time . . . but at manye other times". In Shakespeare only one encounter is involved; the effect of hurry and repentance in IV. iii is thus immeasurably strengthened.

(iv) In Painter, Giletta resides and rules in Rossiglione for some time before she despairs and departs on pilgrimage. In Shakespeare, her departure follows hard upon her arrival.

(*B*) A second class of changes shows Shakespeare concerned to depress Bertram in our estimation, and, correspondingly, to exalt Helena.

(i) In Painter, Giletta is promised, in reward for the cure of the king, any husband the king shall choose for her; it is only after a further request that she is allowed to choose for herself, and even then, when Beltramo turns out to be the chosen one, "the king was very loth to graunt him unto her". The impression we get is that the

1. The theme is, of course, very common in the Renaissance, and its appearance in two separate works cannot, by itself, imply any other connection between them. Cf. Critical Introduction, p. xxxviii, n. 1.

marriage is basically improper. Shakespeare does what he can to reduce this impression. Helena makes only one request; the king shows no hesitation:

> Fair maid, send forth thine eye. This youthful parcel
> Of noble bachelors stand at my bestowing.

When she offers to withdraw, it is he who forces the issue. Moreover, Bertram is informed of the choice in a less brutal way, so his reaction is less excusable.

(ii) In Painter, Beltramo himself "praied license to retourne to his countrye". In Shakespeare, he is not man enough to speak, but will

> write to the king
> That which I durst not speak.

(iii) In Painter, the tasks Helena has to fulfil are imposed in a remote and vague way, and might be taken to imply little more than choleric impatience: "To whom he chorlishly replyed. 'Let her do what she liste. For I do purpose to dwell with her, when...'" etc. Moreover, this is only elicited when Giletta makes a second advance towards him. Shakespeare makes the sentence on Helena seem more cruel, because more deliberate.

(iv) The sordid series of lies and evasions involving Bertram in v. iii is Shakespeare's addition. In Painter, Beltramo is the judge in his own case—a just and magnanimous judge.

(v) In Painter, Giletta is frustrated in her first attempt to win Beltramo, but hearing of the new prohibitions and new conditions she sets about these with a business-like briskness: she "purposed to finde meanes, to attaine the two thinges, that thereby she might recover her husbande". There is nothing of this in Shakespeare: neither her letter to the Countess, nor her soliloquy in III. ii, suggests any purpose for her departure except mortification. A battle of wits is transformed into a struggle with feelings.

(C) Another set of changes seems designed to emphasize the conflict of virtue and nobility in the persons of Helena and Bertram.

(i) In Painter, Giletta is rich, much sought after, and "diligently loked unto by her kinsfolke". In Shakespeare she has only her virtue to recommend her; such relationships as she acquires— the protection of the King, and adoption by the Countess—are acquired through this virtue, without which she would be completely isolated and dependent. There is no question of Helena visiting Bertram in Paris, as Giletta does, before she "repayred to the King".

(ii) Indicative of a similar interest is Shakespeare's treatment of the ring which Bertram gives to Diana. In Painter, where it is the Widow who obtains the ring, we are told only that "he greatly loved that ring . . . for a certaine vertue that he knew it had". Shakespeare makes the ring a positive symbol of Bertram's family honour, so that the bartering it for Diana's chastity is a clearer issue of dishonour.[1] The symbolic importance of the ring is emphasized by the addition of a second ring, which Helena exchanges for the other.[2]

(*D*) Shakespeare tightens up the relationship between the various parts of the story, in particular that between the French scenes and the Italian scenes. There is no political relationship between France and Florence in Painter's tale: Beltramo merely wanders into Italy when he leaves the French court "where understanding that the *Florentines* and *Senois* were at warres, he determined to take the *Florentines* parte". Shakespeare gives reality to both the political and social aspects of the scene, so that his characters are never allowed to stray into an area of moral irresponsibility; the Italian scenes are not merely a background for romantic adventure, but a new setting for the old, accumulating, moral account.

All these modifications may be taken to give a general indication of Shakespeare's attitude to the story he inherited. But larger changes are involved as well; Shakespeare adds a number of important new characters—the Countess (with her clown), Lafew, and (together with the whole business of his sub-plot) Parolles. The Countess, Lafew, and the King—whose part is much expanded by Shakespeare—are used to define a norm of propriety against which the tale of Bertram and Helena is seen in added moral perspective, no longer the brisk contest of wits that Boccaccio devised. Parolles serves to define the reality of Bertram; at the same time he acts as a scapegoat and takes at least some of the blame for Bertram's faults.

The sub-plot of Parolles and his exposure is normally assumed to

1. Cf. IV. ii. 44–5 n.

2. The addition of a ring which the man takes from the woman he has lain with and which is instrumental in reconciling him with the wife he has determined to put away has been thought to show Shakespeare's dependence on Terence's *Hecyra*. In this, a ring is stolen by the hero from a girl he ravished and is the means of identifying his wife (suspected of adultery) as the same girl, and so effecting a reconciliation. There is a general similarity, true enough; but granted that the *Hecyra* and the main source in Boccaccio belong to the same tradition of romance narrative and that Shakespeare also had a wide acquaintance with the tradition, a commonplace motif like the use of a ring to effect recognition cannot be taken to prove direct relationship. The doubling of the rings, like the doubling of the twins in *The Comedy of Errors* may be taken as simply an example of Shakespeare's consistent and typically Elizabethan effort to complicate and elaborate the material of his sources.

be of Shakespeare's own invention. There is a weak parallel in Nashe's *Unfortunate Traveller* (McKerrow, II, 218–25): there a "captain" is persuaded by Jack Wilton that the king desires some-one to steal into the enemy's camp; the captain is flattered into undertaking this mission. He goes over to the enemy pretending to have deserted, and says he is willing to undertake any service against his former masters; but he is too foolish to deceive and is whipped back again. Common to the two stories are (1) the assumption of high rank when the boaster is interrogated: "he answered, that he was a gentleman, a capten commander, a chiefe leader" (p. 223); cf. *All's W.*, IV. iii. 192 ff. (2) Terror at the sight of tortures: "he no sooner sawe the wheele and the torments set before him, but he cryde out like a Rascall" (p. 224); cf. *All's W.*, IV. iii. 119 f. (3) The phrase "Jack Drum's entertainment". These parallels are, however, too commonplace to establish any necessary connection.

4. CRITICAL INTRODUCTION

All's Well that Ends Well is not a play that is often read or per-formed, and on the rare occasions when it is seen or heard it does not seem to give much general pleasure. From this point of view, and it is ultimately the crucial one, criticism of *All's Well* has failed, for it has failed to provide a context within which the genuine virtues of the play can be appreciated. Various palliatives and explanations for the peculiarity of the play have been advanced—ranging from anatomizations of Shakespeare's soul to analyses of his text—and these undoubtedly have their place, but they seem to the present editor not to stick close enough to the play as we have it: a peculiar play, but undoubtedly Shakespearian, and displaying in its several parts qualities that clearly relate it to the more assured successes of the Shakespeare canon.

The problem that presents itself is: how are we to describe the genuine effects of this play so that readers (or audiences) can see it as a whole, or at least as a work with a centre? The play has undoubtedly a strongly individual quality, but it is difficult to start from this, since it is mainly a quality of *strain*, of striving through intractable material for effects which hardly justify the struggle, a quality of harsh discord which seeks resolution, but achieves less than is sought. The usual deductive process of explain-ing the parts of the play by reference to the effect of the whole is especially dangerous here, for integration is difficult to see in terms of the play itself, and assumptions about the harmony towards which the play is supposed to be moving are liable to be arbitrary and unwarranted. An attempt is made to reduce the difficulty by presenting first, in this Introduction, an account (as objective as possible) of the elements of the play which can be isolated, especially those which pull in different directions; only then, when the reader should have some material to check the writer's speculations, do we pass to problems of interpretation and general questions of "meaning".

I. ELEMENTS OF THE PLAY

(a) Structure

A revolution in our attitude to *All's Well* has been brought about by the work of W. W. Lawrence[1] on the genre of the plot-material, and the views of Lawrence have provided a framework for most subsequent discussion. Lawrence points out that the plot is clearly related to folk-tale and fairy-tale, being in fact a combination of two traditional episodes: (1) "the healing of the king", (2) "the fulfilment of the tasks". In folk-tales of the first type a poor or despised person gains a desired end by knowing the secret of a king's illness and by curing him. In tales of the second type a person (often a wife) is set a series of apparently impossible tasks to be performed before she can live happily; against all probability she performs these tasks and claims the reward, which is then granted.

This type of plot, Lawrence points out, demands a simple response to the presentation of good and evil; he assumes, in consequence, that Shakespeare could not have intended Helena to be other than noble, or the ending to be other than a "happy-ever-after" reconciliation; to have done so would have been "to make such sweeping changes in the meaning of traditional stories, in situations made familiar to people by centuries of oral narrative" that the simple audience would be perplexed and baffled (pp. 68 f.). Accordingly, "Shakespeare's aim was to tell, in theatrically effective fashion, a story, the story of a noble woman passing through great afflictions into happiness."

That Lawrence is correct, for at least one level of Shakespeare's intention, and that the dramatic shape he describes is really present are hardly open to doubt, but truth about one element in *All's Well* cannot be trusted to be truth about the whole play, and in fact other elements elaborate and complicate Lawrence's picture.

Even within the framework of the plot described by Lawrence complicating factors arise, for the two elements of traditional folk-tale are not treated from the same point of view. If Helena is the traditional "clever wench" in "the healing of the king", her clever-

1. W. W. Lawrence, *Shakespeare's Problem Comedies* (New York 1931).

ness in "the fulfilment of the tasks" must be granted to be very different; the one is a positive and the other a negative virtue, and our reactions must alter from one to the other, or find a mediating factor which will account for both. But this difference is ignored, not only by Lawrence, but by most critics, so that the real structure of the plot is distorted:

> Helen of Narbonne, having won by a trick the hand of Bertram Count of Rousillon in marriage, with no pretentions to his heart, is repudiated by him after the ceremony. She hears of him presently as in Florence, laying siege to a lady of that city; goes thither herself, and by a second trick wins the ring off his finger and a pledge of his passion for another person: confronting him with which, he is content to take her.
>
> (Maurice Hewlett, *Extemporary Essays* (1922)

In fact, Helena does not hear of Bertram in Florence laying siege to a lady of that city and then go to Florence herself (the implication being that she goes to take advantage of the situation); but more interesting than the error of fact is the frame of mind which prompts it—the assumption that Helena is never passively virtuous, but dominates by her will the course of the plot, and engineers its coincidences. True, in the first half[1] of the play ("the healing of the king") Helena is a positive and competent figure, though to say she won the hand of Bertram "by a trick" is hardly fair to the facts of the play, in which virtue declares itself by divine favour and is found worthy of reward by the divinely allowed arbiter of destiny—the king. But in the second half of the play ("the fulfilment of the tasks") this assumption is clearly untenable. The poor, isolated orphan has now become the favourite of the King and the adopted daughter of the Countess, but it is not by using these advantages that she achieves "the fulfilment of the tasks". She expiates her "ambitious love" by abandoning worldly position, and her journey to Great St Jaques (via Florence) is said unequivocally in the play to be a journey of contrition and abnegation:

> death . . . I myself embrace to set him free.

1. The division of this play (and of *Measure for Measure*) into two halves or movements—one concerned with involved personal relationships leading to an impossible tangle, and the other with loosening the tangle by means less personal and more symbolic, the two halves being clearly separated—is a structural feature which finds its consummation in *The Winter's Tale*. The movement from Sicily to Bohemia, from hate to love, from courtly to pastoral is at once more obvious and more subtle than the move from France to Italy and from love to war in *All's Well*, but the effort in the latter would seem to be in at least the same direction as the achievement of *The Winter's Tale*.

and is accepted as such by the Countess and the two Gentlemen, whose comments seem to reflect a norm Shakespeare intends us to accept. Of course, there are difficulties in the way of this view. In her conversations with the Widow Helena appears as a schemer, and the reader may well feel that no single view of her conduct is possible. In order to apprehend the play we have, however, to accept a heroine of one kind or another, and in making this choice Shakespeare's handling of his source may perhaps help to guide us. We observe that he strives to reduce, not to augment, the activity of Helena in the second half of the play; so that, for example, the conversations with the Widow take place only under the pressure of coincidence, while the first mention of any possible relationship between Diana and Bertram's wife is given to the Widow.

In fact, the dichotomy between Helena active and Helena passive has a false emphasis if we do not see that the second half of the play is less concerned with human will and more with a sense of "All's Well that Ends Well"—things working out under the pressure of forces other than the personal. The objection that this half is too full of "contrivance" and too little irradiated by personality (or even by major speeches) may point to a failure of execution, but it should not conceal from us that the mode in which it is written is not "worse" than that of the first half, but (as in the parallel case of *Measure for Measure*) "different". In terms of structure we find an attempt to darken and deepen the terms of Helena's success-story, so that it falls into place in a pattern of human failures,[1] saved in the end only by coincidence and submission to the supernatural, and this alters in an interesting and subtle way Lawrence's over-simple "passing through great afflictions into happiness". Tillyard speaks of the similar change in *Measure for Measure*, which he supposes to involve a "more abstract"[2] kind of dramatic technique. Certainly the use of this technique in two plays is likely to be deliberate rather than coincidental. Shakespeare is handling traditional motifs, but he makes a new effect out of them by manipulating the viewpoint. In the second half of *All's Well*, Helena is a "clever wench" only in the sense in which Griselda is—clever enough to be virtuous, pious, and patient till Destiny and Justice work things out for her.

The sub-plot of Parolles is yet another complicating factor. This Lawrence dismisses as, on the whole, irrelevant: "This sub-plot is singularly independent of the main action; much more so than is

1. J. Arthos, "The Comedy of Generation", *Essays in Criticism*, v (1955), 97–117, sees the whole play as about "the confounding of love" developed by "the comparison of the failures".

2. E. M. W. Tillyard, *Shakespeare's Problem Plays* (1950), p. 126.

usual with Shakespeare's mature work" (p. 33). This independence is, however, only true of the plots when considered as bare
narrative—the Bertram story could progress without the Parolles
story; but in a more vitally organic sense they are interdependent—
the Bertram story would not mean the same without the Parolles
story. There is continual parody of the one by the other. Parolles
and Helena are arranged on either side of Bertram, placed rather
like the Good and Evil Angels in a Morality. His selfish ostentation
balances her selfless abnegation; both are poor people making
good in a world open to adventurers, but the magical and romantic
actions of Helena are in strong contrast to the prosaic opportunism
of Parolles—the contrast perhaps working both ways, staining the
career of Helena with the imputation of ambition as well as showing
up the degraded mind of Parolles.[1] Parolles wins (temporarily at
least) the battle for Bertram's soul (it is he who ships him off to the
war), and is himself an index to the world of lust and lies into which
Bertram is falling. The Shakespearian view of Bertram and Helena
could hardly, in short, be presented except in the perspective
of Parolles—a perspective which reduces the effects of the folk-
analogues that Lawrence regards as the key to the play. The
gallantry of war is stained by Parolles no less than the erection of
virtue into nobility. The king's laughing adjuration, "Those girls
of Italy . . ." (II. i. 19 ff.) is shown up in sordid reality in Bertram's
intrigue with Diana and in the even sordider counter-intrigue of
Parolles. The pride, pomp, and circumstance of glorious war is
exposed to the same withering realism: "the muster-file, rotten and
sound, upon my life, amounts not to fifteen thousand poll; half of
the which dare not shake the snow from off their cassocks lest they
shake themselves to pieces." The same effect is produced by
Lavatch, for whom the wounds of honour and syphilitic chancres
are indistinguishable.

Indeed it is not only in the relation of sub-plot to main plot but
throughout that the play juxtaposes extreme romantic conventions
with down-to-earth and critical realism. Not only character but
also place is unsparingly observed. Quiller-Couch has said that
"*All's Well* has no atmosphere save that of the stage" ("New Shakespeare", p. xxxiv) but both Rossillion and Paris are in fact acutely
observed. The naturalness of the Countess was repeatedly praised

1. See Clifford Leech, 'The theme of ambition in *All's Well*', *ELH*, xxi (1954),
17–29.

One might even suggest that the placing of the Dumaines' farcical intrigue to
unmask Parolles beside the scenes depicting Helena's intrigue to capture Bertram is designed to reduce the nobility of the latter, though cf. p. xxxv, n. i below
on "parody".

by G. B. Shaw,[1] and has been well described by Legouis[2]: she is a solid and gracious figure and Rossillion her home reflects her personality. Her conversations with the clown and the steward, and with Lafew, give us a convincing picture of the noble household ruled over by this lady. The King's opening remarks and his long speech of reminiscence in I. ii do as much for Paris. The court is not merely the conventional court of Romance; it is far more real than that of Leontes or Theseus or the Duke of Milan, and recalls (as Legouis and Tillyard well point out) the world of *Henry IV*. Indeed it is too realistic politically for the magic Helena practises there.

No less realistic is the Widow of Florence—cautious, shrewd, garrulous. Helena in her negotiations with her is almost subdued to the element she works in, though here we have a realism like that commonly found in folk-tales and fairy-tales where magic and a good eye for the main chance often coalesce. The kind of realism that cuts off this play from the atmosphere of fairy-tale is rather different, and is probably seen best in the presentation of Bertram and Parolles. Critics sometimes complain that there is nothing in *All's Well* of the low-life realism of the Vienna of *Measure for Measure*, but then *All's Well* is not concerned with social corruption. The corruption of honour in Bertram's world is portrayed with a critical and even satirical detachment which is masterly in its kind, and remarkably effective on the stage. But the mastery of critical analysis, discrimination, disintegration of separate attitudes, which we find here, cannot fit into the world of folk-narrative. The vitality of Bertram and Parolles (and it is considerable) fights against the effects that Lawrence perceived.

Moreover, the action of this play is seldom allowed to make simple unimpeded effects, but is complicated throughout by a commentary, implicit as well as explicit, of which the principal agent is the clown. Lavatch has obvious similarities to Touchstone; both undoubtedly play "wise fool" roles designed for Robert Armin,[3] but the differences are just as important. The relationship between Touchstone and Rosalind makes it clear that the satiric wit of the clown is directed from much the same point as the joyous wit of the heroine. Lavatch is as contemptuous of Parolles as Touchstone is of Jaques, but his view does not ally itself in this play to the

1. Shaw was obviously attracted by the Ibsen-like qualities of this play; he calls it a "play that is . . . rooted in my deeper affections". For his appreciation of the Countess see *Our Theatres in the Nineties*, I, 30 ("the most beautiful old woman's part ever written"), and *Pen Portraits*, I, 120 f. I am grateful to H. F. Brooks for pointing out these passages to me.

2. Emile Legouis, 'La Comtesse de Rousillon', *English*, I (1936–7), 399–404.

3. See under "Date", p. xxi.

witty common-sense of the heroine; no central, acceptable, and unified viewpoint is left defined in the midst of the follies and excesses of the rest of the play. The pretensions of the good no less than those of the wicked or foolish are exposed here (as in *Troilus and Cressida*) to continuous criticism.

Much of this effect is produced by parody[1] of the main plot: in I. iii we approach Helena's request to the Countess that she may pursue Bertram by way of Lavatch's request that he may marry Isbel, where "driven on by the flesh" etc. reflects directly on the emotions and ambitions of the heroine. Again in II. ii we find direct satire on the court, reflecting on what happens there in the main plot. In III. ii Lavatch, after a visit to court, adopts court manners so far as to tire of Isbel and seek to reject her, as Bertram has sought to reject Helena; indeed we find him commenting on this alteration at the very moment that the Countess is reading the letter which informs her of Bertram's desertion.

Few, moreover, of the ideas with which the play is concerned pass without derogatory comment from Lavatch; he sees courtliness as a verbal trick, war as a shirking of responsibility, greatness as an obedience to the devil. Lavatch's satire is not, however, merely nihilistic (like that of Thersites). If his speeches are full of bawdry, they are equally full of theology; there seems to be an intimate connection (and not only in this play)[2] between the theological view of man as a fallen creature,

As we are ourselves, what things are we!

and an uninhibited revelling in the sordidness of his fallen state. Few speeches by the clown are without this theological frankness,

1. The word "parody", Dr H. F. Brooks points out to me, may convey to the reader the implication of "farce which degrades the thing it talks about", but the comic treatment of serious subjects was not considered necessarily degrading in either the Middle Ages (e.g. in the Mystery Plays) or the Renaissance (see S. L. Bethell, *Shakespeare and the Popular Dramatic Tradition*). The great popularity of the device no doubt reflects human pleasure in the variousness of experience, and so long as the centrality of one plane of experience is clear, the variety can only enhance its significance (as in Towneley *Secunda Pastorum*, or Marlowe's *Faustus*); but where, as in *All's Well*, the play is searching for a central point of view, the addition of parallel perspectives can only have a critical and even disintegrating effect.

2. The modern association of piety with primness should not make us forget the medieval tradition of religious grotesque, of which (as H. F. Brooks points out) the treatment of the Seven Deadly Sins is the best-known example. The uninhibited descriptions of vice in the sermons and theological controversies of Shakespeare's own day (e.g. in Harsnett or Stubbs or "Martin Marprelate") shows the continuing force of the tradition. We find it not only in Lavatch but also in the Fool in *Lear* and (modified of course to fit in with the pagan background) in Apemantus.

which cannot, in its context, be dismissed as merely cynical. It is notable that among other characters the frailty of man is no less unequivocally allowed, though with them (as Fripp remarks) "the dark clouds of death and bereavement, sickness and anxiety, folly and vice, are illumined by *Faith*. The King, the Countess, Lafeu, the brother Lords, Diana, and above all Helena, are unaffectedly pious"[1] (citing I. i. 64–6; I. iii. 248 f.; II. i. 159; II. iii. 6; IV. ii. 23–9; IV. iii. 18–20). This piety is not confined to explicit comment, nor can it be regarded as something imposed arbitrarily from outside the action. Helena is on one level at least (like Isabella) a minister of Grace "and in her definitive subjection of Bertram she is setting his foot on the path of Christian virtue".[2]

The gnomic and generalizing tendency is reflected in the character of the verse; this is one reason why disintegrators have been so busy with it, for Shakespeare's gnomic style is not generally acceptable today. There is in the verse a continual effort at explicit generalization of the situations which arise and a consequent distortion of the atmosphere of folk-tale.[3]

(b) Themes and Interests

The complexities of this play appear no less in the inner world of its images and interests than in its structure and composition. We find Shakespeare viewing his material in terms of certain distinctions repeatedly displayed and referred to, which indicate an extreme subtlety and delicacy of approach. One of the most important of these distinctions is that of youth and age. In Paris and Rossillion we are in an old folk's world—however gracious—settled, confining, backward-looking to the courtesy and generosity of the dead and departed.[4] The play opens with bereavement, and the sense that we are in a world of shrunken virtue is strong throughout. The moral frailty of the young is specifically associated with the new scientific naturalism which was in Shakespeare's own day[5] replacing the older obedience to supernatural sanctions:

> to make modern and familiar, things supernatural and causeless . . . ensconcing ourselves into seeming knowledge when we should submit ourselves to an unknown fear.   (II. iii. 2–6)

1. E. I. Fripp, 'Shakespeare's Herb of Grace', *Modern Churchman*, XX (1930–1), p. 149.
2. Clifford Leech, art. cit.   3. See below on "Verse".
4. Van Doren states this in an extreme form: "The atmosphere at Rousillon is one of darkness, old age, disease, sadness and death" (*Shakespeare* (1939), p. 211).
5. See Theodore Spencer, *Shakespeare and the Nature of Man* (1942) and Hiram Haydn, *The Counter-Renaissance* (1950).

The magic of Helena is clearly associated with this elder age, but she herself must make her way in the new world of social mobility and opportunism; there is no suggestion that the difficulties of youth can be circumvented, but there is a hint that they can be lived through and their lessons learned. The wisdom of the King, the Countess, and Lafew shows in their tolerance and mellow grace. To present any of these characters (even Lafew) as bumbling comics[1] is to mistake their function; their geniality springs from their humbled wisdom—the knowledge that Parolles is right (for once) when he says

There's place and means for every man alive. (IV. iii. 328)

But even tolerance cannot save the old from desertion and repudiation by the young. Helena, no less than Bertram, has to forget her father and abandon her foster-mother the Countess, as he has to abandon his mother and his foster-father the King. Against France, the ailing kingdom of feudal *courtoisie*, is set Italy, the Renaissance land of opportunity, of opportunities which are ethically dubious it cannot be denied, but where the young can contrive a new relationship by a more naked and unprotected strife than is possible in France, developing their own powers at their own pace, unforced by other people's standards and expectations.

To Italy, in consequence, the action shifts for the vital conflicts of the second half, and only returns to France for the knitting up of the new relationships. There *is* a point where youth and age can meet and marry their different capacities, but the wisdom of age cannot create this point; it can only stand back and endure the coltish but "natural rebellion" of adolescence:

Let me not live . . . to be the snuff
Of younger spirits, whose apprehensive senses
All but new things disdain; whose judgments are
Mere fathers of their garments; whose constancies
Expire before their fashions.   (I. ii. 58–63)

Helena, with all the forces of the elder world massed behind her, cannot achieve more than the limited success of her nominal marriage to Bertram; the point of reconciliation is only reached by self-sacrifice, by an acceptance of oneself as outcast and despised; this acceptance of death, leading to fuller life, is something that Helena, the Countess, the King, Parolles, Diana all have to face in turn; that the pattern is not fully achieved for Bertram is the major

1. As was done at the Old Vic production of 1953–4, on which, however, cf. Richard David in *Shakespeare Survey 8* (1955).

thematic failure of the play. It is this dying into life which in the end redeems the new in the sight of the old, and gives continuing life to the essential perceptions of the old order.

This may be seen as a foreshadow of the world of the last plays. There youth redeems age; here youth has enough to do to find its own diminished world. Yet, as the play insists from its opening words:

> In delivering my son from me, I bury a second husband,

the processes of birth and death are natural complements and cannot be regarded as merely in conflict; "the getting of children" is "the loss of men" as the Clown puts it. The living have to fight their way out of the gracious decline which surrounds them, and the end of the play takes up the final emergence of life out of death as the culmination of the action:

> Dead though she be she feels her young one kick.
> So there's my riddle: one that's dead is quick.
>
> (v. iii. 296 f.)

No less important than such contrasts is a series of intellectual dilemmas which seem to be occupying the author's mind as he writes the play, and which colour both language and character-presentation, problems not derived from the source but imposed upon it. These resemble the *dubbii* of the Italian Renaissance; they appear in the first place as problems of manners, but Shakespeare strengthens and deepens them by suggesting their metaphysical and emotional implications. I wish to refer in particular to two problems: (i) Is disparity of rank an impediment in marriage with a virtuous person?[1] (ii) How can a virgin actively pursue a matter of love without incurring dishonour?

1. This has already been discussed, from a slightly different angle, in M. C. Bradbrook, 'Virtue is the True Nobility', *R.E.S.* (New Series), 1 (1950), 289–301. The conflict between Virtue and Nobility is a very old one (see *J.E.G.P.*, xxiv (1925), 102–24 for G. McVogt's list of commonplaces on the subject) and appears again and again in the extensive courtesy literature of Shakespeare's time—see Ruth Kelso, *Doctrine of the English Gentleman* (1929), and J. E. Mason, *Gentlefolk in the Making* (1935) for surveys of the field. On the specific question of marriage with Nobility see question iii in Boccaccio's *Filocolo* (translated into English by H. G. in 1566)—where the choice is really between wisdom and valiancy—and Edmund Tilney's *Discourse of Duties in Marriage* (1568), sig. B2ᵛ–3ᵛ: "Why then for lack of substance, shall a vertuous wife be repelled, or for want of welth, wisedome be rejected. . . For where vertue aboundeth, all good things doe flowe". A woman's choice of a virtuous husband instead of a noble one is frequently dramatized, e.g. in Medwall's *Fulgens and Lucres*, in *Wily Beguild*, in *Mucedorus* (the most popular play of the whole period), in Webster's *The Dutchess of Malfy*, and elsewhere—the preference of a scholar to a nobleman is a natural theme in Humanist literature. Given the social

(i) Certain antitheses, presented again and again in the early part of the play, indicate that the dramatist sees his action in terms of certain fixed ideas. Bertram and Helena, the two principals, are parallel figures, both being orphans and wards, so that a comparison between them is natural; what indicates the bias of the author's mind is the angle from which this comparison is conducted. Of Helena we learn

> I have those hopes of her good that her education promises her dispositions she inherits—which makes fair gifts fairer . . . she derives her honesty and achieves her goodness. (I. i. 36–42)

i.e. the stock ("inheritance")has been fructified by education and has produced virtue. Bertram, on the other hand, has the nobility of his inheritance stressed throughout the first two scenes *at the expense of* his achievement; "shape", "birthright", and "face" are contrasted with "manners", "goodness", and "moral parts" in such a way as to suggest a real gap between them, and later this failure to improve inheritance into virtue emerges clearly in the action, and is stated unequivocally:

> my son corrupts a well-derived nature (III. ii. 88).

The antithesis between these two in terms of inheritance and achievement is underlined by the handling of the relationship between Helena and the Countess:

> 'Tis often seen
> Adoption strives with nature, and choice breeds
> A native slip to us from foreign seeds. (I. iii. 139–41)

The claim to "honour" by inheritance is weak throughout, for virtue "achieves" its own ancestry as vice defaces its origins:

> But I do wash his name out of my blood
> And thou art all my child. (III. ii. 67 f.)

Honour may be seen as the natural reward for virtue:

> Whose aged honour cites a virtuous youth (I. iii. 205)

or (as very commonly by Shakespeare's contemporaries) as a royal reward for important services.

These terms or axes within which the progress of the play may be plotted are made most explicit in the great speech on honour which the king delivers *ex cathedra* in II. iii. In this, the antithesis of inheri-

---

expectation that men propose but women dispose it is not surprising that the theme is seldom presented as in *All's Well*, where it is the man who has the choice, between a virtuous wife and (potentially at least) a noble one.

tance and achievement, honour and virtue, is extended by association with the dilemma most persistent in Shakespeare—that of
appearance and reality: "virtue" is a reality to which, in its
external and social aspect, we give the "name" and "additions" of
honour. "Name" is what a noble father hands down to his son, but
name is not reality and may be expunged. This contrast between
name and reality is, of course, writ large in the name and character
of Parolles, and is most elaborately dealt with in the painful discovery of his "truth" (see especially IV. iii. 145 ff.) in Act IV—
where we see the resplendent "bubble" of words shrink to its
infinitesimal though honest reality: "even the thing I am". Bertram, however, as he comes under the sway of Parolles also becomes
the victim of words estranged from reality, as Diana points out:

> 'Tis not the many oaths that makes the truth,
> But the plain single vow that is vow'd true.   (IV. ii. 21 f.)

and he is defeated by the very confusion between appearance and
reality that he himself has built up, by

> wicked meaning in a lawful deed,
> And lawful meaning in a lawful act   (III. vii. 45 f.).

Words only acquire sanction when they are backed by actions or at
least by faith in their meaning. Helena's promise to cure the king
involves genuine risk and sacrifice; for the real commerce of the
virtuous is at the level of action:

> If thou proceed
> As high as word, my deed shall match thy deed (II. i. 208 f.).

Bertram's promise to marry Diana is based on nothing but words,
and his unmasking in V. iii, no less than Parolles' in IV. iii, is a
stripping away of the screen of words with which he, no less than
Parolles, has concealed himself from his own deeds (see especially
V. iii. 179–85).

The superiority of virtue to honour as of realities to names is a
point the play makes without qualification,[1] but the simple contrast
of Helena and Bertram as virtue-without-honour and honour-
without-virtue[2] leading up to the climactic speech in II. iii is not

---

1. It may be thought that there is something to be said on the other side, in-
sofar as Bertram's immature nature (unimproved by art) is unfairly forced by
Helena and the King into responsibilities for which he is not yet prepared—thus
he is married off without ever having "had his fling". Nature may truly be said
to be violated if forced to produce fruit before time has matured it—but this
point does not receive any clear emphasis in *All's Well*.

2. Or "ungentle gentle" and "gentle ungentle" as *The Institution of a Gentleman* (1555) puts it.

continued beyond this point. In the second half of the play the treatment of these concepts seems to alter. "Honour" is something Bertram not only assumes but actually achieves in Florence, though at the same time we are shown a new antithesis—that to "honesty"—and the complementary meaning of the word "honour", as in

> the honour of a maid is her name, and no legacy is so rich as honesty. (III. v. 12 f.)

The two "honours" are brought face to face most obviously in Diana's request for the ring which is the external sign of Bertram's family honour, as her virginity is the seal of *her* family honour, and the exchange which takes place indicates the extent to which they are interdependent. Diana's honour can only be bought by Bertram's dishonour, who

> in this action contrives against his own nobility, in his proper stream o'erflows himself. (IV. iii. 23 f.)

For all his military prowess, Bertram's honour cannot be complete till Helena reveals that this complementary dishonour is not real; by saving the ring she can be said, in a symbolic sense at least, to save family honour, and by revealing the role she has played she restores meaning to the words that Bertram has sworn.

(ii) On the other side, the history of Helena shows virtue seeking a name and not knowing how to acquire it. We see Helena frustrated by lack of name:

> If she be
> All that is virtuous, save what thou dislik'st—
> A poor physician's daughter—thou dislik'st
> Of virtue for the name. (II. iii. 121-4)

We also see her defeated by mere name—Parolles. Virtue, the royal fiat, signs of heaven's favour—these are insufficient: that which is sought is not found. The search for a means by which a woman's virtue can become effective in society is obviously another of the major themes of the play.

Early in I. i we find a long dialogue on the use of virginity which has puzzled commentators.[1] It is Helena who sets the pace and

---

1. The usual explanation is that the passage is an interpolation or relic of an old play (cf. on "Text" above). Tillyard (*Problem Plays*, pp. 98 f.) has defended its genuineness on stylistic grounds and compares *R 3*, I. iv (on conscience), *I H 4*, v. i (on honour). H. F. Brooks compares also *John*, II. i (on commodity). In each case a witty paradox is presented, praising what is normally dispraised or dispraising what is normally praised, and the manner adopted is rather like that of the formal Paradox—as in Lando, Munday, Donne, etc.

tone of this, so that Shakespeare obviously intends it to represent an interest germane to *her* situation. Notice, too, that the dialogue separates two soliloquies, one full of doubt and despair, the other inspired by determination to win; something has happened to Helena's mind in the interval between them; one would expect the dialogue to refer to this movement of opinion. I think it does refer to it, as a free and frothy play upon the ideas which are fermenting beneath it in Helena's (or rather Shakespeare's) mind, and the topic it turns upon—the use of virginity, and the manner in which it can be laid out to best advantage—is obviously germane to the situation of a virgin yearning for honest marriage to a young nobleman.

Certainly Shakespeare does not fail to involve Helena's virgin state in the episode in which she cures the king; it is as an attractive young virgin that she is introduced to him:

> I am Cressid's uncle
> That dare leave two together.   (II. i. 96 f.)

and it is the loss of maiden-status that she stakes against the king's recovery. It is not, however, merely the sexual aspect of virginity that Shakespeare is emphasizing here; the traditional association of virginity with magic power and priesthood is also involved in the priestess-like incantations for the recovery; and there is no sense that there is a discontinuity between the two aspects. Later in the play the idea of dedicated virginity gives way to that of natural fertility, and here again there is a strong sense, throughout the treatment of Helena, of essential connection with Divine Grace (an idea taken up and developed in the last plays); Helena claims Bertram eventually not only by virtue of the symbolic ring but also by virtue of the child within her.

We may say that it is by the judicious and, as far as the play goes, uncriticized use of her virginity that Helena is enabled to choose the husband of her desire; the achievement of a husband in name is, however, as we have noted above, only the watershed of the play, at which the ideas begin to change their direction. Virginity has to be used in other ways before the final reconciliation can be achieved. A pointer to the later ideas about the "use of virginity" may be found in a curious passage in which Helena appeals to the countess:

> but if yourself
> Whose aged honour cites a virtuous youth,
> Did ever, in so true a flame of liking,
> Wish chastely and love dearly, that your Dian
> Was both herself and love ...   (I. iii. 204–8)

where the combination of Dian and love points to the later combination of Diana and Helena (in itself the heroine's name is almost a synonym for "love"). To be chaste and yet adventure in love, to risk all for love in a way of penance and privation, to "embrace" Death instead of Bertram—these are to be the sacrifices that the use of virginity imposes on Helena; but in the sacrifice lies the achievement. The final use of her virginity is the purchase of honour not only for herself, but also, as a ransom, for her husband.

In the development of both these themes the idea of Nature, accepted and yet transformed by "labouring art" into a power capable of subduing Fortune (to use the standard Renaissance antithesis), is important; here is relevant the recurrent star-imagery of the play—to which Caroline Spurgeon has pointed[1]—for the stars are seen throughout as the representatives of a fate which must be yielded to at first, but which can, after judicious yielding, be moulded to the will, and so overcome.

The words "virtue", "honour", "nature", "fortune", and their derivatives, appear continually in the play; more important than mere recurrence, however, is the variety of meaning that is wrung out of them: "virtue" is military *virtus*, the achievement of a virtuoso, chastity, as well as moral perfection; "honour" is military fame, it is blue blood, it is chastity, it is civil reputation; "fortune" is the governor of social distinction no less than of individual fate; "nature" is the author of love as well as the destroyer of virginity, the preserver of social order as well as the prompter of revolt.

The importance of these terms and of the ideas based on them is inherent in the text; they belong to Shakespeare's conception as clearly as the story he chose, and they show how far from simple was the perspective in which he viewed the simple materials out of which he made his play.

II. PROBLEMS OF THE PLAY

Enough elements have probably been collected now to indicate the main kinds of difficulty which impede total interpretations of our play. Lawrence's basic interpretation of the play in terms of plot-material is just and cannot be ignored, but other elements, though to some extent they confirm his interpretation, in other ways complicate it out of recognition. Critical realism accompanies fairy-tale, satire shadows spirituality, complex moral perceptions deny us a simplicity of approach, complex intellectual interests demand an analytical and detached attitude to the characters.

1. *Shakespeare's Imagery* (1935).

I wish to examine now some of the traditional "problems" of the play—the bed-trick, and the characters of Bertram, Parolles, and Helena—to see how far standard critical interpretations of these involve a coalescence of the elements described, and how far interpretation has been obliged to omit or discount in its attempts to produce unity.

(a) The Bed-trick

The trick of substituting one bride for another is entirely derivative in this play: it is an essential part of the *novella* of Boccaccio and (as Lawrence has shown) is a common feature of folk-tales dealing with "the clever wench" and "the fulfilment of the tasks". But the play contains more elements, levels, stimuli, than any folk-tale would, and some of these would seem to explain and even justify the critical execration which the bed-trick calls forth here. The psychological reality of Helena and the realism of the background make the facile substitution of one body for another seem irrelevant and tasteless, while the satiric stratum of the play seems to underline those elements in the trick which modern moral criticism finds abhorrent. The Christian and gnomic overtones of the play again seem to raise issues which cannot easily be resolved by plot-manipulation—unless there is an understanding that plot-movements stand for spiritual developments. Usually scholars have not seen this distaste, however, as requiring any solvent as extreme as symbolism, and most have invoked the undoubted difference of manners between modern "reality" and Elizabethan. There was little sense among Shakespeare's contemporaries that this was a degrading and unsatisfactory way of getting a husband, either in real life or on the stage. No doubt an age which saw matrimony as a matter of social convenience rather than personal emotion accepted such means of obtaining a husband or wife as a smaller violation of the spirit of marriage than we can today. Fripp[1] gives a reference to Francis Osborne's *Memoires* and here we seem to find a roughly contemporary attitude to the same trick in real life. Osborne writes of

> . . . the last great *Earle of Oxford*, whose *Lady* was brought to his bed under the notion of his *Mistris*, and from such a virtuous deceit she [sc. Pembroke's wife] is said to proceed
>
> (1658 ed., p. 79)

This is a close parallel from the court-life of Shakespeare's time, and it shows only moral admiration for the trick.[2] In the literature

1. *Shakespeare Man and Artist* (1938), ii, 601.
2. H. F. Brooks cites a distant but not uninstructive parallel in the assumption

of the time the trick is, of course, very common. R. S. Forsythe's *The Relations of Shirley's Plays to the Elizabethan Drama* (1914) cites twenty-one plays of the period in which the trick is used; but as one reads through the list of plays there cited one comes to realize that the reasons for offence given above do not occur outside Shakespeare, ıor nowhere else are the emotions of the people involved made so real to us. It is obvious that the trick is not one that would, *ipso facto*, shock an Elizabethan, but we cannot lose the existing facts of the text to conciliate an imaginary Elizabethan, and the fact is that elements in this play fight strongly against any facile acceptance of the bed-trick.[1]

(b) Bertram

The problem of Bertram's role in the play involves much the same bifurcation of evidence. The plot requires him to be high-spirited, but faulty, rash and hasty, but admirable; Shakespeare, however, complicates our reaction to youthful impetuosity by considering it in the whole context of youth versus age, and by dwelling with moral weight on his flaws as typical of fallen humanity:

> The web of our life is of a mingled yarn, good and ill together.
> (IV. iii. 68 f.)

he makes us less willing to accept them as flashes of excessive spirit.

Again, it is possible to point out many historical accidents which impede modern understanding of the role. Time has diminished the respect we feel for blue blood as a good in itself, and has dimmed also our sense of soldiership as involving "virtue" in its original meaning:

> valour is the chiefest virtue and
> Most dignifies the haver; (*Cor.*, II. ii. 82–3)

The critic who remarked, "His bravery is only that of a lower animal, a bulldog, a fighting cock"[2] was obviously failing to make this historical allowance. Another factor that is often overlooked is Bertram's age, again perhaps because we think of maturity in different terms from our Elizabethan predecessors.[3] We might sup-

---

that a man made an "honest woman" of the girl he had seduced once he married her. Behind the assumption that this is right and desirable lies something of the same disregard of personal compatibility as troubles us in the bed-trick.

1. Cf. Leech, art. cit.

2. J G. A. Dow, 'Notes on *All's Well*', *New Shakespeare Society Transactions 1881*, p. 240.

3. Essex, for example, distinguished himself at Zutphen when he was nineteen, and was Master of the Horse to Queen Elizabeth when he was twenty. The careers of contemporary Italians were even more precocious.

pose that his military prowess and independence argued maturity of mind, but we find that he is treated without much respect at home, and if we collect the references to him in the play we notice that he is most often a "boy"—a "rude boy", a "proud scornful boy", a "lascivious boy", a "rash and unbridled boy", an "unbaked and doughy youth"—his faults remain those of immaturity. Even his defiance of the king is ascribed to nothing worse than "youth and ignorance". Together with this sense of immaturity goes a sense that he may develop into something better. The king remarks

> Thy father's moral parts
> Mayest thou inherit too!   (I. ii. 21 f.)

as though morality was something possible in the future, but which could hardly be expected in the present. Tillyard has recently remarked that the growth of the hero (and moral perception is surely the major part of any such growth) is a common feature of the problem plays.

The problem of Bertram's immaturity is illumined by a comparison with another of Shakespeare's immature orphan heroes—Coriolanus. In both we see the same petulant wilfulness coupled to military prowess, the same scorn for unaristocratic virtues, and the same sense of duty to a noble mother; but the very similarity of these characteristics only underlines the different treatment they are given. Coriolanus' unbalance of nature is seen as part of a personal tragedy in which psychological weaknesses are a cause and explanation of the political and moral chaos. The whole play hinges upon the personality of Coriolanus, and the intellectual and moral interests it raises, as well as the interest of the other characters presented, relate back to this fulcrum. Bertram, however, is enmeshed in a different kind of play; he is not the central character; he illustrates ideas and tendencies that the play develops elsewhere and in other (sometimes more striking) ways. No character in *All's Well* bulks as large as Coriolanus, for the view of life our play presents shows characters as changing, developing, striving within a framework of values too large and shadowy and complex to be distilled into any individual personality. In such a context Bertram cannot be given the psychological depth of Coriolanus; what he is given is an extremely realistic surface, and at the level of Jonsonian caricature he is a brilliant success.

The Jonsonian method is, however, more suited to the exposure of follies than to the creation of sympathies. The noble part of his nature, which the plot demands, lacks emphasis; as he is shown, he is hounded into happiness, and the Achillean stubbornness of the soldier is melted into mere slipperiness. A historical understanding of Bertram in an Elizabethan context cannot remove the failure of technique that a total view of the play reveals. As the representative of "honour" in the thematic aspect of the play, tempted, falling, and saved, he is possible; as the realistic picture of the "unlicked" Renaissance nobleman he is credible; but when the moral dimension of natural man choosing Sin but saved by Grace is added, and the different kind of reality in Helena is juxtaposed against him, the superstructure of meaning becomes too heavy for the basis of character and the whole topples dangerously near incoherence, and virtually separates out into its constituent elements.

(c) Parolles

Legouis has suggested that Parolles is the real failure of the play, and that all would have ended better if Bertram's vices had been more adequately attributed to the influence of this "counterfeit module". Here again historical criticism intervenes and suggests that Parolles is not such a failure in Elizabethan terms as he appears in ours. Some confirmation of this is found in one of the few bits of royal criticism handed down—the words "Monsieur Parolles" written against the title of our play in the "catalogue" of Charles I's copy of the second folio now preserved in Windsor Castle. Charles's view that Parolles is the central attraction of *All's Well* (and that Malvolio is the central attraction of *Twelfth Night*) is not unreasonable; such theatrical success as the play has enjoyed has largely depended on Parolles; he is drawn with considerable care and his role as tempter is worked out in detail. Too often he is regarded as a watered-down Falstaff, but, as Krapp points out,[1] he is not essentially a *miles gloriosus* (in many ways he is nearer to the classical parasite).[2] The "words" which give him his name and his success are not so much boastful words (though he does use these) but rather words of the newest cut; the latest slang, the latest fashionable attitudes, the latest clothes are Parolles' stock-in-trade. He is

1. G. P. Krapp, 'Parolles', *Shakesperian Studies*, ed. J. B. Matthews and A. H. Thorndike (1916), pp. 291–300.

2. H. B. Charlton in his *Shakespearian Comedy* (1938) has made an extensive comparison of Parolles with Falstaff and considers that in many respects he is a similar figure, only seen from a different standpoint, that of an antipathetic, unhedonistic morality. The very fact that Parolles is consistently censured in the play makes his exploits very different. His ebullience is nervous; he does not really believe in himself. The lines that Charlton quotes (IV. i. 37–9) only show what Parolles would like to be able to carry off; what he does achieve is rather different, something more like Lucio or Thersites—a guttersnipe eloquence in detraction.

(like Osric) appearance without reality, in any of the roles in which he appears, a nut without a kernel, a word without a meaning.

Parolles is constructed elaborately, but modern readers are liable to miss this elaboration for it belongs to a genre that we associate with Jonson rather than Shakespeare. He is built round an idea by a series of images and attitudes which are constant and make their effect by their consistency and accumulation. The very first mention we hear of him sets the key-note:

> Yet these fix'd evils sit so fit in him
> That they take place when virtue's steely bones
> Looks bleak i' th' cold wind.   (I. i. 100–102)

Parolles is the "superfluous" man that Lear inveighs against: the clothes-imagery is a constant means in Shakespeare (as in Swift and Carlyle) of expressing appearance without reality, and here no doubt was emphasized by a theatrical appearance that showed him to be a "nut" in the modern sense. This and the lexical absurdity of his speech build up to a Jonsonian excess and a Jonsonian deflation in the cruel horseplay of IV. iii. There is no temptation to feel for Parolles here, as we do for example for Falstaff or Shylock, a sense that Fate has been unjust, for there is no psychological depth to his follies; the follies *are* the character. Even the "simply the thing I am shall make me live" speech appears as a further access of meaning granted to a Morality figure, not as a revelation of life that makes us revalue all that has gone before.

To see the Jonsonian success of Parolles is not, however, to make him fit into this play; in particular it does not enable us to balance him against the different kind of reality that we see in Helena.

(d) Helena

To fit Helena into the play or adapt the play to Helena is obviously the central problem of interpretation in *All's Well*. Here we can see a distinction, largely historical, between those who have preferred the first of these alternatives and those who have preferred the second. The nineteenth-century critics, following Coleridge's "loveliest creation" and Mrs Jameson's "the beauty of the character is made to triumph over all", concentrate on the effect of Helena as an individual and strive to see the rest of the play as a "vehicle" for her personality. This, for example, was the avowed view of Karl Elze who in his essay on *All's Well* (1872, translated 1874) sees Helena as the starting-point and heart of the drama, and the other features as derived from Shakespeare's primary interest in her: "What was it that tempted him to dramatize it [sc. "Giletta of Narbonne"]? It was evidently only the character

of Giletta".[1] Herford, in his introduction to the Eversley edition
(1899) takes a similarly central view of Helena, but (with the
clouding of romanticism)[2] sees her nobility as flawed by "something fundamentally irrational in the nature of love itself". E. K.
Chambers (1908) takes this still further; he sees Helena's development as a degradation of nobility: "the meanness [sc. of the bed-
trick] . . . is a measure of the spiritual straits to which the instinct of
sex has reduced the noblest of women."[3] It would seem fairly obvious that this is carrying the "problem" of Helena too far; the
attempt to explain the play in terms of the heroine's personality has
produced only a theory which distorts both play and personality.

More modern criticism (or rather scholarship) has tended to
react to an opposite extreme, and, viewing Helena as the "clever
wench" of a "simple" folk-tale, has been liable to sacrifice the personality to the plot; this may produce over-emphasis as gross as
Chambers':

> The only "problem" in it [sc. *All's Well*] is Helena's problem of
> getting the man she wants for a husband. There is nothing
> gloomy or bitter either about the problem or about its solution.
> It is a problem in wit, not in manners or morals. The clue to it
> is in Boccaccio's heading to the tales of the third day . . . "dis-
> course is had of the fortune of such as have painfully acquired
> some much-coveted thing, or, having lost, have recovered it."[4]

This seems to me a comment on an abstract of the plot, but not
on the play as we have it; there may be nothing bitter about the
problem, but there is plenty bitter about the play. To ignore the
context in which the bed-trick is presented, the parallel with
Parolles, the Clown's comments and parodies—the various elements pointed out by Professor Leech[5]—is to ignore the pervasive
atmosphere of the play. Helena is undoubtedly, in some ways, a
fairy-tale heroine, with a background of spiritual or magical power,
but neither the atmosphere of France or Florence nor the poetic
tone of her most effective speeches (for instance I. iii. 186 ff.) allows
the emphasis to rest here. Her role is a complex one, but there is an
absence of adequate external correlatives to justify this complexity;
we are drawn to regard her as an isolated complex individual—
Shakespeare's "loveliest heroine" in his unloveliest comedy—and

---

1. *Essays on Shakespeare*, p. 122.

2. Cf. however, G. B. Shaw writing in 1895: ". . . the sustained transport of
exquisite tenderness and impulsive courage which makes poetry the natural
speech of Helena" (*Our Theatres in the Nineties*, I, 30).

3. "Red Letter Shakespeare" edn, p. 13, rept. in *Shakespeare, A Survey* (1925),
p. 207.

4. Madeleine Doran, *Endeavours of Art* (1954), p. 251.   5. Art. cit.

the consequent disproportion throws the play out of gear, as the Romantic view of Shylock throws *The Merchant of Venice* out of gear. We are drawn to see the psychological probability of a noble infatuation (shades of Dorothea Casaubon!) in a way which explains, if it does not justify, Chambers' anachronisms.

To reconcile the different levels of reality we can see in Helena, in Bertram and Parolles, in Countess, King, and Lafew is perhaps impossible without too great a sacrifice of all that is worthwhile in the play. It is possible, however, to notice that this problem is one that is not confined to *All's Well*. The specific problem of reconciling a simple magical heroine derived from the source with a realistic background reappears not only in the equally vexed figure of Isabella, but also, more helpfully, in Marina in *Pericles* and in the last plays in general. Traversi remarks of Marina in the brothel scenes:

> Her motives . . . are inflexibly simple, self-consistent, and therefore, in terms of the dramatic objectivity with which Boult, Pandar and their like are presented, artistically incompatible. The fault lies in the attempt to adapt the realism of Shakespeare's earlier manner to symbolic purposes still in the process of elaboration.[1]

The relation of the inflexibly simple and self-consistent actions of Helena to the dramatic objectivity of Bertram and Parolles, and indeed to much of her own plot-material (e.g. the bargaining with the widow) has just this flaw. Whether the reason Traversi gives for the fault can be adapted to serve for *All's Well* is a problem whose consideration must be postponed. Certainly, if we compare the use of Trinculo or Autolycus and consider the relation of their realism to the fairy-tale princesses of their plays we can see a direction of advance, which achieves a reconciliation of the jarring elements of *All's Well* by presenting them in a new poetic dimension.

III. THE UNITY OF THE PLAY

All the problems of interpretation discussed here seem to spring from the same disunity between different aspects of the play (discussed in the first part of this Introduction): interpretations of single characters fail to convince because other aspects demand different treatment. Moreover, they elicit responses in which scholars and critics are opposed to one another, throughout the entire series. The scholars can point to good reasons why modern responses are untrustworthy and can make out a good case for the

1. *Shakespeare: the last phase* (1954), p. 33. The same general approach to the last plays had appeared earlier in Tillyard, *Shakespeare's Last Plays* (1938).

play's unity and normality as an Elizabethan pot-boiler. But is the game worth the candle? "Do we not feel," the critics may justly reply, "a power and a spirit in the play very different from that of *The Honest Whore* or *The Wedding*?" The critics can point to the "facts" of powerfully realized moral commentary and searching analysis which can hardly be accidental (since they are absent from the source, and reappear in *Measure for Measure*) and to instances of that sense of being involved in a universal experience, which cuts off Shakespeare from his lesser contemporaries.[1] But even so, they are left with a series of unco-ordinated impressions of power and the apparent alternatives of fitting these "facts" to a modern and anachronistic framework or ignoring them, pushing them outside the reduced unity of a pot-boiler.

One important attempt to unify critical perceptions has been made in this century and should be mentioned here. *All's Well* has been seen (together with *Measure for Measure* and *Troilus and Cressida*) as a play whose unity is different from that of either comedies or tragedies, and whose aim is to discuss or expose the problems it raises rather than to lead them to a conclusion. But the genus "problem-play" does not seem to have been satisfactorily defined. The person who first applied the term to Shakespeare— F. S. Boas[2]—obviously had the analogy of plays like some of Ibsen's and Shaw's in mind and the analogy of their sociological drama has continued to affect the idea. But none of Shakespeare's plays are problem plays in the sense in which *The Doll's House* or *Mrs Warren's Profession* are—plays in which problems and iniquities of contemporary society are exposed and the dilemmas of human beings oppressed and (to some extent) shaped by these situations discussed. The injustice that appears in Shakespeare's "problem-plays" is not social—the unfair pressure of social hypocrisy on human beings—but the injustice of life which prevents inner ideals from being realized, the same injustice that appears in all his serious plays. Professor Charlton has suggested that a Shakespearian "problem-play" is rightly so called because it "presents the problem. It does not provide the answer"[3] and he compares these plays with Shaw's *Man and Superman*, supposing that the common factor is the dominance of the artist's apprehension by an intellectual view of the human situation. But the intellectual schematism behind *Man and Superman* is quite different from the unco-ordinated intellectualism of Shakespeare's problem-plays. Helena certainly could be presented as a victim of the life-force,

1. There is an excellent treatment of this point in H. S. Wilson, 'Dramatic Emphasis in All's Well', *Huntington Library Quarterly*, xiii (1949–50), 217–40.
2. In *Shakspere and his Predecessors* (1896).　　3. *Op. cit.*, p. 245.

driven to possess the best-bodied fighting-man available; but in Shakespeare she is not. She is not seen as struggling to achieve what the twentieth century calls "personal fulfilment", but is viewed as part of a larger and vaguer search for meaning, a search on the part of the whole play for a meaning which will interrelate the various levels of experience. It is not the heroine who is unfulfilled but the play itself, which seems intellectual because it is unfulfilled, and has failed to find human terms to express its vision, leaving the rough ends of its intellectual promptings still exposed.

Alternatively, we might attempt to unify our perceptions of *All's Well* along the lines indicated for *Measure for Measure* by O. J. Campbell.[1] We might call our play a satire and consider it as a satiric onslaught on the aristocratic vices of Bertram (shadowed by Parolles). On this reading the King, the Countess, and Lafew would be essentially normative characters, Lavatch a satiric commentator, and Helena the main agent in Bertram's exposure. But too much is omitted here; Helena is not simply a satiric figure who outgrows her humours function; from the very beginning she is, as Tillyard puts it, more than "the humour of predatory monogamy". With her the detachment essential to Jonsonian comedy is not only not achieved; it is never attempted.

It is undoubtedly true that plays which discuss or expose problems can be successfully unified, but only, it would seem, if the plot (or rather, the thematic structure) dominates the characters. That Shakespeare was making some attempt to recapture the balance of the *débat* and the Morality in these plays is perhaps true.[2] The symbolic quality of many characters in the problem plays has often been remarked: Pandarus, Troilus, and Cressida were already symbolic when Shakespeare took them in hand; the duke in *Measure for Measure* has obvious symbolic overtones; in this world even the names of characters become significant as an index to function. The names in *Measure for Measure* have already been anatomized[3] and certainly many of the names in *All's Well* are suspiciously meaningful—*Parolles, Lafew* (or La Feu), *Lavatch* (or La Vache), *Diana (Fontybell)* all have obvious connection with character, and perhaps even *Helen* ought to be added to these. Yet, in spite of the traces of morality plays in these dramas, the characters are not subordinate enough to make them mere vehicles for the

1. *Shakespeare's Satire* (1943).

2. M. C. Bradbrook, 'Authority, Truth and Justice in *Measure for Measure*', *R.E.S.*, XVII (1941), 385–99; cf. D. G. James, *The Dream of Learning* (1951), p. 84.

3. M. C. Bradbrook, *R.E.S.* (1941) and R. W. Battenhouse, 'Measure for Measure and the Christian Doctrine of the Atonement', *PMLA*, LXI (1946).

problems involved (or alternatively, the ideas are not sufficiently dominant). There is a sense of solidity, an opaque humanity about Helena's desire for Bertram (as about Isabella's condemnation of Claudio) which makes the reader wish to know what the human outcome can be. To think of this play as a problem-play (or a Morality, or a satire) is not to make it a satisfactory play; the further problem always remains: "Why try to write thus?"

It is normal to explain the problem-plays in terms of Shakespeare's development. The older version of this presented the development in terms of the author's psychology: a dark lady, or middle-age, or King James caused a clouding of Shakespeare's vision. This is not widely believed today. A more modern version explains the development in terms of changing theatrical taste; the effort to keep up with the public drove Shakespeare from Comedy to History, to Tragedy, to Romance. In this view the problem-plays are not (as with the psychological school) a grim effort to write comedy while feeling tragically, but an effort to catch up with the satire of Marston, cater for a new taste in bitter bawdry. Both of these theories have plausibility, but both err by seeing the creative activity as too passive, as the plaything of forces outside its creativeness; neither allows sufficiently for the creative interplay between author and environment, the fact that the feelings of the author are a creative part of the climate of opinion in which he lives. An author records his feelings (however obliquely) but this does not mean that he is thereby debarred from speaking to his contemporaries in the mode they enjoy. Neither the view that Shakespeare was trying in *All's Well* to write a comedy like his early ones, nor the view that he was trying to be as "unhealthy" as Marston, will explain the peculiar force that invests both the idealism and the satire of this play, or indeed the dramatic perversity of many of its devices.

Another possible answer to this question, "Why so perverse?" appears when we examine in detail the most obviously perverse section of the play—the dénouement. On the face of it the action of the last scene of our play (as in *Measure for Measure*) appears a wanton elaboration of theatrical suspense. The dénouement in the source would have provided an easy and effective end to the tale that Shakespeare had conducted up to that point. Tillyard rightly emphasizes the series of hammer-blows that Bertram sustains in iv. iii. In this scene we hear of the angry letter of his mother, the estrangement of the king, the death of his virtuous wife; we see the disapproval of his comrades the two French officers, and witness the unmasking of his only supporter—Parolles. At this point, as

Tillyard says, "Bertram has achieved the utmost self-assertion of which he is capable"; and this self-assertion has led directly to his complete estrangement from all sources of love and power. When we hear that his mother's letter has changed him "al¬ost into another man" and that he now intends to return home we might think that the stage was adequately set for (what would be much nearer Boccaccio) an effective return of the repentant prodigal to the forgiveness which Helena can secure for him. But no! Shakespeare invents a labyrinthine series of accusations and lies for the last scene, protracting the reconciliation into a tedious lawsuit. Tillyard links this with the blows to Bertram's morale in IV. iii and assumes that "panic" is the explanation of Bertram's behaviour, a panic which culminates when Helena appears "now his saviour" and which then spills over into gratefulness. This, however, does not touch the central dilemma—why, when reconciliation is aimed at, Bertram is made so unpleasant. If personal reconciliation is really the end of this scene, we can only say that Shakespeare has been extraordinarily clumsy. If, as E. E. Stoll would have it: "As he squirms and lies and slanders he prolongs the dénouement and adds to the stagy excitement"[1] Shakespeare is still a poor dramatist for any performance after the first (Stoll's Shakespeare seems frequently indistinguishable from Fletcher).

That Shakespeare was not primarily interested in personal reconciliation would seem to be indicated by the virtual absence of personal, non-formal speech. But is "theatrical effect" the only alternative? The case is obviously parallel to *Measure for Measure* in which Angelo's wickedness is emphasized just before he is married off and forgiven. In both cases Shakespeare seems to aim at emphasizing the virtue of forgiveness; the greater the crime to be forgiven the greater the virtue of the person forgiving. The major victory at the end of the play is not the achievement of a husband but the ransom of wickedness by the overflowing power of mercy—and this is what the Countess forecasts:

> He cannot thrive,
> Unless her prayers, whom heaven delights to hear
> And loves to grant, reprieve him from the wrath
> Of greatest justice.   (III. iv. 26–9).

The effect described here is not clear in either *All's Well* or *Measure for Measure*, for in these plays the strand of psychological realism makes the absence of personal reconciliation seem wanton and careless; but the less equivocal parallels of *Pericles*, *Cymbeline*, and

1. E. E. Stoll, *From Shakespeare to Joyce* (1944), p. 248.

The Winter's Tale seem to show that the elaboration of dénouement may well be deliberate, for reasons other than the merely
theatrical.

There is a strong case for avoiding the traditional separation of
"problem-plays" from "romances" and considering as a group the
"later comedies"—*All's Well, Measure for Measure, Pericles, Cymbeline*, and the rest. Viewed in this context, much that seems perverse
in *All's Well* begins to fall into focus: in particular, the handling of
the dénouement shows a clear relationship to that in the other
plays. The paradoxical and judicial dénouements of *All's Well* and
Measure for Measure are less comprehensive than those of *Pericles* and
Cymbeline, and that of *All's Well* is less obviously ritualistic and less
pervaded by the sense of forgiving than any of the other three.
Nevertheless, in its symbolism (e.g. the use of the ring), in its tor-
tuousness, in its "escape into ritual", in its juxtaposition of birth
and death, in the muting of personal emotion, it clearly fore-
shadows the endings of the romances.

Much of the perversity of the dénouement disappears if we see it
as an attempt at the effects gradually mastered in the intervening
comedies, and triumphantly achieved in *The Winter's Tale*, an
attempt foiled in *All's Well* by stylistic and constructional methods
inappropriate to the genre. The same theory explains much else
that is perverse in the play. We have noticed again and again the
odd combination of attitudes in the play—its fairy-tale plot, its
realistic and satirical elements, its brooding concern with problems
of nature and nurture, innocence and action, birth and death, and
its Christian (or at least spiritual) colouring. We find the same
elements in the last plays, but there so disposed as to convey, not
stress, but the multimundity of life. There, a subtle ingenuousness
of treatment convinces us that such strange juxtapositions are
inevitable and, in a sense, proper; in *All's Well* Shakespeare's resource is too often merely to dilute his realistic technique, to stay
silent where expressive speech would be inappropriate. Thus in the
later episodes of both *All's Well* and *Measure for Measure* we find
that Shakespeare avoids (surely deliberately) the power of personal expressiveness which was his above all other authors'. No
doubt the sense of Destiny working out its purposes in human lives
would be lost if personal reconciliation were too powerfully expressed, but the mere substitution of Bertram's cryptic fustian or
Isabella's silence for the elaborate recognitions of the earlier
comedies does not remove from our minds the desire for some
expression of what is being resolved.

When we turn to *Pericles* we find that transposition to a new poetic key allows the recognition scene to be human without infringing the symbolic power of the event:

Thaisa. The King my father gave you such a ring. [*Shows a ring.*
Pericles. This, this! No more, you gods! your present kindness
    Makes my past miseries sports. You shall do well
    That on the touching of her lips I may
    Melt and no more be seen. O, come, be buried
    A second time within these arms! (*Per.*, v. iii. 40–5)

The power which will eventually harmonize the jarring elements of *All's Well* is the power of a new poetic vision. In terms of this, the substantiality and self-consciousness of Helena becomes the exalted and yet warm purity of Imogen; the all-too-true nastiness of Bertram turns into the overwrought heroic folly of Posthumus or Leontes; the vices of Parolles, stubbornly relevant and antipathetic in our play, become the irreducible and irrepressible element (Autolycus or Caliban) which is accepted because it is part of a vision in which daffodils and doxies, larks and "aunts" are all equally natural, in which (there more surely than here):

    There's place and means for every man alive.

5. THE VERSE

The characteristic verse of *All's Well* is laboured and complex, but not rich. This is not a play which is rewarding to those who look to Shakespeare for a luminous tissue of striking images. On the other hand the quality of the verse does not support the idea propounded by Lawrence and supported by Middleton Murry[1]—the idea that Shakespeare's attitude to the play was "perfunctory", that here for once he condescended to produce a pot-boiler. The verse is not "thin" in the manner of a weak or uninterested writer, but contorted, ingrown, unfunctional.

Both the maturity of the style and at the same time the failure to organize its complexity into a unified expression can be seen in a comparison of a workaday passage from an earlier play with a similarly workaday passage from *All's Well*. Here is Demetrius explaining why he changed his love from Hermia to Helena:

    But, my good lord, I wot not by what power—
    But by some power it is—my love to Hermia,
    Melted as the snow, seems to me now
    As the remembrance of an idle gaud
    Which in my childhood I did dote upon;

1. J. M. Murry, *Shakespeare* (1936), ch. xiii.

> And all the faith, the virtue of my heart,
> The object and the pleasure of mine eye,
> Is only Helena. To her, my lord,
> Was I betroth'd ere I saw Hermia.
> But, like a sickness, did I loathe this food;
> But, as in health, come to my natural taste,
> Now I do wish it, love it, long for it,
> And will for evermore be true to it.   (*MND.*, iv. i. 161–73)

Compare Bertram's explanation of a similar change of heart:

> *King.*   You remember
>   The daughter of this lord?
> *Ber.* Admiringly, my liege. At first
>   I stuck my choice upon her, ere my heart
>   Durst make too bold a herald of my tongue;
>   Where, the impression of mine eye infixing,
>   Contempt his scornful perspective did lend me,
>   Which warp'd the line of every other favour,
>   Scorn'd a fair colour or express'd it stol'n,
>   Extended or contracted all proportions
>   To a most hideous object. Thence it came
>   That she whom all men prais'd, and whom myself
>   Since I have lost, have lov'd, was in mine eye
>   The dust that did offend it.   (v. iii. 42–55)

The loosely strung together appositions and similes of the earlier passage and the easy charm of the images invoked must be set against the complex network of unvisual metaphors drawn from widely different levels of experience found in the latter. The regular flow of the repetitions (e.g. ll. 166–8, 170–2) is replaced by a telescoped, asymmetrical construction, the expression no longer being achieved by a series of easy, logical, or rather rhetorical, steps (ll. 161–5: refutation; 166–8: confirmation; 168–9: narration; 170–3: conclusion) but mainly by means of a complex of metaphors presented in one rapid involved sentence. It is easy to see that a more intense mental activity lies behind the later passage; but the intensity is not thoroughly realized in terms of dramatic rhetoric; the complexity is self-defeating. A complex relationship of objects is presented: *heart*, *eye*, and *tongue* are related to each other and to the *I* which should control them, and we are asked to imagine not only a right relation between these but also a distortion of that relation. The amount of mental energy required is out of all proportion to any dramatic illumination of the context; the images invoked remain obstinately intellectual, separate from one another, obstinately particular, do not combine to provide a difficult but genuine illumination, as often in *Hamlet*.

In *All's Well*, the rhetorically organized forward flow of the verse seen in the earlier passage is sacrificed, but no other dynamic is supplied in its place; the parallelisms in ll. 48–52 of the passage cited summon up too many disparate images to carry the reader forward. The thought seems to revolve round a number of small points, worrying at them and their implications, and a syntactical conclusion is reached without bringing any reduction in the verbal tension.

The peculiarly irritating quality in many of the couplet passages in *All's Well* (as against those in earlier plays) derives in part at least from this opposition between syntax and meaning. Take,

> It is not so with Him that all things knows
> As 'tis with us that square our guess by shows;
> But most it is presumption in us when
> The help of heaven we count the act of men.
> Dear sir, to my endeavours give consent;
> Of heaven, not me, make an experiment.
> I am not an impostor, that proclaim
> Myself against the level of mine aim,
> But know I think, and think I know most sure,
> My art is not past power, nor you past cure.   (II. i. 148–57)

There is an appearance here of neat rhetorical balance within couplets of simple construction; but the intellectual complexity of the antitheses is such that the neatness of structure is felt as cramping and frustrating: the relation between human ignorance and human presumption is too complex to be expressed satisfactorily by the trite *But most* in l. 150. The problems of knowing which are the emphatic words in the lines (e.g. *most* or *us* in l. 150), what are the exact relations of words (e.g. of the first *know* in l. 156) and of bringing into focus phrases whose rhetorical surface is deceptive (e.g. the two uses of *past* in l. 157)[1] are all part of the same failure of the couplet organization to express the thought.

Throughout *All's Well* there is an attempt to express complex thought within the limits of normal syntax and versification; in this field, as in others, we have to look to the last plays to see a solution of the problem of technique and a resolution of the stylistic tensions set up. The extremely loose parenthetical syntax employed in the last plays allows an expression of complex relationships and contradictory levels of experience without tying them to set forms; thus the relationships are suggested and implied, not pursued through labyrinthine detail. In the more relaxed style the positive[2]

---

1. Cf. II. i. 167 (free . . . freely) and IV. iii. 217.
2. Notice the extent to which definition in *All's Well* (e.g. in v. iii. 42–55

evocation of value in images of sensuous warmth and the communication of emotional drive behind the words becomes a possibility. The bare and dissonant intellectuality of search which we find in *All's Well* breaks down into something less nervous and less brittle, but richer and more satisfying; the particular references no longer (as so often in *All's Well*) move to generalities which illuminate only the particulars from which they started, but combine to evoke a world of values, sensuously apprehended though beyond the power of logic to express.

There is a general failure in *All's Well* to establish a medium in verse which will convey effectively the whole tone of the play (as is done, for example, in *Troilus and Cressida* and *Coriolanus*), but one cannot pretend that every speech is a failure or that there is no great Shakespearian poetry in the play. There are two or three great speeches (e.g., I. iii. 186 ff., II. iii. 149 ff., III. ii. 99 ff.) in which there emerges a complex and bitter music,[1] the identification and appreciation of which is probably, on one level, the last reward of a study of *All's Well that Ends Well*.

---

quoted above) is achieved by a negative process of exclusion. We learn most often and with greatest vividness what people cannot, will not, or do not wish to do.

1. See on this the excellent treatment in Professor Ellis-Fermor's 'Some functions of verbal music in drama', *Shakespeare Jahrbuch*, xc (1954), 37–48.

ALL'S WELL THAT ENDS WELL

DRAMATIS PERSONAE[1]

KING OF FRANCE.

DUKE OF FLORENCE.

BERTRAM, *Count of Rossillion.*

LAFEW, *an old lord.*

The two brothers DUMAINE,[2] *French lords, later captains serving the Duke of Florence.*

PAROLLES, *a follower of Bertram.*

A French gentleman.[3]

RYNALDO, *steward to the Countess of Rossillion.*

LAVATCH, *clown in her household.*

A page.

COUNTESS OF ROSSILLION, *mother to Bertram.*

HELENA, *an orphan protected by the countess.*

WIDOW CAPILET *of Florence.*

DIANA, *daughter to the widow.*

VIOLENTA,[4]⎫
MARIANA, ⎬ *neighbours and friends to the widow.*

Lords, Attendants, Soldiers etc., French and Florentine.

SCENE: *Rossillion; Paris; Florence; Marseilles.*

1. Dramatis Personae] First given (more or less) in Rowe[1]; not in F.
2. The two brothers Dumaine] See Introduction pp. xv ff. and iv. iii. 171 n.
3. A French gentleman] See v. i. 6 n.
4. Violenta] See iii. v. Entry n.

ALL'S WELL THAT
ENDS WELL

ACT I

SCENE I.—[*Rossillion. The Count's palace.*]

Enter young BERTRAM, *Count of Rossillion, his mother* [*the* COUNTESS], *and* HELENA, LORD LAFEW, *all in black.*

Count. In delivering my son from me, I bury a second
    husband.

Ber. And I in going, madam, weep o'er my father's death
    anew; but I must attend his majesty's command, to
    whom I am now in ward, evermore in subjection.   5

Laf. You shall find of the king a husband, madam; you,

ACT I

Scene I

Act I Scene I] *Actus primus. Scoena Prima* F.   *Rossillion. The Count's palace.*]
The Countess of Rousillon's House in France. Theobald[1]; *not in* F.   *Enter . . . mother
the Countess, and*] *Eneer . . . Mother, and* F.   1. *Count.*] *Mother.* F.   3. *Ber.*]
Ros. F (*and at 30, 32, 55; Ro. 71*).

S.D. Rossillion] the French Rousillon, "an old province of France,
separated from Spain by the Pyrenees.
Perpignan was the capital, as it is of
the modern department of Pyrénées-
Orientales, which occupies nearly the
same territory" (Rolfe). The English
form, here retained, Professor H. G.
Wright (*M.L.R.* L (1955), 47) takes to
be an Elizabethan anglicization of the
French form "Rossillon" found in
early editions of le Maçon's Boccaccio
(cf. Chatillion for Chatillon in *John*
[Folio text]) rather than an attempt at
Italian "Rossiglione" found in Boccaccio and Painter. "The County
Rossilion" was one of Charlemagne's

paladins, and is a character in Greene's
Orlando Furioso.

1–2. *In delivering . . . husband*] The
intimate connection of birth and death
is one of the leading ideas of the play.
Here, by a quibble on *delivering*, they
are juxtaposed with the sense "the
delivery of a son into the world of
responsibility is as a death to the
mother, though as a birth to the son."
See Intro., pp. xxxvii ff.

5. *in ward*] The heirs to feudal
estates, if left orphan, became the
wards of the king, who acted as guardian while they were still minors, i.e.
under twenty-one.

6. *of*] in the person of (On.).

3

sir, a father. He that so generally is at all times good
must of necessity hold his virtue to you, whose
worthiness would stir it up where it wanted, rather
than lack it where there is such abundance.   10

Count. What hope is there of his majesty's amendment?

Laf. He hath abandon'd his physicians, madam; under
whose practices he hath persecuted time with hope,
and finds no other advantage in the process but only
the losing of hope by time.   15

Count. This young gentlewoman had a father—O that
"had", how sad a passage 'tis!—whose skill was
almost as great as his honesty; had it stretch'd so far,
would have made nature immortal, and death
should have play for lack of work. Would for the   20
king's sake he were living! I think it would be the
death of the king's disease.

Laf. How call'd you the man you speak of, madam?

Count. He was famous, sir, in his profession, and it was his
great right to be so: Gerard de Narbon.   25

Laf. He was excellent indeed, madam; the king very

11. *Count.*] *Mo. F (so to 70).*

7. *generally*] most probably = to all
men.

8. *hold*] *N.S.* takes the word here
(and at I. i. 75, II. iii. 224, III. ii. 91) to
have the meaning, unique in Shakespeare, of "uphold". I do not think
that the word has the same meaning in
all four passages, nor does "uphold"
seem to be the best equivalent in any
one of them. Here, as at I. i. 75, and
II. iii. 224, I take the meaning to be
"maintain", "continue", a usage
common in Shakespeare. For III. ii. 91
see the note there.

8–10. *whose worthiness . . abundance*]
Your worth is such as will incite virtuous treatment from one who is not
good; you are not likely then to have to
forgo such treatment from the King,
who is good to all men.

10. *lack*] Theobald's emendation
"slack" has found favour with editors,
but surely F is correct, allowing that
the subject is not *He*, but *worthiness*.

12–15.] Thiselton detects a legal
metaphor here. He cites Minsheu
(1617) who explains "practice" as
"*exercitatio forensis*" and "process" as
"the manner of proceeding in every
cause", and presumes that *persecuted*
means "followed justice". It seems
more probable, however, that *practices* should be "medical treatment"
(cf. *sweet practiser* below, II. i. 184) and
persecuted time with hope mean "stretched out his days painfully in the hope of
a cure".

17. *passage*] Onions takes the meaning to be "occurrence, incident" as in
Cym., III. iv. 90, "no act of common
passage", but the idea of "having
passed away" (as in *1 H 6*, II. v. 108:
"the passage of your age") must be
present. For a similar ambiguity in
a similar context cf. *Ham.*, IV. vii.
112.

18. *honesty*] uprightness, integrity,
honour.

lately spoke of him admiringly—and mourningly;
he was skilful enough to have liv'd still, if knowledge
could be set up against mortality.

Ber. What is it, my good lord, the king languishes of?   30

Laf. A fistula, my lord.

Ber. I heard not of it before.

Laf. I would it were not notorious. Was this gentlewoman
the daughter of Gerard de Narbon?

Count. His sole child, my lord, and bequeathèd to my   35
overlooking. I have those hopes of her good that her
education promises her dispositions she inherits—
which makes fair gifts fairer; for where an unclean
mind carries virtuous qualities, there commendations go with pity; they are virtues and traitors too.   40
In her they are the better for their simpleness: she
derives her honesty and achieves her goodness.

Laf. Your commendations, madam, get from her tears.

Count. 'Tis the best brine a maiden can season her praise
in. The remembrance of her father never approaches   45

37. promises] *F;* promises; *Rowe*[3]+.

27. *admiringly—and mourningly*] won-
dering at his skill while living, and
mourning his death.

30–3.] Notice that Bertram's first
part in this conversation is a humble
question. *I would it were not notorious,*
remarks Lafew somewhat patroniz-
ingly, as if to imply "you may not have
heard of it yet, boy, but you will when
you grow up", and then returns
abruptly to his conversation with the
Countess.

31. *a fistula*] "A fistula at the present
day means an abscess external to the
rectum, but in Shakespeare's day it
was used in the more general signi-
fication for a burrowing abscess in any
situation" (Bucknill, *Medical Knowledge of Shakespeare*, p. 96).

35–6. *bequeathed to my overlooking*]
Helena is also in ward.

36–8. *that her education . . . fairer*] I retain F punctuation, against the textus
receptus. As Thiselton points out,
what makes *fair gifts* (= *dispositions*)

fairer is *education*. One must suppose a
"which" to be omitted after *dispositions*, but this is a common Shakespearian ellipsis (Abbott §244).

39. *virtuous qualities*] The antithesis
between *mind* and *virtuous qualities* is
between inherited nature and the
qualities imparted by training. *Virtuous qualities* does not mean "fine
moral qualities", but "the qualities of
a virtuoso, skill, capacity, technical
prowess". Hoby translates Castiglione's *virtuose qualità* by "vertuous
qualities" (Everyman edn, p. 72)
where the modern translator has "admirable accomplishments" (Opdyke,
p. 61).

40. *they are virtues and traitors too*] The
virtuous qualities are traitors when they
do not serve virtue (in the common
sense), but use their powers in the service of evil.

41. *their simpleness*] their being un-
mixed.

44. *season*] preserve, as in brine.

her heart but the tyranny of her sorrows takes all
livelihood from her cheek. No more of this, Helena;
go to, no more; lest it be rather thought you affect a
sorrow than to have—

Hel. I do affect a sorrow indeed, but I have it too.   50

Laf. Moderate lamentation is the right of the dead; excessive grief the enemy to the living.

Count. If the living be enemy to the grief, the excess makes
it soon mortal.

Ber. Madam, I desire your holy wishes.   55

Laf. How understand we that?

Count. Be thou bless'd, Bertram, and succeed thy father

49. have—] *F;* have it. *Warburton;* have. *Var. '73.*   53–6.] *As in F; Count.*
If . . . mortal. *Laf.* How . . . that? *Ber.* Madam . . . wishes. *conj. Theobald;*
Count. How . . . that? If . . . mortal. *Ber.* Madam . . . wishes. *N.S.*

47. *livelihood*] animation, life (On.).
On the other hand, the image of sorrow as a tyrant suggests that "main-
tenance, victuals" (*O.E.D.* 1.2) may
be the central meaning.

49. *have*—] The dash in F suggests
that Helena interrupts the Countess,
which is improbable enough, and one
is tempted to replace it by a period, as
many editors have done, giving a
harsh but not unShakespearian ellipsis. On the other hand dashes are rare
enough in F to suggest deliberate intention when they are used. At I. iii.
148 the dash seems to imply a pause in
the speech, and we may suppose that
the Countess pauses here, oppressed by
the return of her discourse to true sorrow (such as her own).

50.] Helena's riddling reply cannot
be fully understood till her soliloquy
(ll. 77 ff); she is affecting grief for her
father, but she is feeling real grief for
Bertram. As the Clarkes point out,
Helena's remarks in this scene are
consistently enigmatic, and inevitably
misunderstood by those about her.
The effect of uncertainty gradually
resolving itself into purpose seems to
be what is aimed at.

51–2.] Noble compares Ecclesiasticus, xxxviii. 17 and 20–22. Verse 17
reads: "make lamentation expedi-

ently, and be earnest in mourning, and
vse lamentation as he is worthie, and
that a day or two, lest thou bee euill
spoken of: and then comfort thy selfe,
because of heauinesse." The topic is
also commonplace in classical "conso-
lations" such as those of Seneca and
Plutarch. Cf. *Ham.*, I. ii. 89–100, *Rom.*,
III. v. 72–3. Notice again, the reference
to life emerging from death and cf.
Intro., pp. xxxvii f.

53–4.] "If the living do not indulge
grief, grief destroys itself by its own
excess" (Johnson).

55.] "Bertram abruptly checks this
tedious discussion about the grief of a
waiting-gentlewoman" (*N.S.*).

56.] The relevance of this remark is
not obvious, and various rearrangements have been proposed. Kinnear
supposes that there is a "humorous"
reference to the possibility of the
Countess's wishes being anything else
but holy, but this is a fairly desperate
explanation. Lafew may be commenting on Bertram's rude interruption of
the conversation about Helena, and
drawing the audience's attention to
this early symptom of his coltishness.
Coleridge believed that ll. 55 and 56
were spoken simultaneously.

57–60.] *and succeed . . . birthright*]
shape, blood, and *birthright* are what one

In manners as in shape! Thy blood and virtue
Contend for empire in thee, and thy goodness
Share with thy birthright! Love all, trust a few,   60
Do wrong to none. Be able for thine enemy
Rather in power than use, and keep thy friend
Under thy own life's key. Be check'd for silence,
But never tax'd for speech. What heaven more will,
That thee may furnish and my prayers pluck down,   65
Fall on thy head! Farewell. My lord,
'Tis an unseason'd courtier; good my lord,
Advise him.

Laf.   He cannot want the best
That shall attend his love.

Count. Heaven bless him! Farewell, Bertram.   [*Exit.*]   70

Ber. The best wishes that can be forg'd in your thoughts
be servants to you!
[*To Helena*] Be comfortable to my mother, your
mistress, and make much of her.

Laf. Farewell, pretty lady; you must hold the credit of   75
your father.   [*Exeunt Bertram and Lafew.*]

Hel. O, were that all! I think not on my father,
And these great tears grace his remembrance more

70. S.D. *Exit.*] *F2; not in F.*   73. S.D. *To Helena*] *N.S., conj. Nicholson;* (*71*)
Rowe[1]+ *; not in F.*   76. S.D. *Exeunt Bertram and Lafew.*] *Rowe*[1]*; not in F.*

inherits; *manners, virtue,* and *goodness*
are what one achieves.

60. *Share*] share the empire, divide
the rule.

60–6. *Love all . . . head*] The Countess's speech of farewell draws on the
traditional topics of the "advice to a
son", which stretch back at least as far
as the *ad Demonicum* of Isocrates, and
inform many examples of the genre in
Shakespeare's day, including Polonius' advice to Laertes. See *Sh. Q.,* VIII
(1957), 501–6.

67. *unseason'd*] immature (On.). We
say, "raw".

68. *the best*] It is not clear what *best*
refers to. I suggest it means "the best
things", the whole sentence meaning,
"he cannot lack the best things, if he
shows love". This would be in accord

with the rather patronizing tone
adopted towards Bertram in Lafew's
other speeches. Thiselton takes it to
mean "the best advice", but it is not
clear why *advice* should depend on *love*.

71–2.] Earlier editors took these
words to be addressed to Helena, but
Brinsley Nicholson (*apud* Thiselton) is
undoubtedly correct in thinking that
only ll. 73–4 are spoken to her. Bertram nowhere in this scene shows any
affability to Helena.

73. *comfortable*] comforting.

77. *O, were that all*] Would that the
effort not to disgrace my father were
the only effort I was involved in.

78–9. *And these . . . for him*] The antithesis turns, I think, on the distinction
between the grace given to her father's
memory by the great tears shed now,

Than those I shed for him. What was he like?
I have forgot him; my imagination   80
Carries no favour in't but Bertram's.
I am undone; there is no living, none,
If Bertram be away; 'twere all one
That I should love a bright particular star
And think to wed it, he is so above me.   85
In his bright radiance and collateral light
Must I be comforted, not in his sphere.
Th' ambition in my love thus plagues itself:
The hind that would be mated by the lion
Must die for love. 'Twas pretty, though a plague,   90
To see him every hour; to sit and draw
His arched brows, his hawking eye, his curls,
In our heart's table—heart too capable
Of every line and trick of his sweet favour.
But now he's gone, and my idolatrous fancy   95

85. me.] me: *Rowe*[1]; me *F*.   91. hour; to] hour, to *Pope;* houre to *F*.

and the (smaller) grace given by the (smaller) tears she shed when he died. Brigstocke supposed the antithesis to lie between *his* (Bertram's) remembrance and *him* (the father), but the name of Bertram has not been introduced into the speech yet, and consequently could not be understood by an audience. Cf. "biggest tears" in *Per.*, IV. iv. 26. Shakespeare may have known Martial's epigram (I. xxxiii) on a girl who weeps for her father only in public.

81. *favour*] (1) feature, face; (2) love-token.

83–4. *'twere . . . star*] Cf. Polonius to Ophelia: "Lord Hamlet is a prince out of thy star" (*Ham.*, II. ii. 140).

83–7. *'twere . . . sphere*] There appears to be some reminiscence of these lines in Aimwell's soliloquy in Shirley's *The Witty Fair One*, Act I, Scene ii.

86. *collateral*] In Ptolemaic astronomy the spheres moved "collaterally", i.e. in parallel motion. Hence, "I must be content with the parallelism of our careers, for they belong to different levels and can never come

into contact." The light of the upper spheres was visible in the lower spheres, but no other contact was possible.

89–90. *The hind . . . love*] T. W. Baldwin sees a reference to the fable of the mouse and the lion (*Small Latin*, I, 630).

90–1. *'Twas pretty . . . hour*] Cf. Boccaccio's *Tancred and Gismunda*, "it was pleasure ynoughe, to see thee every hower" (Painter, ed. Miles, I, 151). See Intro., p. xxvi.

92. *hawking*] "hawk-like, keen" (Schmidt).

93. *table*] "board or flat surface on which a picture is painted" (On.). For the conceit of the heart as a *table* cf. Sonn. XXIV, 1–2.

capable] (1) (as a heart) susceptible; (2) (as a table) easy to draw on.

94. *line and trick of his sweet favour*] the contour and characteristic expression of his dear face.

95–6. *and my . . . relics*] There is a contradiction between *idolatrous* and *sanctify;* she worships, and despises herself for it.

Must sanctify his relics. Who comes here?

Enter PAROLLES.

One that goes with him; I love him for his sake,
And yet I know him a notorious liar,
Think him a great way fool, solely a coward;
Yet these fix'd evils sit so fit in him   100
That they take place when virtue's steely bones
Looks bleak i' th' cold wind; withal, full oft we see
Cold wisdom waiting on superfluous folly.
Par. Save you, fair queen!
Hel. And you, monarch!   105
Par. No.
Hel. And no.
Par. Are you meditating on virginity?
Hel. Ay. You have some stain of soldier in you; let me ask

102. Looks] *F;* Look *Rowe*[1]+.

99. *a great . . . coward*] largely a fool, a complete coward.

101. *take place*] Different glosses have been offered for this: "take up their quarters", "find acceptance", "are received as equals in high society". The basic figure on which the passage is built is the antithesis between the *superfluous* clothes which *sit so fit* on Parolles and *take place*, and the *cold wisdom* whose *steely bones Looks bleak i' th' cold wind*. Within this framework it seems likely that the idea of social acceptance is the primary one in *take place*. See Tillyard, *Shakespeare's Problem Plays*, pp. 91–2, for an admirable critique of the poetry of this passage. See *Shakespeare Quarterly*, v (1954), 281–6 for a history of the overclothed/ underclothed antithesis which is used here to divide Parolles and Helena.

steely bones] "unyielding, uncomplying virtue" (Schmidt). Thiselton takes *steely bones* to be the same as "hard bones" as in *Euphues* (Arber, p. 297): "wasted to the harde bones".

104–60.] See Intro., pp. xli f.

104. *queen*] perhaps with a quibble on "quean".

104–5. *Save you . . . monarch*] Cf. Erasmus' colloquy "Proci et Puellae" (which has many parallels with the following debate): "Ego tibi rex ero, tu mihi regina" (*Works* (1703), 1, 696). Melbancke's *Philotimus* (1593), p. 50, translates the relevant parts of Erasmus.

105. *monarch*] There may be a reference here to "Monarcho", a crazy Italian at Queen Elizabeth's court, who is probably referred to in *LLL.*, IV. i. 92. This might explain Parolles' immediate disclaimer.

107. *And no*] I am no more a queen (or quean) than you are a monarch (or Monarcho).

109. *Ay*] Helena's reply is non-committal, and the military and usurious images which follow conceal, especially for an age that does not think of love in these terms, the process of her thought. Yet her questions indicate clearly enough the drift of her ideas: how can a virgin, straitened by her modesty, pursue her love?

stain] similar to the modern "tincture": some qualities, at least superficial, of a soldier (so Johnson). Some

you a question. Man is enemy to virginity; how may 110
we barricado it against him?

Par. Keep him out.

Hel. But he assails; and our virginity, though valiant, in
the defence yet is weak. Unfold to us some warlike
resistance.   115

Par. There is none. Man setting down before you will
undermine you and blow you up.

Hel. Bless our poor virginity from underminers and
blowers-up! Is there no military policy how virgins
might blow up men?   120

Par. Virginity being blown down man will quicklier be
blown up; marry, in blowing him down again, with
the breach yourselves made you lose your city. It is
not politic in the commonwealth of nature to preserve virginity. Loss of virginity is rational increase, 125
and there was never virgin got till virginity was first

113–14. valiant, in the defence] *F; valiant in the defence, Var. '85.*

commentators, taking this with the
red-tail'd humble-bee in IV. v. 6, see a
reference to the red breeches they presume to be worn by Parolles.

113–14. *our virginity . . . weak*] The F
punctuation gives the best sense here,
for if, with later editors, we read
"though valiant in the defence, yet is
weak" we contradict the presupposi-
tion of the sentence following, i.e. that
virginity cannot make warlike resistance, i.e. is not valiant in the defence.

116. *setting down*] laying siege. The
comparison of wooing to besieging is,
of course, commonplace.

122. *blown up*] Partridge (*Shakespeare's Bawdy*) says that this refers to
sexual orgasm.

123. *breach*] Cf. *2 H 4*, II. iv. 50.
your city] your virginity. Cf. *Lucr.*,
469.

123–9. *It is not politic . . . ever lost*] In
this passage and below (ll. 143–6) the
basis of the imagery is commercial.
The woman who invests her virginity
in matrimony is seen to be drawing a
yearly interest in the form of children.
city, commonwealth, rational increase,

mettle (= metal), *ten times* all seem to be
connected to the same central idea of
the allowed ten per cent interest on
moneys invested. The connection of
love and usury is a commonplace of the
time; cf. *Sonn.* IV and VI; Marlowe,
Hero and Leander, I, 232–6; Erasmus,
"Proci et Puellae". Cf. *Mer. V.* (New
Arden edn), pp. liii ff.

126–7. *and there was . . . to make virgins*] Cf. the arguments of Ferardo in
Lyly's *Euphues*: "If thy mother had
bene of that minde when she was a
mayden, thou haddest not nowe bene
borne, to be of this minde to be a virgin. Way with thy selfe what slender
profit they bring to the common
wealth . . ." (Arber, p. 86). Tilley
(M 1196) quotes earlier examples of
the same argument from Erasmus'
colloquies ("Proci et Puellae") and
Pettie. Cf. also *Ven.*, 203–4:

O had thy mother borne so hard
    a mind,
She had not brought forth thee,
    but died unkind!

The idea probably goes back to
Jerome's "Laudo nuptias, laudo con-

lost. That you were made of is mettle to make virgins.
Virginity, by being once lost, may be ten times
found; by being ever kept it is ever lost. 'Tis too cold
a companion. Away with't!   130

Hel. I will stand for't a little, though therefore I die a
virgin.

Par. There's little can be said in't; 'tis against the rule of
nature. To speak on the part of virginity is to accuse
your mothers, which is most infallible disobedience.   135
He that hangs himself is a virgin; virginity murthers
itself, and should be buried in highways out of all
sanctified limit, as a desperate offendress against
nature. Virginity breeds mites, much like a cheese;
consumes itself to the very paring, and so dies with   140
feeding his own stomach. Besides, virginity is peev-
ish, proud, idle, made of self-love which is the most
inhibited sin in the canon. Keep it not; you cannot
choose but lose by't. Out with't! Within the year it

144–5. the year . . . two] *Harrison, conj. Anon;* ten yeare . . . two *F;* ten years . . .
ten *Hanmer;* two years . . . two *Collier²*, conj. *Steevens;* ten months . . . two *Singer²*,
conj. *Malone;* one year . . . two *Grant White.*

iugium, sed quia mihi virgines
generant" (Epistle xxII §20).

127. *mettle*] F "mettall". The Elizabethans did not distinguish between
the spellings of "mettle" and "metal",
and since the ideas of "coin" and "substance" are both present here no
modernization can be completely
satisfactory.

131.] There are probably the usual
obscene quibbles on *stand* and *die* for
which cf. *Sonn.* 151 and *Lr.*, IV. vi. 200.

133. *in't*] on its behalf.

136–7. *He that . . . murthers itself*] To
remain a virgin is equivalent to suicide,
for virginity murders virginity by re-
fusing to procreate children who are
virgins. Cf. Erasmus' "epistola sua-
soria" from *De conscribendis epistolis,*
trans. T. Wilson in *The arte of rhetorique*
(1560): "you shall be coumpted a
Parricide, or a murtherer of your
stocke" (1909 rept., p. 61).

140–1. *dies . . . stomach*] The virgin's
obstinacy against marriage kills her (in

the sense given above) by *feeding* (i.e.
maintaining) her *stomach* (i.e. pride).

143. *inhibited sin in the canon*] pro-
hibited in the scriptures. Noble cites
Deut., vi. 4–5, Lev., xix, 18, and
Mark, xii, 29–33. Tillyard has remarked that the whole passage may be
regarded as a parody of St Paul on
Charity, but the parallels seem very
weak.

143–4. *Keep . . . with't*] Do not hoard
your principal, for that is the way to
lose it; put it out to interest.

144–5. *the year . . . two*] The emendation adopted is the most plausible in
point of sense, though the error two
(tow)/ten is easier graphically. The F
reading is possible in terms of money
(10 per cent p.a.—the allowed rate—
doubles the capital in ten years) but
could hardly be called *a goodly increase*
in terms of human reproduction. Cf.
Marlowe, ". . . being put to loan / In
time it will return us two for one"
(*Hero and Leander*, I, 235 f) and Lyly,

will make itself two, which is a goodly increase, and 145
the principal itself not much the worse. Away with't!

Hel. How might one do, sir, to lose it to her own liking?

Par. Let me see. Marry, ill, to like him that ne'er it likes.
'Tis a commodity will lose the gloss with lying; the
longer kept, the less worth. Off with't while 'tis 150
vendible; answer the time of request. Virginity, like
an old courtier, wears her cap out of fashion, richly
suited but unsuitable, just like the brooch and the
toothpick, which wear not now. Your date is better
in your pie and your porridge than in your cheek; 155
and your virginity, your old virginity, is like one of
our French wither'd pears: it looks ill, it eats drily;
marry, 'tis a wither'd pear; it was formerly better;
marry, yet 'tis a wither'd pear. Will you anything
with it?   160

---

154. wear] *Capell;* were *F.*

"he made her of one, two" (*Gallathea*,
v. i. 22). Cf., however, Lyly's *Love's
Metamorphosis*: "I hate that Marchant,
who, if he find my beautie worth one
pennie, will put it to vse to gaine ten"
(III. ii. 32 f).

148. *Marry . . . likes*] "Parolles, in
answer to the question, 'How one
shall lose virginity to her own liking?'
plays on the word *liking*, and says, '*she
must do ill, for* virginity, to be so lost,
must like him that likes not virginity"
(Johnson). Cf. a similar paradox in
Erasmus' *Proci et Puellae*: "violanda
virginitas, ut discatur" (*Works*, I, 695).

149–50. *'Tis . . . worth*] It is like mer-
chandise which deteriorates with
keeping.

150–1. *Off with't . . . request*] Tilley
quotes this as an example of the proverb, "As the market goes, wives must
sell" (M 670). Cf. *AYL.*, III. v. 60.

151. *vendible*] Cf. *Mer. V.*, I. i. 112:
"a maid not vendible".

153. *the brooch*] At some point in sar-
torial development the brooch in the
hat became démodé, but it is not easy
to date exactly the period of its eclipse.
In Jonson's *Christmas* (1616) it belongs

clearly to the dress of the past; the
reference in *Poetaster* (1601), I. ii. 161
may well be satirical (since it is spoken
by Tucca). The passage in *LLL.*, v. ii.
610–11 cited by *N.S.* cannot be regarded as truly parallel—see Tilley
T 434.

153–4. *the toothpick*] Toothpicks were
at one time taken as a sign of travelled
gentility (see *John*, I. i. 190), and were
consequently worn prominently, e.g.
in the hat; see Overbury's "Character
of a Courtier": "If you find him not
here, you shall in Paul's, with a pick-
tooth in his hat." Cf. Shirley, *The
Witty Fair One*, IV. ii: "Lay it out in
toothpicks, I will wear them in my
hat."

154. *wear not now*] are not now in
fashion.

154–5. *Your date . . . porridge*] with a
pun on *date* (1) age, (2) fruit (cf. *Troil.*,
I. ii. 248, 249). To comprehend the
curious mixture of dates and porridge
we should remember that the Elizabethans often used dates for general
sweetening where we use sugar.

155. *in your cheek*] The reference is to
the withered cheek of age or *date*.

Hel. Not my virginity; yet . . .
    There shall your master have a thousand loves,
    A mother, and a mistress, and a friend,
    A phoenix, captain, and an enemy,
    A guide, a goddess, and a sovereign,   165
    A counsellor, a traitress, and a dear;
    His humble ambition, proud humility,
    His jarring-concord, and his discord-dulcet,

161. virginity;] *This edn;* virginity *F*+.   yet . . .] yet: *F*.   168. jarring-concord . . . discord-dulcet] *This edn;* iarring, concord . . . discord, dulcet *F*.

161. *Not my virginity; yet . . .*] The break in sense and metre here is usually said to be due to textual corruption. It may be so, but Helena is "fooling the time" (like Desdemona in *Oth.*, II. i): the words that pass have (for her) a deeper frame of reference than Parolles can understand; in this context abrupt transitions of thought may be expected. *Will you anything with it* (your virginity)? says Parolles. "No," replies Helena (in effect), "I shall not exchange my virginity." Suddenly, with only a *yet* to bridge the gap, she starts to talk about the court and its cult of love. It is possible that Shakespeare expected his original audience to understand the connection that is suppressed, for it is not hard to imagine that Helena's refusal to trade on her virginity leads to the sense that others elsewhere may be less scrupulous, which leads directly to her evocation of the amorous dialect of the court. The reason why Helena suppresses the intermediate idea is also fairly obvious: the words would be too intimate to be spoken to Parolles—perhaps too intimate to be spoken at all. Throughout this scene broken and ambiguous language is characteristic of Helena, though nowhere else are her ellipses as harsh as here.

163–6.] Helena suggests the varieties of love available to Bertram at court by listing the conceited titles given to the beloved in contemporary poetry. For the general idea, cf.

He calls her his deare heart, his
  sole beloued
His joyful comfort, and his sweet
  delight
His mistress and his goddess, and
  such names
As louing knights apply to louely
  dames
       (*Orlando Furioso*,
    tr. Harrington, XXIX, 8)

For *phoenix* cf. Drayton's *Idea*, 16; for *captain* cf. Humfrey Gifford, *A Posie of Gilloflowers*: "His Friend W.C. to Mistres F. K. whom he calls his Captaine"; for *enemy* cf. Tottel (Arber), p. 151, and *Wint.*, I. ii. 167; for *sovereign* cf. Constable, *Diana*, decade IV, sonnet II; for *counsellor* cf. "statesman" in *Wint.*, I. ii. 168; for *traitress* cf. Linche, *Diella*, VII and Petrarch "Datemi pace . . ."; for *guide* cf. Barnes, LVII. The other words, *mistress, friend, goddess, dear* are obvious enough, but *mother* seems out of place. Herford suggested "mauther", a dialectical word for maiden, but any rusticity seems inappropriate here. It may be that Helena begins *A mother, and a mistress, and a friend* meaning "every kind of love" (cf. *Ancrene Riwle* [E.E.T.S., O.S. 225, p. 179]) and only then goes on to the variations in nomenclature.

167–9.] These oxymorons are again characteristic of the love-poetry of the court.

168.] F is probably using the comma as we today use the hyphen—"to join words that represent a single idea";

His faith, his sweet disaster; with a world
Of pretty, fond, adoptious christendoms   170
That blinking Cupid gossips. Now shall he—
I know not what he shall. God send him well!
The court's a learning-place, and he is one—
Par. What one, i' faith?
Hel. That I wish well. 'Tis pity—   175
Par. What's pity?
Hel. That wishing well had not a body in't
Which might be felt, that we, the poorer born,
Whose baser stars do shut us up in wishes,
Might with effects of them follow our friends,   180
And show what we alone must think, which never
Returns us thanks.

Enter Page.

Page. Monsieur Parolles, my lord calls for you.   [*Exit.*]
Par. Little Helen, farewell. If I can remember thee I will
       think of thee at court.   185
Hel. Monsieur Parolles, you were born under a charitable
       star.
Par. Under Mars, I.
Hel. I especially think under Mars.
Par. Why under Mars?   190
Hel. The wars hath so kept you under, that you must
       needs be born under Mars.

---

169. disaster] *F;* distaster *conj. this edn.*   183. Monsieur Parolles, . . . you.] *As Capell;* Monsieur *Parrolles,* | . . . you. | *F (as verse).*   S.D. *Exit.*] *Theobald[1]; not in F.*

see also *Ham.,* III. iii. 89 (Q2); *Troil.,* III. ii. 23 (QF), v. iii. 28 (F), v. x. 33 (QF).

169–71. *with a world . . . gossips*] Such dainty and foolish nicknames are bestowed upon mistresses, as if they were Christian names (*christendoms*) for which blind (*blinking*) Cupid stands as godfather (*gossips*).

173. *he is one—*] What is suppressed must be something like "all too apt to learn courtly ways".

179. *baser stars*] our having been born, by destiny, into a base or humble

family. Cf. *homely stars* below, II. v. 75.

180–2. *Might . . . thanks*] Would that such as I were able to show effects of our wishing in terms of physical action, for as long as we can only *think* good for those to whom we wish well, so long we must do without gratitude.

188. *Under Mars, I*] perhaps should be modernized as: "Under Mars, ay".

188–92.] The point of this exchange is, of course, that Parolles says "under *Mars*" while Helena emphasizes the *under.*

Par. When he was predominant.

Hel. When he was retrograde, I think rather.

Par. Why think you so?   195

Hel. You go so much backward when you fight.

Par. That's for advantage.

Hel. So is running away, when fear proposes the safety;
but the composition that your valour and fear makes
in you is a virtue of a good wing, and I like the wear 200
well.

Par. I am so full of businesses I cannot answer thee
acutely. I will return perfect courtier; in the which
my instruction shall serve to naturalize thee, so thou
wilt be capable of a courtier's counsel, and understand 205
what advice shall thrust upon thee; else thou diest in
thine unthankfulness, and thine ignorance makes
thee away. Farewell. When thou hast leisure, say
thy prayers; when thou hast none, remember thy
friends. Get thee a good husband, and use him as he 210
uses thee. So, farewell.   [*Exit.*]

Hel. Our remedies oft in ourselves do lie,

198–9. So . . . away, . . . safety; but] *As Pope;* So . . . away, / . . . safetie: / But F.
211. S.D. *Exit.*] F2; *not in* F.

193–4.] Parolles, trying to give his meaning less ambiguously, says that Mars was in the ascendant when he was born. Helena replies with another astrological term, which is used of planets moving in an unfavourable direction or *backward*.

199. *composition*] the make-up of your character (with perhaps a glance at the meaning "truce, conditional surrender").

200. *of a good wing*] Rolfe glosses: "equivalent to 'strong in flight', but here used with a quibbling reference to the other sense of *flight*". There may also be a reference to flaps or "wings" (*O.E.D.* sb. II. 8) on Parolles' costume; by 1604, according to Linthicum's *Costume in Shakespeare*, these were "little and diminutive", so that conspicuous ones on Parolles' costume would be a proper subject for ridicule (cf. Jonson, *E.M.O.*, III. v. 5).—*N.S.* gives "wings"

to Osric in *Ham.*, v. ii. *I like the wear well* has an obvious reference if this is true; for a metaphorical use of *wear*, however, cf. *Meas.*, III. ii. 68–9.

204. *naturalize*] familiarize (On.).

205–6. *capable . . . thee*] The collocation of three words often subject to obscene quibbles (*capable, understand,* and *thrust*) is, presumably, not accidental. Cf. *LLL.*, IV. ii. 75.

206–8. *else . . . away*] repeating the ideas of ll. 136 ff above.

208. *leisure*] opportunity, especially for religious duties. Cf. *Meas.*, III. ii. 231, *H 8*, III. ii. 140.

209–10. *when . . . friends*] i.e. only think of them when you have no opportunity; don't remember them at all.

212–25.] The couplets here seem designed to raise the sense of inevitability and of supernatural confidence. See Intro., p. xxi.

Which we ascribe to heaven; the fated sky
Gives us free scope; only doth backward pull
Our slow designs when we ourselves are dull.   215
What power is it which mounts my love so high,
That makes me see, and cannot feed mine eye?
The mightiest space in fortune nature brings
To join like likes, and kiss like native things.
Impossible be strange attempts to those   220
That weigh their pains in sense, and do suppose
What hath been cannot be. Who ever strove
To show her merit that did miss her love?
The king's disease—my project may deceive me,   224
But my intents are fix'd, and will not leave me.   *Exit.*

[SCENE II.—*Paris. The King's palace.*]

Flourish cornets. Enter the KING OF FRANCE *with letters, and divers
attendants.*

King. The Florentines and Senoys are by th' ears;

219. like likes] *F4;* like, likes *F.*

Scene II

Scene II] *Capell; not in F.*   *Paris. The King's palace.*] *Paris. A Room in the King's
Palace. Capell; not in F.*

213. *the fated sky*] the fateful sky; the
sky to which we ascribe the power of
fate.

217. *makes . . . eye*] The word *mounts*
in the line preceding makes it probable
that the image is derived from hawking. Helena can see her prey (Bertram) but yet holds back from pursu-
ing him to Paris. The lines following
makes it probable that the answer to
her question is "Nature".

218–19. *The mightiest . . . things*] "the
affections given us by nature often
unite persons between whom fortune
or accident has placed the greatest
distance or disparity; and cause them
to join, like likes (instar parium) like
persons in the same situation or rank of
life" (Malone). Cf. *Tim.,* IV. iii. 385,
386.

221. *That weigh their pains in sense*]
"Who estimate the pains they take by
the amount of trouble and suffering
involved . . . and also . . . who calculate
the difficulties of their strange attempts
(unusual undertakings) by reason and
common-sense probability of success"
(Clarkes).

Scene II

S.D. Flourish Cornets] W. J. Lawrence thinks that cornets were only
used at the Blackfriars Theatre, and
that their mention in a text implies a
production later than 1609 (*Shakespeare's Workshop,* p. 60). Cf. below
II. i. S.D.

1. *Senoys*] natives of Siena. For the
bearing of this gallicism on the question of source, see Intro., p. xxv.

by th' ears] quarrelling, at variance;

  Have fought with equal fortune, and continue
  A braving war.
First Lord.   So 'tis reported, sir.
King. Nay, 'tis most credible. We here receive it
  A certainty, vouch'd from our cousin Austria,   5
  With caution that the Florentine will move us
  For speedy aid; wherein our dearest friend
  Prejudicates the business, and would seem
  To have us make denial.
First Lord.   His love and wisdom,
  Approv'd so to your majesty, may plead   10
  For amplest credence.
King.   He hath arm'd our answer,
  And Florence is denied before he comes;
  Yet, for our gentlemen that mean to see
  The Tuscan service, freely have they leave
  To stand on either part.
Second Lord.   It well may serve   15
  A nursery to our gentry, who are sick
  For breathing and exploit.
King.   What's he comes here?

Enter BERTRAM, LAFEW, *and* PAROLLES.

First Lord. It is the Count Rossillion, my good lord,
  Young Bertram.
King.   Youth, thou bear'st thy father's face;

3, 9, 18. *First Lord.*] *Rowe*[1]; 1. *Lo. G.* | *F* (1. *Lor. G. 18*). 15, 67. *Second Lord.*]
Rowe[1]; 2. *Lo. E.* | *F* (*L. 2. E. 67*). 18. Rossillion] *Rosignoll F.*

the proverbial metaphor (Tilley E 23) is derived from the fighting tactics of certain animals.

 3. *A braving war*] one in which each defies the other. See *Tit.*, II. i. 26 S.D.: "*Enter Chiron and Demetrius, braving.*"

 5. *cousin*] fellow sovereign.

 7. *our dearest friend*] There is no clear reason in history or the text why Austria should be called France's *dearest friend*, but he seems to be the only person who can be referred to here. H. F. Brooks suggests that Shakespeare is re-membering *John*, where Austria *is* the ally of the King of France.

 11. *arm'd*] *O.E.D.* Arm v.[1] 5. "To ...furnish with a protective covering".

 17. *breathing*] exercise, activity. Cf. below II. iii. 252.

 18. *Rossillion*] The curious Folio reading, "Rosignoll" is, suggests H. G. Wright, "probably to be explained as a momentary aberration on the part of one who knew French and before whom an association of sounds conjured up the nightingale" (*M.L.R.*, L (1955), 47, Note 1).

Frank nature, rather curious than in haste,   20
Hath well compos'd thee. Thy father's moral
    parts
Mayest thou inherit too! Welcome to Paris.
Ber. My thanks and duty are your majesty's.
King. I would I had that corporal soundness now,
As when thy father and myself in friendship   25
First tried our soldiership. He did look far
Into the service of the time, and was
Disciped of the bravest. He lasted long,
But on us both did haggish age steal on,
And wore us out of act. It much repairs me   30
To talk of your good father; in his youth
He had the wit which I can well observe
Today in our young lords; but they may jest
Till their own scorn return to them unnoted
Ere they can hide their levity in honour.   35
So like a courtier, contempt nor bitterness
Were in his pride or sharpness; if they were,
His equal had awak'd them, and his honour,

---

20. *Frank*] liberal, bounteous (On.). *curious*] fastidious, careful.

26-7. *He did ... time*] Herford paraphrases, "he had keen insight in the affairs of war", or it may be that the reference is to length of service rather than insight.

28. *Disciped of*] Probably means "had as pupils" rather than "taught by" (Brigstocke).

30. *wore ... act*] wore us down so that we could not act.

31-5. *in his ... honour*] He had as much wit as our young lords, but his wit was balanced by noble action, so that he never became a mere jester, and so the proper object of other men's wit. "Jocose follies, and slight offences, are only allowed by mankind in him that over-powers them by great qualities" notes Johnson. Cf. *Disticha Catonis*, III, 7:

Alterius dictum aut actum ne
    carpseris umquam
Exemplo simili ne te dirideat alter.

and Spenser, *Mother Hubberd's Tale*, 711-26. Castiglione's *Courtier*, bk 2, is probably the best-known example of a traditional topic—illustrating the witticisms proper to courtiers.

34. *unnoted*] may mean that they have scoffed so much that they cannot recognize their own taunts when returned by others or (more probably) that they become so associated with scoffing that no one is surprised when they too are scoffed at.

36. *like a courtier*] Courtesy is often defined in this period as the power of being affable to all estates. See below, IV. v. 101, 102; cf. the whole conduct of *Faerie Queene*, bk VI, and Ashley, *Of Honour*: "For how can Honour be sooner gotten, or being gotten already better agree with vertue, then by being kind, affable, gentle and courtuous vnto all; yf you must needs offend on th' one part, lett yt rather be in geving every man more then his due" (ed. Heltzel, p. 58).

Clock to itself, knew the true minute when
Exception bid him speak, and at this time   40
His tongue obey'd his hand. Who were below him
He us'd as creatures of another place,
And bow'd his eminent top to their low ranks,
Making them proud of his humility
In their poor praise he humbled. Such a man   45
Might be a copy to these younger times;
Which, followed well, would demonstrate them now
But goers backward.

Ber.   His good remembrance, sir,
Lies richer in your thoughts than on his tomb;
So in approof lives not his epitaph   50
As in your royal speech.

King. Would I were with him! He would always say—
Methinks I hear him now; his plausive words
He scatter'd not in ears, but grafted them

52. him!] *Theobald¹;* him *F.*

39. *true minute*] The clock of his honour is *true* (cf. below, II. v. 5), i.e. tells him the exact moment to respond.

40. *Exception*] disapproval, as in "take exception to".

41. *His tongue . . . hand*] As the clock-chime does not sound till the hand is at the right place, so he did not let his tongue say more than his hand could answer for.

42. *of another place*] We may paraphrase "as though they were not below him in rank" or "with the courtesy due to strangers"; in either case the implication is the same.

43–5. *And bow'd . . . he humbled*] The general sense is clear: "he made the humble proud of the fact that he was humbling his own eminence in praising them." The paradox of courteous behaviour is expressed elliptically; the natural object of *humbled* is *top*, and though this construction is strained, it is possible by a combination of two common Shakespearian ellipses: a "which" omitted after *humility*, and a reference by this "which" to the idea

of *top* implicit in *humility* (by bowing he turned his top into his humility); for the second of these elliptical constructions cf. below, II. iii. 149. Cf. *R 2*, III. iii. 190 f:

> Fair cousin, you debase your
>   princely knee
> To make the base earth proud with
>   kissing it.

50. *So in . . . epitaph*] "the truth of his epitaph is in no way so fully confirmed" (On.).

52. *Would . . . him*] H. F. Brooks compares *H 5*, II. iii. 7.

53. *plausive*] fit to be applauded.

54–5. *He scatter'd . . . bear*] Shakespeare very commonly puns on *ears* as (a) organs of hearing, (b) seed-boxes of cereals. Knight compares: "Grant, we beseech thee . . . that the words which we have heard this day with our outward ears may . . . be so grafted inwardly in our hearts, that they may bring forth in us the fruit of good living" (*The Book of Common Prayer.* Collects at the end of the Communion.)

To grow there and to bear—"Let me not live",   55
(This his good melancholy oft began
On the catastrophe and heel of pastime,
When it was out) "Let me not live", quoth he,
"After my flame lacks oil, to be the snuff
Of younger spirits, whose apprehensive senses   60
All but new things disdain; whose judgments are
Mere fathers of their garments; whose constancies
Expire before their fashions". This he wish'd.
I, after him, do after him wish too,
Since I nor wax nor honey can bring home,   65
I quickly were dissolved from my hive
To give some labourers room.

Second Lord.   You're loved, sir;
They that least lend it you shall lack you first.

King. I fill a place, I know't. How long is't, count,
Since the physician at your father's died?   70
He was much fam'd.

Ber.   Some six months since, my lord.

King. If he were living I would try him yet—
Lend me an arm—the rest have worn me out
With several applications; nature and sickness

---

57. *catastrophe and heel*] a good example of the Metaphysical quality in many Shakespearian doublets. Both words mean "latter end", but are drawn from divided and distinguished worlds of apprehension.

57–8. *pastime . . . out*] *it* may refer to *pastime*, so that *out* means "at an end" (cf. *Tp.*, III. ii. 1), or to *heel*, so that the pastime is being said to be "out at heel" (cf. *Cas.*, I. i. 17 ff).

59. *After . . . oil*] Cf.
My oil-dried lamp and time-
    bewasted light
Shall be extinct with age and
    endless night
                    (*R 2*, I. iii. 221–2)
See Tilley O 29.

59. *snuff*] The black, burned-out portion of a wick which, not removed by trimming (as an old man is removed by death) prevents the *younger*

or lower wick from burning brightly.

60. *apprehensive*] quick to perceive or "soak up".

61–2. *whose . . . garments*] "who have no other use of their faculties, than to invent new modes of dress" (Johnson).

64.] The first *after* = "later than", the second "in harmony with".

65–7. *Since . . . room*] The aptness of the metaphor is increased if we remember that the Elizabethans assumed the queen bee to be a king.

68. *lend it you*] *it* may mean "love", but Thiselton's suggestion that it refers back to *room* is supported by the King's answer. For sentiment and general expression cf. *AYL.*, I. ii. 171–3: "only in the world I fill up a place, which may be better supplied when I have made it empty".

74. *several*] separate and individual to each doctor.

Debate it at their leisure. Welcome, count;   75
My son's no dearer.

Ber.   Thank your majesty. *Exeunt. Flourish.*

[SCENE III.—*Rossillion. The Count's palace.*]

Enter COUNTESS, STEWARD, *and* CLOWN.

Count. I will now hear. What say you of this gentlewoman?
Stew. Madam, the care I have had to even your content
          I wish might be found in the calendar of my past
          endeavours; for then we wound our modesty, and
          make foul the clearness of our deservings, when of   5
          ourselves we publish them.
Count. What does this knave here? get you gone, sirrah.
          The complaints I have heard of you I do not all
          believe; 'tis my slowness that I do not; for I know
          you lack not folly to commit them and have ability   10
          enough to make such knaveries yours.
Clo. 'Tis not unknown to you, madam, I am a poor fellow.
Count. Well, sir.

76. S.D. *Exeunt.*] *Exit. F.*

Scene III

Scene III] *Capell; not in F.   Rossillion. The Count's palace.*] *Rosillion. A Room in the
Count's Palace. Capell; not in F.   1. hear. What] heare, what F.*

Scene III

The verses by William Cartwright prefixed to the first (1647) Beaumont and Fletcher Folio may refer to this scene or to *Tw. N.*, I. v:

> *Shakespeare* to thee was dull, whose best jest lyes
> I' th' Ladies questions, and the Fooles replyes;
> Old fashion'd wit, which walkt from town to town
> In turn'd Hose, which our fathers call'd the Clown;
> Whose wit our nice times would obsceannesse call,
> And which made Bawdry passe for Comicall.

2. *even*] "even v.4. To make (accounts etc.) even" (*O.E.D.*). The word is apt for a steward, as is *calendar* (record, register).

6. *publish*] Thiselton takes this word to be "a strong hint to her (sc. the Countess) to dismiss the clown", but the hint is surely too oblique to convey this to any auditor; what the steward hesitates to publish is not Helena's confession but his own merit. Admittedly the steward's preamble is very wordy and it is possible to believe that he is playing for time till the Countess notices the clown's presence.

9–11. *for . . . yours*] He is accused of being both a fool and a knave.

Clo. No, madam, 'tis not so well that I am poor, though
      many of the rich are damn'd; but if I may have your   15
      ladyship's good will to go to the world, Isbel the
      woman and I will do as we may.

Count. Wilt thou needs be a beggar?

Clo. I do beg your good will in this case.

Count. In what case?   20

Clo. In Isbel's case and mine own. Service is no heritage,
      and I think I shall never have the blessing of God till
      I have issue a' my body; for they say barnes are
      blessings.

Count. Tell me thy reason why thou wilt marry.   25

Clo. My poor body, madam, requires it; I am driven on
      by the flesh, and he must needs go that the devil
      drives.

Count. Is this all your worship's reason?

Clo. Faith, madam, I have other holy reasons, such as   30
      they are.

Count. May the world know them?

Clo. I have been, madam, a wicked creature, as you and
      all flesh and blood are, and indeed I do marry that I
      may repent.   35

14. No, madam, 'tis] *Capell;* No maddam, / 'Tis *F.*

14. *No, madam, 'tis*] Hinman (*Sh. Q.*
vi, 262) points to F division of the line
(the last on the page) as typical of
compositor's "space-losing".

16. *go to the world*] get married. Cf.
"Thus goes every one to the world but
I, and I am sun-burnt; I may sit in a
corner and cry 'Heigh-ho for a husband!'" (*Ado,* ii. i. 286–8). The phrase
must derive from the Catholic view of
the essential carnality of marriage.

17. *as we may*] as well as we can, with
probably a glance at the obscene sense
of "do".

21. *Isbel's case*] Kökeritz (p. 119)
sees an obscene pun.

Service . . . heritage] Tilley (S 253)
quotes many examples of this proverb
from the fifteenth century forward.
Kelly (1721) calls it "an argument for
Servants to seek out some new settle-
ment".

23–4. *barnes are blessings*] Tilley
quotes examples from 1585 onwards.
The now mainly northern form
"barnes" for "children" was formerly
current all over England.

27–8. *he must . . . drives*] proverbial
(see Tilley D 278). Note that though
the clown's speech is largely composed
of proverbial scraps, his courtly wit
brings these up only to be mocked at.

30. *other holy reasons*] *N.S.* notes that
marrying to beget children can be
called *holy* because it is mentioned in
the marriage-service. Partridge and
Kökeritz point out the obscene
quibbles on both *holy* (cf. Bale's *King
Johan* (M.S.R.), 890 ff) and *reasons*
(= raisings), the latter as in *Sonn.* cli
and *Shr.,* Ind. ii. 122.

34–5. *marry . . . repent*] "In allusion to
the old proverb 'marry in haste, and
repent at leisure'" (Halliwell).

Count. Thy marriage, sooner than thy wickedness.

Clo. I am out a' friends, madam, and I hope to have
   friends for my wife's sake.

Count. Such friends are thine enemies, knave.

Clo. Y'are shallow, madam, in great friends; for the   40
   knaves come to do that for me which I am aweary of.
   He that ears my land spares my team, and gives me
   leave to in the crop; if I be his cuckold, he's my
   drudge. He that comforts my wife is the cherisher of
   my flesh and blood; he that cherishes my flesh and   45
   blood loves my flesh and blood; he that loves my
   flesh and blood is my friend; ergo, he that kisses my
   wife is my friend. If men could be contented to be
   what they are, there were no fear in marriage; for
   young Charbon the puritan and old Poysam the   50
   papist, howsome'er their hearts are sever'd in religion, their heads are both one; they may jowl horns
   together like any deer i' th' herd.

Count. Wilt thou ever be a foul-mouth'd and calumnious
   knave?   55

Clo. A prophet I, madam; and I speak the truth the next
   way:

40. madam, in] *F3;* Madam in *F;* Madam; e'en *Hanmer;* madam—in *Alexander.*

40. *in great friends*] "you cannot
fathom the depth of a great friendship" (Thiselton). Perhaps there
ought to be a pause after *madam,* so
that the impudence of the words preceding may be allowed to make a
separate point before the words following explain it.

42–4. *He that...drudge*] Tilley (L 57)
quotes Torriano, *The Proverbial Phrases*
(1666): "To dig anothers garden ... to
Cuckold one, to do his work and
drudgery, as they say for him."

42. *ears*] ploughs.

43. *in the crop*] bring in the crop.

44–8. *He that comforts ... wife is my
friend*] This mock sorites is probably
traditional. Tiessen (*Archiv* LVIII)
cites Rabelais: "Si tu es cocu, ergo ta
femme sera belle; ergo tu seras bien
traicté d'elle; ergo tu auras des amis

beaucoup; ergo tu seras saulvé."
(Bk III, cap. xxviii). Cf. Jonson, Chap-
man, Marston, *Eastward Ho,* v. v.
187 ff.

48–9. *be what they are*] i.e. cuckolds.

50–2. *young ... one*] cuckoldry, being
universal, unites the young and the
old, the *Charbon* (chair bonne)-eating
puritans and the *Poysam* (poisson)-
eating papists. Behind the expression
would seem to lie the proverb "Young
flesh and old fish are best" (Tilley
F 369).

51–2. *howsome'er ... one*] Presumably
this is a comic inversion of a proverb:
"Hearts may agree though heads
differ" (Tilley H 341).

52. *jowl*] dash, knock (On.). Cf.
Ham., v. i. 76.

56–7. *the next way*] the nearest way.
Presumably the phrase glances at the

> *For I the ballad will repeat*
> *Which men full true shall find:*
> *Your marriage comes by destiny,*   60
> *Your cuckoo sings by kind.*

Count. Get you gone, sir; I'll talk with you more anon.

Stew. May it please you, madam, that he bid Helen come
    to you; of her I am to speak.

Count. Sirrah, tell my gentlewoman I would speak with   65
    her—Helen I mean.

Clo.   *Was this fair face the cause, quoth she,*
> *Why the Grecians sacked Troy?*
> *Fond done, done fond,*
> *Was this King Priam's joy?*   70
> *With that she sighed as she stood,*
> *With that she sighed as she stood,*
> *And gave this sentence then:*
> *Among nine bad if one be good,*

58–61.] *Verse (2 lines) Rowe³; prose F.*   69. *Fond done, done fond*] Fond done,
done, fond *F;* Fond done, fond done;—for *Paris* he *Theobald¹, conj. Warburton;*
om. Pope.   69–70.] *As Var. '73; one line F.*   71–2. *With . . . stood, | . . . stood,*]
With that she sighed as she stood, *bis F.*   73–6.] *As Rowe³; prose F.*

theory of prophetic inspiration as proceeding from direct contact with the
Divine Author of truth.

58–61.] The last two lines of this
stanza would seem to be traditional.
Steevens points out that something
similar is found in a poem in John
Grange's "Garden" (*The Golden Aphro-
ditis* (1577), sig. R2): "A newe
Married man being stung with wedlocke, declareth his minde *Cantico
more*, upon this text:

> Content yourself, as well as I, let
>   reason rule your minde,
> As Cuckoldes come by destinie, so
>   Cuckowes sing by kinde."

61. by kind] according to nature, i.e.
more fundamentally than "by destiny" above.

67–76.] A hiatus has sometimes been
assumed in this ballad-fragment; certainly l. 69 is defective metrically
(though it is possible that four long
syllables (together with the pause due
to the inversion) may be thought

equivalent to the required tetra-
meter); it gives neither rhyme nor
any obvious sense. What was "fond
(i.e. foolishly) done" was presumably
the receiving of Paris into Troy, and
some reference to Paris seems necessary to explain the numbers. Ballad
stanzas need not, however, make sense
by themselves, if presented to audiences who know the whole ballad. The
most probable "she" to say all this is
Hecuba, and "The lamentations of
Hecuba and the ladies of Troye"—a
ballad—entered in the Stationers'
Register on 1 Aug. 1586, but not now
known, seems a probable source for the
lines. The comparison with Helen of
Troy (especially in the decade of
Troilus and Cressida) can hardly be
complimentary, but whether this reflects more on Helena (so Clifford
Leech) or on the clown (so W. W.
Lawrence) remains doubtful. F's *bis* at
l. 71 is a clear indication of the stanza
having been set to music.

> *Among nine bad if one be good,*   75
> *There's yet one good in ten.*

Count. What, one good in ten? You corrupt the song,
   sirrah.

Clo. One good woman in ten, madam, which is a purify-
   ing a' th' song. Would God would serve the world so   80
   all the year! We'd find no fault with the tithe-
   woman if I were the parson. One in ten, quoth'a!
   And we might have a good woman born but or every
   blazing star or at an earthquake, 'twould mend the
   lottery well; a man may draw his heart out ere 'a   85
   pluck one.

Count. You'll be gone, sir knave, and do as I command
   you?

Clo. That man should be at woman's command, and yet
   no hurt done! Though honesty be no puritan, yet it   90
   will do no hurt; it will wear the surplice of humility

83. And] *F;* an *Pope.*   but or] *Capell;* but ore *F;* but o'er *Rowe*[1]*;* but one
Collier[2]*;* but for *Craig;* before *Alexander.*

77. *You corrupt the song*] In the original, Hecuba is more likely to have
said:

   If one be bad among nine good,
   There's yet one bad in ten.

i.e. even if Priam had nine good sons
and only one bad one (Paris), he still
had one bad one. The Countess claims
that the clown "corrupts" the song because he increases the badness; the
clown replies that he means women,
not men, and so he has increased the
proportion of good (women).

81–2. *We'd find . . . parson*] If the proportion of good women were in fact as
high as a tithe (or tenth) the parson
would be satisfied from the point o.
view both of ethics and of self-interest
(*tithe-woman* being considered as analogical to tithe-pig). Cf. for the general
idea: "This tree is *Castanea,* from
whence take away N.E.A. and there
remains *casta,* of which chaste thinges,
the parson of the parishe maye well
tithe the Tenthes to eke forthe his
liuinge, and neyther the towne em-
payred, nor hee enriched by this extor-

tion" (Melbancke's *Philotimus* (1583),
p. 33).

83. *but or*] This, Capell's reading, is
usually explained as a variant of "but
(i.e. only) ere", but it is not clear why
"*ere* a star", though "*at* an earthquake". It would be better to take the
or . . . or as equivalent to "either
. . . or" (*O.E.D.* s.v. Or conj.[2] B.3), as
e.g. in *Cæs.,* v. iv. 24.

84–5. *the lottery*] the normal odds
against finding a good woman.

85–6. *draw . . . pluck*] both terms
derived from the idea of *lottery.*

89–91. *That man . . . do no hurt*] There
is probably a strain of bawdy double-
talk in this. Presumably *honesty* means
"chastity", and is *no puritan* because
celibacy is a papistical virtue; the *hurt*
involved is loss of chastity, which
chastity itself cannot encompass—
H. F. Brooks points to the parallel
phrase in *Wint.,* iv. iv. 195–8. There
may be in this an oblique reference to
Helena's dilemma.

91–2. *wear . . . heart*] conform out-
wardly, as the Puritans did, obeying

over the black gown of a big heart. I am going, for-
sooth; the business is for Helen to come hither.   *Exit.*
Count. Well, now.
Stew. I know, madam, you love your gentlewoman   95
    entirely.
Count. Faith, I do. Her father bequeath'd her to me, and
    she herself, without other advantage, may lawfully
    make title to as much love as she finds; there is more
    owing her than is paid, and more shall be paid her   100
    than she'll demand.
Stew. Madam, I was very late more near her than I think
    she wish'd me; alone she was, and did communicate
    to herself her own words to her own ears; she
    thought, I dare vow for her, they touch'd not any   105
    stranger sense. Her matter was, she loved your son.
    Fortune, she said, was no goddess, that had put such
    difference betwixt their two estates; Love no god,
    that would not extend his might only where qualities
    were level; [Diana no] queen of virgins, that would   110
    suffer her poor knight surpris'd without rescue in the
    first assault or ransom afterward. This she deliver'd
    in the most bitter touch of sorrow that ere I heard

---

109. might only] might onelie, *F*; might, only *F4*.   110. level; Diana no
queen] *Theobald*[1]; leuell, Queene *F*.

the law by wearing the surplice, but
preserving a sign of their pride in independence by wearing also the black
Geneva gown, the Calvinist's natural
garb, under it. *N.S.* points out that the
reference would be especially apposite
in 1605, but cf. Intro., p. xxii.

    97–101. *Her father . . . demand*]
Helena is presented as a capital sum,
which by itself, without *advantage* (i.e.
interest) gives her the legal right to the
payment of love.

    105–6. *they . . . sense*] that no
stranger's ear could hear them.

    107–8. *Fortune . . . estates*] The dif-
ference of rank is due to chance and
not to divine dispensation. The denial
of godhead to Fortune is of great
antiquity; cf. "ex hominum questu
facta Fortuna est dea" (*Adagia Pub-*

lilii Syri) and Juvenal *Sat.* x, 365 f.

    109–10. *only . . . level*] would do so
only in cases where there was equality
of rank; *only* seems to have the sense of
"except" (*O.E.D.* adv. B.2), and the
Folio punctuation may be designed to
convey this sense.

    110. *level . . . virgins*] Theobald's in-
terpolation makes sense of a passage
which is inexplicable in the Folio, and
is supported by:
    Pardon, goddess of the night,
    Those that slew thy virgin knight.
          (*Ado*, v. iii. 12–13)
Cf. also *Two Noble Kinsmen*, v. i. 146.

    113. *touch*] usually explained as
"feeling", but *touch* is used of "expression" in both music and painting
and it may well have the same sense
here.

virgin exclaim in, which I held my duty speedily to
acquaint you withal, sithence, in the loss that may   115
happen, it concerns you something to know it.

Count. You have discharg'd this honestly; keep it to yourself. Many likelihoods inform'd me of this before,
which hung so tott'ring in the balance that I could
neither believe nor misdoubt. Pray you leave me;   120
stall this in your bosom; and I thank you for your
honest care. I will speak with you further anon.

Exit Steward.

Enter HELENA.

Count. Even so it was with me when I was young;
If ever we are nature's, these are ours; this thorn
Doth to our rose of youth rightly belong;   125
Our blood to us, this to our blood is born:
It is the show and seal of nature's truth,
Where love's strong passion is impress'd in youth.
By our remembrances of days foregone,
Such were our faults, or then we thought them none.   130
Her eye is sick on't; I observe her now.

Hel. What is your pleasure, madam?

Count.   You know, Helen,
I am a mother to you.

---

122. S.D. *Enter Helena*] *Enter Hellen F; Singer*[2] (*after 130*).   132–3. You know
... you.] *As Capell; one line F.*

---

114. *which*] = which thing. See
Abbott §271, Franz §347.

115. *sithence*] since.

122. S.D. Enter Helena] The Folio
direction for the entry of Helena at this
point is separated by more lines than
usual from the first words recognizing
her presence, and many editors have
postponed the entry. However, as the
Cambridge editors remark, "The
Countess may be supposed to be observing Helena earnestly as she enters
with slow step and downcast eyes. Her
words have thus more force and
point." At the same time, as *N.S.*
notes, there is a change of speech-
prefixes in the Folio. *Cou.* becoming
Old Cou. between this point and l. 181.
N.S. takes this to indicate "patching"

of later-written verse on to an earlier
prose dialogue, but it may indicate no
more than a different section of the
foul-papers which lie behind the
Folio text.

124. *these*] situations like this, these
difficulties, illustrated visually for the
audience by the "slow step and downcast eyes" of Helena.

126. *blood*] usually glossed as "passion", but may mean no more than
"natural disposition".

128. *impress'd*] as by a seal (or
thorn).

130. *or then . . . none*] or rather, we
can hardly call them faults, for then
they did not seem faults to us.

131. *observe*] not merely "see", but
"see through".

Hel. Mine honourable mistress.
Count.   Nay, a mother.
    Why not a mother? When I said "a mother",   135
    Methought you saw a serpent. What's in
        "mother"
    That you start at it? I say I am your mother,
    And put you in the catalogue of those
    That were enwombed mine. 'Tis often seen
    Adoption strives with nature, and choice breeds   140
    A native slip to us from foreign seeds.
    You ne'er oppress'd me with a mother's groan,
    Yet I express to you a mother's care.
    God's mercy, maiden! does it curd thy blood
    To say I am thy mother? what's the matter,   145
    That this distempered messenger of wet,
    The many-colour'd Iris, rounds thine eye?
    —Why, that you are my daughter?
Hel.   That I am not.
Count. I say I am your mother.
Hel.   Pardon, madam;
    The Count Rossillion cannot be my brother.   150
    I am from humble, he from honoured name;
    No note upon my parents, his all noble.
    My master, my dear lord he is; and I

134-5. Nay ... "a mother",] *As Pope; one line F.*   148. —Why,] *F;* Why—
Rowe[1].

140-1. *and choice ... seeds*] We choose
a scion (or *slip*) which we graft (by
adoption) on to our own stock, and
though the seed from which the scion
was grown is foreign to us, yet, after
grafting, the scion becomes native to
us.

146. *distempered*] contains ideas of
both emotional distraction and incle-
ment weather. Henley compares

  And round about her tear-
    distained eye
  Blue circles stream'd, like rainbows
    in the sky.

        (*Lucr.*, 1586-7)
148. —*Why*] Thiselton takes the
dash in the Folio to indicate a pause,

while the Countess waits for a reply.

  That I am not] To understand the
full force of this and the other ambigu-
ities in this dialogue we should remember that the Elizabethans used
"mother", "daughter", etc. to mean
"mother-in-law", "daughter-in-law",
etc. Thus Helena is able to reply "I
weep that I am not your daughter-in-
law" while seeming to say "I weep
that I am not your daughter."

  152. *note*] distinction. Cf. "For
Nobilitie is as much to say, as a note or
marke, and a noble man, as a man
more noted, and knowne, then any
others" (*Nennio, or a Treatise of
Nobilitie*, tr. Jones (1595), fol. 55).

His servant live, and will his vassal die.
He must not be my brother.
Count.   Nor I your mother?   155
Hel. You are my mother, madam; would you were—
So that my lord your son were not my brother—
Indeed my mother! or were you both our mothers
I care no more for than I do for heaven,
So I were not his sister. Can't no other   160
But, I your daughter, he must be my brother?
Count. Yes, Helen, you might be my daughter-in-law.
God shield you mean it not! daughter and mother
So strive upon your pulse. What! pale again?
My fear hath catch'd your fondness; now I see   165
The myst'ry of your loneliness, and find
Your salt tears' head. Now to all sense 'tis gross:
You love my son. Invention is asham'd
Against the proclamation of thy passion
To say thou dost not. Therefore tell me true;   170
But tell me then, 'tis so; for, look, thy cheeks
Confess it t'one to th'other, and thine eyes

159.] I care . . . for, then . . . for heauen *F;* I care . . . for than . . . fore heaven *conj. Thiselton;* I care . . . for't than . . . for heaven *N.S.*   166. loneliness] *Theobald¹;* louelinesse *F.*   172. t'one to th'other] *F2* ('ton); 'ton tooth to th'other *F.*

---

158. *both our mothers*] the mother of both of us. Cf. *Rom.*, II. iii. 51.

159. *I care . . . heaven*] I desire it and Heaven to the same extent; the ambiguity of this way of saying "I desire it very much" is characteristic of Helena. J. C. Maxwell points out to me that the difficulty arises from a double use of *care for*, used with a negative to mean "I don't object to", and then, in relation to *heaven*, to mean "I am devoted to". Cf. Nashe, "I was persuaded I should not be more glad to see heaven than I was to see him" (II, 242).

160. *Can't no other*] can it not be otherwise (Brigstocke).

165. *fondness*] may either mean "love of Bertram" or "foolishness".

166. *loneliness*] Thiselton defends F *louelinesse,* taking it to mean "the state

of being in love"; but if the Countess had known Helena was in love, before the steward revealed the fact, why did her ensuing observations (ll. 123–31) take up the idea of love in general as if this was the point of the revelation, and not the idea of love for one's master? Cf. similar errors in *Ham.*, III. i. 46 (Q2: *lowliness* and F: *lonelinesse*) and *Wint.*, v. iii. 18; in fact, the confusion of "u" (often equivalent to modern "v") with "n" is the commonest of errors.

167. *gross*] obvious.

168. *Invention*] here means "the faculty for inventing lying excuses". "Invention" was that section of rhetoric which dealt with the production of arguments.

171. *But . . . 'tis so*] But then your truth must be that you love Bertram.

See it so grossly shown in thy behaviours
That in their kind they speak it; only sin
And hellish obstinacy tie thy tongue,   175
That truth should be suspected. Speak, is't so?
If it be so, you have wound a goodly clew;
If it be not, forswear't; howe'er, I charge thee,
As heaven shall work in me for thine avail,
To tell me truly.
Hel.   Good madam, pardon me.   180
Count. Do you love my son?
Hel.   Your pardon, noble mistress.
Count. Love you my son?
Hel.   Do not you love him, madam?
Count. Go not about; my love hath in't a bond
Whereof the world takes note. Come, come, disclose
The state of your affection, for your passions   185
Have to the full appeach'd.
Hel.   Then I confess,
Here on my knee, before high heaven and you,
That before you, and next unto high heaven,
I love your son.
My friends were poor, but honest; so's my love.   190
Be not offended, for it hurts not him
That he is lov'd of me; I follow him not
By any token of presumptuous suit,
Nor would I have him till I do deserve him;
Yet never know how that desert should be.   195
I know I love in vain, strive against hope;

188–9.] *As Pope; one line F.*

174. *in their kind*] according to their
nature.
176. *That . . . suspected*] Sin and Hell
encourage Helena to an obstinate
silence so that their enemy, Truth,
may be brought into disrepute.
177. *wound . . . clew*] A *clew* is a ball of
twine. The whole phrase is proverbial,
and is used, remarks Howell (*apud*
Tilley, T 252) "in derision when a
business hath sped ill".
183. *Go not about*] Do not talk obli-

quely and circuitously, avoiding a
plain answer. Cf. *Mer. V.*, II. ix. 37,
Ado, IV. ii. 23, *Wint.*, IV. iv. 690.
186. *appeach'd*] confessed against
you.
190. *friends*] relatives.
192–3. *I follow . . . suit*] Helena has
been accused of deceiving the Countess about her intentions; but she is not
speaking of intentions here, only of the
fact that she has not communicated
with Bertram since he left Rossillion.

Yet in this captious and inteemable sieve
I still pour in the waters of my love
And lack not to lose still. Thus, Indian-like,
Religious in mine error, I adore   200
The sun that looks upon his worshipper
But knows of him no more. My dearest madam,
Let not your hate encounter with my love,
For loving where you do; but if yourself,
Whose aged honour cites a virtuous youth,   205
Did ever, in so true a flame of liking,
Wish chastely and love dearly, that your Dian
Was both herself and love—O then, give pity
To her whose state is such that cannot choose
But lend and give where she is sure to lose;   210
That seeks not to find that her search implies,
But riddle-like lives sweetly where she dies!

Count. Had you not lately an intent—speak truly—
    To go to Paris?

Hel.   Madam, I had.

Count.   Wherefore? tell true.

Hel. I will tell truth, by grace itself I swear.   215

197. inteemable] intemible *F*; intenible *F2*+.

197. *captious and inteemable sieve*] The
lover's hope is like a sieve, which,
though *captious* (i.e. capacious enough
to absorb every bit of feeling one can
pour into it) is *captious* in another
sense (*O.E.D. a.*1 = deceitful), for
what has been poured in cannot be
"teemed" (i.e. poured out again).
This use of "teem" is still common in
dialect, and does not require emendation into Standard English.

199. *lack . . . still*] either (a) fail not
to go on pouring, and so losing;
or (b) lack not reserves to go on
losing. Cf. *AYL.*, IV. i. 189.

Indian-like] The Indians are most
probably the West-Indians or abori-
gines of America, as in *LLL.*, IV. iii.
218. Sun-worship seems however at
this time to be imputed to non-
Christians fairly indiscriminately.

203. *encounter with*] meet in an encounter or fight.

205. *cites*] proves, as by "citing"
witnesses or authorities.

207–8. *that your Dian . . . love*] so that
you remained true to the ideal of
chastity in spite of feeling the force of
love. Cf. Lyly, *Gall.*, III. i. 2 and v. iii. 27.

209.] *state*, not an understood "she",
is the subject of *cannot choose*; though
her *state* imposes passivity on Helena,
she chooses action.

209–10.] H. F. Brooks points to the
close parallel in *Sonn.* LXIV, 13 f.

212. *riddle-like*] without ever revealing the cause of her condition, the
object of her desires. Cf. Viola's tale of
her who never told her love (*Tw. N.*,
II. iv. 109–14). We may, on the other
hand, regard *riddle-like* as a parenthesis, describing the paradox which
follows: "to express it as a riddle,
lives . . ."

lives . . . dies] remains still, in one
place, instead of searching.

You know my father left me some prescriptions
Of rare and prov'd effects, such as his reading
And manifest experience had collected
For general sovereignty; and that he will'd me
In heedfull'st reservation to bestow them,   220
As notes whose faculties inclusive were
More than they were in note. Amongst the rest
There is a remedy, approv'd, set down,
To cure the desperate languishings whereof
The king is render'd lost.

Count.   This was your motive   225
For Paris was it? Speak.

Hel. My lord your son made me to think of this;
Else Paris and the medicine and the king
Had from the conversation of my thoughts
Haply been absent then.

Count.   But think you, Helen,   230
If you should tender your supposed aid,
He would receive it? He and his physicians
Are of a mind; he, that they cannot help him;
They, that they cannot help. How shall they
       credit
A poor unlearned virgin, when the schools,   235

225–6. This . . . Speak.] *As Capell; one line F.*   226. it? Speak.] *Var.* '*73;* it,
speake? *F.*

218. *manifest*] The normal meaning
of the word is perfectly possible here,
but rather weak. Some have taken the
meaning to be "well-known". *N.S.*
suggests that *manifest experience* may
mean "knowledge of manifestations"
[i.e. symptoms]. This is attractive,
though *O.E.D.* does not support manifestations = symptoms at this date.
The use of an adjective in places where
we would expect a genitive construction is common in Shakespeare's English (see Abbott §§4 and 374, and
cf. "valued file" (*Mac.,* iii. i. 94) for
"file of value", "modest evidence"
(*Ado,* iv. i. 36) for "evidence of
modesty", "experimental seal" (*Ado,*
iv. i. 166) for "seal of experimenta-
tion").

219. *general sovereignty*] as master
medicines, panaceas.

220. *In heedfull'st . . . them*] to keep
them back carefully till an emergency.

221–2. *As notes . . . in note*] usually
taken to mean "prescriptions more
powerful than was generally known",
an interpretation which stretches the
meaning of *inclusive* rather far. Perhaps
we ought rather to paraphrase: "as
prescriptions whose power was to be
taken as more comprehensive than if
they were famous", assuming the
second *were* to be hypothetical.

223. *approv'd*] tried out.

225. *render'd lost*] said to be dying.

229. *conversation*] interchange, movement to and fro.

Embowel'd of their doctrine, have left off
The danger to itself?
Hel.   There's something in't
More than my father's skill, which was the great'st
Of his profession, that his good receipt
Shall for my legacy be sanctified   240
By th' luckiest stars in heaven; and would your honour
But give me leave to try success, I'd venture
The well-lost life of mine on his grace's cure
By such a day, an hour.
Count.   Dost thou believe't?
Hel. Ay, madam, knowingly.   245
Count. Why, Helen, thou shalt have my leave and love,
Means and attendants, and my loving greetings
To those of mine in court. I'll stay at home
And pray God's blessing into thy attempt.
Be gone tomorrow; and be sure of this,   250
What I can help thee to, thou shalt not miss.   *Exeunt.*

244. day, an] *F;* day, and *F3+.*

236. *Embowel'd*] = disembowelled, emptied.

left off] abandoned as incurable. *O.E.D.* quotes "left off by a very honest and able Doctor" from 1662.

242. *try success*] test the outcome.

243. *The well-lost life*] It is worth risking my life in such an attempt.

245. *knowingly*] I know what I'm doing.

ACT II

[SCENE I.—*Paris. The King's palace.*]

Enter the KING *with divers young Lords taking leave for the Florentine war;* BERTRAM *and* PAROLLES[*; Attendants*]. *Flourish cornets.*

King. Farewell, young lords; these warlike principles
    Do not throw from you; and you, my lords, farewell;
    Share the advice betwixt you; if both gain all,
    The gift doth stretch itself as 'tis receiv'd,
    And is enough for both.
First Lord.   'Tis our hope, sir,   5

ACT II

Scene I

Act II Scene 1] *Rowe*[1]; *Actus Secundus F.*   *Paris. The King's palace*] *Paris. A Room in the King's Palace. Capell; not in F.*   *Enter . . . Bertram and Parolles; Attendants*] *Enter . . . Count, Rosse, and Parrolles F.*   1, 2. lords . . . lords] *F;* lord . . . lord *Hanmer.*   3. you;] you, *F.*   gain all,] *Johnson;* gaine, all *F.* 5. *First Lord.*] *Rowe*[1]; *Lord. G. | F.*

S.D. Enter the King . . .] *N.S.* adds to the Folio's "Enter the King", "borne by attendants in his chair"; cf. the use of a chair in *Lr.*, IV. vii. Lafew's words in l. 64 of this scene may imply the King unable to stand; I prefer, however, to take *so stand up* to mean "stand up from a kneeling position with the same sprightliness as I do", to remove the chair as superfluous, and leave the S.D. as in the Folio. The King's *Give me some help here* at l. 208 would be more appropriate for support than for transportation.

1–2. . . . *lords . . . lords* . . .] This, the Folio reading, is plausible enough if we allow that the "divers young Lords" are divided into two groups (perhaps according to their destina-

tion—Florence or Siena) and that the King turns from one to the other.

3–5. *Share . . . both*] The F punctuation of l. 3 might be regarded as placing *if both gain* in parenthesis, so that *all* referred to *you*; i.e. "betwixt you, that is you all if both sides gain"; but the construction would be a very strained one. It would also be possible to convert the first comma to a semi-colon, retain the second comma, and attach the *all* to *The gift*; but the expression of *all* being *enough* is unhappy. Punctuated as here, I take the passage to mean: "share my advice, but there is no need to divide it—both sides may be able to accept *all* my maxims; the more people who take my advice, the further it will stretch."

34

After well-ent'red soldiers, to return
And find your grace in health.
King. No, no, it cannot be; and yet my heart
　　Will not confess he owes the malady
　　That doth my life besiege. Farewell, young lords.   10
　　Whether I live or die, be you the sons
　　Of worthy Frenchmen; let Higher Italy—
　　Those bated that inherit but the fall
　　Of the last monarchy—see that you come
　　Not to woo honour, but to wed it, when   15
　　The bravest questant shrinks: find what you seek,
　　That fame may cry you loud. I say farewell.
First Lord. Health at your bidding serve your majesty!
King. Those girls of Italy, take heed of them;

---

13. bated] *F;* bastards *Hanmer.*   15–16. it, when . . . shrinks:] *F;* it; when . . .
shrinks, *Pope.*   18. *First Lord.] Rowe¹; L. G. | F; Second Lord. Rowe³.*

---

6. *After well-ent'red soldiers*] Abbott
(§418) notes this as a Latin construction (e.g. post urbem conditam) and
compares Milton,

He, after Eve seduced, unminded
　　slunk
Into the wood fast by
　　　　(*Paradise Lost*, v, 322–3).

9. *owes*] owns.

12. *Higher*] From the use of the same
epithet in IV. iii. 40 it is probable that
this reference is to a region of Italy,
not to a social class. Thiselton takes it
to mean "further"; *O.E.D.* s.v.
"High" (A.I.3) gives "upper (in-
land)"; perhaps Rome and the Papal
states are meant (see next note).
Cf. *The Weakest Goeth to the Wall*
(M.S.R. l. 1712): "as ye trauel vp
into high Fraunce" (i.e. from Picar-
dy).

13–14. *Those bated . . . monarchy*]
Two major difficulties are involved in
this much-discussed passage: (*a*) the
meaning of *bated*; (*b*) the meaning of
the last monarchy. Johnson took *bated* to
mean "depressed, dejected" and Holt
White "excepted"; the former seems
to have more point (especially if we
interpret *Higher* geographically) and

cf. "abated" in *Cor.*, III. iii. 134. *the last
monarchy* has been variously interpreted but more or less conjecturally,
without finding any particular relevance in the words used. It sounds,
however, like a direct reference to the
doctrine of the four monarchies or
empires, derived from Daniel, ii. 31 ff
and common in Christian historio-
graphy. In the standard form (available to Shakespeare in the Prologue to
Gower's *Confessio* (ll. 595–848) for example) the last monarchy would be
the (Holy) Roman Empire. In the
Protestant form given in Sir David
Lyndsay's *Monarche* the Papal monarchy was the last.

15–16. *wed it, when . . . shrinks*]
Editors usually change the comma to
a semi-colon, but the clause *when . . .
shrinks* can refer back to *wed* as well as
forward to *find*; the *questants* can be
suitors as easily as soldiers. Accordingly it seems best to leave the Folio
pointing.

19. *girls of Italy*] The charms of
Italian courtezans were proverbial in
Shakespeare's England. Cf. Imogen's
reference to "some jay of Italy" in
Cymb., III. iv. 47.

They say our French lack language to deny   20
If they demand; beware of being captives
Before you serve.
Both Lords.   Our hearts receive your warnings.
King. Farewell. [*To Some Lords*] Come hither to me.

[*Retires.*]

First Lord. O my sweet lord, that you will stay behind us!
Par. 'Tis not his fault, the spark.
Second Lord.   O, 'tis brave wars!   25
Par. Most admirable! I have seen those wars.
Ber. I am commanded here, and kept a coil with
   "Too young", and "The next year" and "'Tis too
   early".

---

23. S.D. *To Some Lords*] *This edn; To Attendants Theobald*[1]; *not in* F.   S.D.
Retires.] *retires to a Couch; Capell; Exit. Pope; not in* F.   24. *First Lord.*] 1. *Lo.* G. |
F *(and at 34, 37).*   25. *Second Lord.*] 2. *Lo.* E. | F *(and at 35, 38).*

21–2. *beware . . . serve*] beware of becoming a captive (in love) before you
have begun your military career. The
Clarkes point out the "elegant pun"
on *serve* ((*a*) militarily, (*b*) in servi-
tude).

23. S.D.] There is no S.D. in the
Folio, but the King's *Come hither* implies
some kind of retirement. Editors are
not able to agree (*a*) with whom the
King retires, (*b*) whither he retires.
(*a*) I , as some have supposed, the King
addresses Bertram in l. 23, we have
surely a remarkable case of disobedience in Bertram and forgetfulness in
the King, unmotivated and undramatic. If the King faints here or calls for
attendants to bear him away, the inso-
lence of Bertram and the lords who
ignore this is again undramatic and in-
consequent. It seems best to suppose
that the King should speak in l. 23 to a
section of the assembled lords, allowing the four or so who take part in the
following episode to detach themselves
from the public events and conduct a
private conversation. For the "consult
apart" convention H. F. Brooks compares *Cæs.*, II. i. 100–11 and v. i. 69–92.
(*b*) If the King disappears from the
stage here, why does the Folio mark

neither exit nor entrance? It is, moreover, hard to find any point at which
the King can return conveniently. An
entry after l. 48 gives Parolles too long
a speech before the King's presence is
acknowledged—a difficulty which is
accentuated if he is carried in a chair:
the *N.S.* directions seem to require
that he be borne round the stage like
the ark of the covenant. An entry after
l. 59 makes Lafew's speech sudden and
unceremonious; when Shakespeare
shows characters entering together he
usually breaks in upon their conversation after some words can be imagin-
ed to have been spoken. The easiest
solution of the problem would seem to
be the following: the King and the
lords he summoned in l. 23 retire to
one side of the stage. At l. 59 Lafew
enters and kneels; the King then
leaves the lords and turns to Lafew.

25. *the spark*] perhaps an affectation.
O.E.D.'s first example in this sense
comes from the anon. *Timon* (c. 1581 <
> 90). Cf. below, l. 40.

26. *admirable*] King (p. 167) notes
this as an affectation (cf. Jonson,
Poet., III. iv. 243).

27. *kept a coil with*] fussed. Cf. *Two
Noble Kinsmen*, II. iv. 17–18.

Par. And thy mind stand to't, boy, steal away bravely.

Ber. I shall stay here the forehorse to a smock,   30
　　Creaking my shoes on the plain masonry,
　　Till honour be bought up, and no sword worn
　　But one to dance with. By heaven, I'll steal away!

First Lord. There's honour in the theft.

Par.　　　　　　　　　　　　　Commit it, count.

Second Lord. I am your accessary; and so farewell.   35

Ber. I grow to you, and our parting is a tortur'd body.

First Lord. Farewell, captain.

Second Lord. Sweet Monsieur Parolles!

Par. Noble heroes, my sword and yours are kin. Good
　　sparks and lustrous, a word, good metals. You shall   40
　　find in the regiment of the Spinii one Captain Spurio,
　　with his cicatrice, an emblem of war, here on his
　　sinister cheek; it was this very sword entrench'd it.
　　Say to him I live, and observe his reports for me.

First Lord. We shall, noble captain.   [*Exeunt Lords.*]   45

---

29. And . . . boy, . . . bravely.] *As Pope;* And . . . boy, / . . . brauely. / *F.*
42. with his cicatrice, an emblem] *Theobald¹;* his cicatrice, with an Embleme *F.*
45. *First Lord.*] *Rowe¹; Lo. G. | F.*　　　S.D. *Exeunt Lords.*] *Collier¹; Theobald¹*
(after 48); Capell (after 46); not in F.

29. *bravely*] The ambiguous tone of this word here and below, II. iii. 295, suggests that it was capable of an undertone of irony now inaudible—perhaps connected with the obsolete meaning of "brave" (= overdressed).

30. *forehorse to a smock*] "the leader in a team of horses driven by a woman" (*N.S.*). As *N.S.* further remarks, the situation depicted here is essentially that of the young courtiers of Elizabeth (see *Fragmenta Regalia* (Arber), pp. 32 f); it does not follow, however, that the play "can scarcely have been written after 1603". Shakespeare, as might be expected, depicts the unknown by means of the known, but the known need not be contemporary. Staunton says that the forehorse "was gaily ornamented with tufts and ribbons and bells".

31. *Creaking . . . masonry*] making a useless noise on smoothly tiled floors.

32–3. *no sword . . . dance with*] Lighter swords, not intended for fighting, were worn by Elizabethan dancers. Cf. *Ant.*, III. xi. 35 f.

36. *I grow . . . body*] This parting is as painful to us as being torn apart on the rack is to a human body. The elaborateness of this expression, together with the affected phrases, *sweet lord, admirable*, etc. suggest that Shakespeare is here expressing a contemptuous view of courtly affectation.

38. *Sweet*] One of the most generally ridiculed affectations of courtly language.

39.] Capell adds S.D. "measuring Swords with them".

40. *metals*] The idea of "spirit" is present no less than that of "sword" (cf. above, I. i. 127 n.).

41. *Spurio*] The name is significant; see Florio, *Worlde of Wordes* (1598), s.v. Spurio: "used . . . for a counterfeit".

Par. Mars dote on you for his novices!
     [*to Bertram*] What will ye do?
Ber. Stay the king.
Par. Use a more spacious ceremony to the noble lords;
     you have restrain'd yourself within the list of too cold   50
     an adieu. Be more expressive to them, for they wear
     themselves in the cap of the time; there do muster
     true gait, eat, speak, and move, under the influence
     of the most receiv'd star; and though the devil lead
     the measure, such are to be followed. After them, and   55
     take a more dilated farewell.
Ber. And I will do so.
Par. Worthy fellows, and like to prove most sinewy
     sword-men.   *Exeunt* [*Bertram and Parolles*].

      Enter LAFEW. [*The* KING *comes forward.*]

Laf. [*kneeling*] Pardon, my lord, for me and for my tidings. 60
King. I'll fee thee to stand up.

47. S.D.] *Capell; not in F.*　　47. ye] *F;* you *Hanmer.*　　48. Stay] *F;* Stay: *F2.*
59. S.D. *The King comes forward.*] *This edn; seeing him rise. Capell (after 48); Re-enter*
King. Camb. (after 48); not in F.　　60. S.D. *kneeling*] *Johnson; not in F.*　　61. fee]
Theobald[1]; see F.

47. *ye*] This seems to be addressed to
Bertram rather than the Lords, but no
emendation is necessary: *ye* was a correct (if somewhat old-fashioned) form
of the polite plural (cf. modern "you").

48.] Editors who think of the King
as re-entering at this point (see above,
l. 23 n.) naturally prefer F2 punctuation here, with the sense: "stop talking; the King's coming"; F2 punctuation may, alternatively, mean: "(I
shall) stay; (for some reason connected
with) the King". I take the phrase,
with F punctuation, to be a direct
answer to Parolles' question, and to
mean: "I shall remain in court to stay
(support) the King." This interpretation has been queried because it contradicts *I'll steal away* above (l. 33) but
Bertram is a difficult character upon
whom to base arguments from psychological inconsistency.

50. *list*] the selvage of cloth; hence,
limit, boundary.

51–2. *wear . . . time*] a typical
Parolles periphrasis (in terms of
clothes and fashion) for "are notable"
(like jewels, ribbons, etc.).

52–4. *there do . . . star*] The image of
the lords "mustering" true gait in the
cap of time is a little ridiculous, but
may well have been intended to be so.
Mrs 'Espinasse suggests "there they
display the proper way of proceeding"
as a paraphrase of *there . . . gait*; this interpretation of *gait* (for which cf. *Ham.*,
I. ii. 31) has the advantage of avoiding a tautology between *gait* and *move.*

55. *measure*] dance.

61. *fee*] Theobald's emendation,
though not entirely satisfactory, is
probably better than F "see", and
(given the similarity of long 's' and 'f')
represents a very easy mistake; what is
wanted is some antithesis to *pardon*, and
this *fee* to some extent provides:
Lafew asks for a *Pardon*; the King does
not grant this but offers payment (or

Laf. Then here's a man stands that has brought his pardon.
    I would you had kneel'd, my lord, to ask me mercy,
    And that at my bidding you could so stand up.
King. I would I had; so I had broke thy pate   65
    And ask'd thee mercy for't.
Laf.   Good faith, across!
    But, my good lord, 'tis thus: will you be cur'd
    Of your infirmity?
King.   No.
Laf.   O, will you eat
    No grapes, my royal fox? Yes, but you will
    My noble grapes, and if my royal fox   70
    Could reach them. I have seen a medicine
    That's able to breathe life into a stone,
    Quicken a rock, and make you dance canary
    With sprightly fire and motion; whose simple touch
    Is powerful to araise King Pippen, nay,   75
    To give great Charlemain a pen in's hand
    And write to her a love-line.
King.   What "her" is this?
Laf. Why, Doctor She! My lord, there's one arriv'd,

66–71.] *As Capell;* ... for't. / ... thus, / ... infirmitie? / ... No. / ... foxe? /
... and if / ... medicine / *F.*   70. and] *F;* an *Theobald*[1].   75. Pippen] *F;*
Pepin *Theobald*[1].

bribe) if he will only stand up; "then",
says Lafew, "I will stand up a par-
doned man, for I have already
brought my pardon (Helena)". The
sense of *fee* as "a physician's remunera-
tion" is probably also present.

64.] See note on II. i Entry.

66. *across*] a term from the combats
of chivalry. It implies that the King's
jest has hit him very clumsily, as a
lance handled clumsily might be
snapped across by the impact, and not
shivered or splintered from the point
backwards, in the approved fashion.
Cf. *Ado*, v. i. 136–7.

70. *My noble grapes*] The words *my*
and *noble* are emphatic, the latter possibly reinforced by a play on *noble* and
royal as coins (cf. *R 2*, v. v. 67 f). In
Aesop's fable the fox said that the
grapes were sour because he could

not reach them; so, says Lafew, the
King decries the idea of recovery because he thinks recovery out of reach.

71. *medicine*] seems to be used here in
its normal sense, though the change to
"her" (the point that surprises the
King) is facilitated by the existence of
O.E.D. medicine sb.[2]: a physician.
Cf. *Mac.*, v. ii. 27.

73. *canary*] a lively dance.

74. *simple touch*] mere touch; but
also perhaps with the sense: the touch
of whose simples or medicines.

75. *araise*] *N.S.* notes that no later
examples of this word are given in
O.E.D. and suggests that Shakespeare
used an archaic word to suit Pepin and
Charlemagne, cited here for their antiquity. Cf. Webster, *D.M.*, II. i. 111

Pippen] common Elizabethan form
of Pepin, reigned in France 741–68.

If you will see her. Now by my faith and honour,
If seriously I may convey my thoughts   80
In this my light deliverance, I have spoke
With one that in her sex, her years, profession,
Wisdom and constancy, hath amaz'd me more
Than I dare blame my weakness. Will you see her,
For that is her demand, and know her business?   85
That done, laugh well at me.

King.   Now, good Lafew,
Bring in the admiration that we with thee
May spend our wonder too, or take off thine
By wond'ring how thou took'st it.

Laf.   Nay, I'll fit you,
And not be all day neither.   [*Lafew goes to the door.*]   90
King. Thus he his special nothing ever prologues.
Laf. Nay, come your ways.

Enter HELENA.

King.   This haste hath wings indeed.
Laf. Nay, come your ways.
This is his majesty; say your mind to him.
A traitor you do look like, but such traitors   95
His majesty seldom fears; I am Cressid's uncle
That dare leave two together. Fare you well.   *Exit.*
King. Now, fair one, does your business follow us?
Hel. Ay, my good lord.
Gerard de Narbon was my father,   100

---

90. S.D. *Lafew goes to the door.*] *This edn; Exit. Theobald*[1] + ; *not in F.*   92, 92
S.D. *Laf.* Nay . . . ways. *Enter Helena*] F (*Enter Hellen*); *Laf. Returns.* Nay . . .
ways. *Bringing in* Helena. *Theobald*[1]+.

81. *light deliverance*] jesting manner of speaking (Craig *apud* Brigstocke).

82. *profession*] what she professes to be able to do.

83–4. *more . . . weakness*] I cannot think it is only my partiality (or age) that makes me think her so wonderful.

87. *admiration*] wonder.

88. *take off*] abate or reduce; as in *Ham.*, III. ii. 244, *Cym.*, V. ii. 2.

89. *I'll fit you*] supply to your satisfaction . Cf. *Spanish Tragedy*, IV. i. 69.

90 ff.] In F there is no exit for Lafew when he goes to fetch Helena, and the entry for Helena is for her alone. This may indicate that Shakespeare did not intend Lafew to *leave* the stage; if so, l. 91 will be spoken as he walks back to the stage door, and *This . . . ways* as he returns to the fore-stage with Helena. Cf. the movements of Charmian in *Ant.*, II. v. 81–4 (see New Arden edn).

96. *Cressid's uncle*] Pandarus, the eponym of pandars.

      In what he did profess, well found.
King.   I knew him.
Hel. The rather will I spare my praises towards him;
      Knowing him is enough. On's bed of death
      Many receipts he gave me; chiefly one,
      Which, as the dearest issue of his practice,   105
      And of his old experience th' only darling,
      He bade me store up as a triple eye,
      Safer than mine own two; more dear I have so,
      And hearing your high majesty is touch'd
      With that malignant cause, wherein the honour   110
      Of my dear father's gift stands chief in power,
      I come to tender it and my appliance,
      With all bound humbleness.
King.   We thank you, maiden;
      But may not be so credulous of cure,
      When our most learned doctors leave us, and   115
      The congregated college have concluded
      That labouring art can never ransom nature
      From her inaidible estate. I say we must not
      So stain our judgment or corrupt our hope,

108. two; more dear I] *F;* two, more dear. I *Var. '78.*

101. *In . . . found*] found to be good at what he professed—medicine.

105–6.] the only cure he had produced which he continued to think very highly of at the end and summit of his life.

107. *triple*] third. Cf. *Ant.*, I. i. 12.

110. *cause*] disease (On.). Cf. *Cor.*, III. i. 235: "Leave us to cure this cause".

110–11. *wherein . . . power*] the honourable gift of my father has most power to deal with this very complaint. The exact sense of *honour* is not clear; the gift may be so termed because it comes from Gerard, or the word may be used proleptically; but the general sense is clear enough and does not require the reversal of *honour* and *power* conjectured by Johnson, a reading which also ignores the fact that the remedy, obviously, is not famous.

112. *appliance*] (1) service, (2) treatment.

116. *The congregated college*] Thiselton sees in this a reference to the Royal College of Physicians. Mr R. R. Simpson tells me that such an important matter as withdrawal from a case (involving the reputation of the whole profession) would, in both the London College of Physicians and the Faculty of Medicine in Paris, be decided only in congregation. Cf. Jonson, *Volp.*, II. vi. 26–8: ". . . they have had / (At extreme fees) the college of physicians / Consulting on him."

117. *labouring art*] the endeavours of human skill. The extent to which this speech generalizes the King's *inaidible estate* as something true of *nature* in general is notable.

119. *stain*] taint.

corrupt our hope] ill-founded *hope* is *corrupt* because contrary to sense.

To prostitute our past-cure malady   120
To empirics, or to dissever so
Our great self and our credit, to esteem
A senseless help, when help past sense we deem.
Hel. My duty then shall pay me for my pains.
I will no more enforce mine office on you,   125
Humbly entreating from your royal thoughts
A modest one to bear me back again.
King. I cannot give thee less, to be call'd grateful;
Thou thought'st to help me, and such thanks I give
As one near death to those that wish him live.   130
But what at full I know, thou know'st no part;
I knowing all my peril, thou no art.
Hel. What I can do can do no hurt to try,
Since you set up your rest 'gainst remedy.
He that of greatest works is finisher   135
Oft does them by the weakest minister.
So holy writ in babes hath judgment shown,
When judges have been babes. Great floods have flown
From simple sources, and great seas have dried
When miracles have by the great'st been denied.   140

120–3. *To prostitute . . . deem*] to allow
quacks to meddle with my incurable
disease, or to behave in a way different
from what my reputation would lead
people to expect, trusting in cures
beneath reason when in fact only
something beyond reason could cure
me.

127. *A modest one*] "a simple admis-
sion that her offer, though declined,
was not out of place" (Herford); more
specifically, I think, the entreaty raises
the possibility of her offer having
brought her maidenly "modesty" into
question.

129 ff.] The transition to couplets
here marks the change to a more formal and less purely personal exchange,
leading up to the invocation of the
supernatural.

134. *set up your rest*] derived from the
gambling card-game called Primero;
similar to the modern "stake your all".

135–6.] Noble compares 1 Corin-

thians, i. 27: "God hath chosen the
weake things of the worlde, to con-
found the things which are mightie".
Cf. below, II. iii. 33–4.

137–8. *So . . . been babes*] This is most
probably a reference to the judgment
of Daniel in the case of Susannah and
the Elders; but, as *N.S.* points out,
holy writ is full of such babes.

138–9. *Great floods . . . sources*] In
view of the Biblical references in the
context it seems probable that Henley
is right in finding an allusion here to
Moses' striking water from the rock
(Exodus, xvii), but the sentence says
no more, in fact, than "great rivers
begin as little springs".

139–40. *great seas . . . denied*] refers
most probably to the drying of the Red
Sea to allow the Israelites to escape
from Egypt; *the great'st* is presumably
Pharaoh whose heart was hardened to
pursue the Israelites before the miracle
took place.

Oft expectation fails, and most oft there
Where most it promises, and oft it hits
Where hope is coldest and despair most fits.
King. I must not hear thee. Fare thee well, kind maid.
Thy pains, not us'd, must by thyself be paid;   145
Proffers not took reap thanks for their reward.
Hel. Inspired merit so by breath is barr'd.
It is not so with Him that all things knows
As 'tis with us that square our guess by shows;
But most it is presumption in us when   150
The help of heaven we count the act of men.
Dear sir, to my endeavours give consent;
Of heaven, not me, make an experiment.
I am not an impostor, that proclaim
Myself against the level of mine aim,   155
But know I think, and think I know most sure,
My art is not past power, nor you past cure.
King. Art thou so confident? Within what space
Hop'st thou my cure?
Hel.   The greatest Grace lending grace,

143. fits] *Collier*[1], *conj. Theobald;* shifts *F;* sits *Pope.*   154. impostor] *F3;*
Impostrue *F;* imposture *Capell.*

143. *fits*] Theobald's emendation
supplies the rhyme and is probably
correct, though F "shifts" is more
vivid. One can see how the corruption
could have arisen if the copy had
"ffitts"—a spelling consistent with the
habit of doubling final consonants
observed in hand D's contribution to
Sir Thomas More.

145.] Since your efforts have not
been of use to anyone else, another
person cannot pay you for them; your
own (?virtue) must be your sufficient
payment, together with thanks from
me.

147.] The contrast between breathing in (inspiration from God) and
breathing out (human speech) is used
to sharpen the contrast between
Helena's spiritual and positive mission
and the King's human and negative
response.

149. *square ... shows*] "form our con-
jectures according to appearances"
(the Clarkes).

154. *impostor*] F "Impostrue" is
obviously a mistake for "Imposture"
an earlier spelling of F3 and modern
"impostor".

154–5.] Though I am stating pub-
licly, even before I take aim, that I
shall hit the target, do not take me for
a bragging charlatan, for I know
my own mind, and my mind tells
me that it is certain that my skill can
deal with your disease. *against* most
probably means "in expectation
of", though "in regard to" is also
possible.

157. *past power*] The most likely
meaning of *past* here is *O.E.D. prep.*
and *adv.* A.3 "incapable of".

159–67.] The periphrases of Helena's reply are probably designed
to produce an effect of incantation
against sickness.

Ere twice the horses of the sun shall bring   160
Their fiery coacher his diurnal ring,
Ere twice in murk and occidental damp
Moist Hesperus hath quench'd her sleepy lamp,
Or four and twenty times the pilot's glass
Hath told the thievish minutes how they pass,   165
What is infirm from your sound parts shall fly,
Health shall live free and sickness freely die.

King. Upon thy certainty and confidence
What dar'st thou venture?

Hel.   Tax of impudence,
A strumpet's boldness, a divulged shame,   170
Traduc'd by odious ballads; my maiden's name
Sear'd otherwise; ne worse of worst, extended

---

161. coacher] *This edn, conj. Anon. (Fras. Mag. 1853)*; torcher *F.*   163. her] *F;*
his *Rowe[1]+.*   172. Sear'd otherwise; ne worse of] Seard otherwise, ne worse
of *F;* Seard otherwise, no worse of *F2;* Sear'd otherwise; nay, worse of *Singer[2];*
Sear'd otherwise; nay worse—of *conj. Perring;* Seared; otherwise—ne worse of
N.S.   worst, extended] *Sisson, conj. Perring;* worst extended *F;* worst extended,
Rowe[1].

---

161. *coacher*] Though universally
accepted, F reading "torcher" has
little to recommend it: it is otherwise
unknown (though an easy analogical
formation); "fiery torcher" would
seem to be a tautology and the whole
image of "their fiery torcher" running
in a ring is distressingly unrelated to
anything in experience. The anon.
emendation *coacher* has more probability: *O.E.D.* quotes examples of the
word from 1587–1609; Shakespeare
elsewhere (*Rom.*, III. ii. 2) uses the
parallel formation "waggoner", and
of course the whole idea of the sun's
horses as coach horses is commonplace. Moreover, the *ductus literarum*
shows that one word could easily be
mistaken for the other in Elizabethan
script, the confusion c : t being one of
the commonest of the period.

162. *murk and occidental damp*] the
thick gloom and ṣog of sunset.

163. *Hesperus . . . lamp*] Editors usually change F *her* to "his"; but the
"error" may well be Shakespeare's—

deriving from his knowledge that Hesperus is in fact the planet Venus. Bion,
in fragment 11, speaks of "Hesperus,
golden lamp of the lovely daughter of
the foam".

164. *pilot's glass*] From this and
Mer. V., I. i. 25 it appears that Shakespeare thought of the nautical glass as
an hour and not (as it was later) a half-
hour glass. There is no evidence that
he was wrong about the practice of his
own time. Cf. also *Temp.*, I. ii. 240 and
v. i. 223 and New Arden note at latter
place.

166. *sound*] proleptic adjective; i.e.
which will become sound.

169. *Tax*] charge, accusation (On.).

172–3. *ne . . . ended*] *ne worse of worst,*
if it is correct, must be a deliberate
archaism, not improper, of course, in
oracular speeches of this kind. The
only other appearance of the archaic
ne (= nor) in Shakespeare is in the
pseudo-medieval prologue of Gower
in *Pericles* (2 Prol. 36); *ne . . . ended* I
take to mean: nor will it make *the*

With vildest torture, let my life be ended.
King. Methinks in thee some blessed spirit doth
      speak
    His powerful sound within an organ weak;   175
    And what impossibility would slay
    In common sense, sense saves another way.
    Thy life is dear, for all that life can rate
    Worth name of life in thee hath estimate:
    Youth, beauty, wisdom, courage—all   180
    That happiness and prime can happy call.
    Thou this to hazard needs must intimate
    Skill infinite, or monstrous desperate.
    Sweet practiser, thy physic I will try,
    That ministers thine own death if I die.   185
Hel. If I break time, or flinch in property
    Of what I spoke, unpitied let me die,
    And well deserv'd. Not helping, death's my
      fee;
    But if I help, what do you promise me?
King. Make thy demand.

---

180. courage] courage, virtue *Theobald*[1]; courage, honour *Collier*[2]; courage, health and *conj. Brigstocke.*

---

worst (a divulged shame) any worse if I die on the rack. Brigstocke takes *extended* to mean "seized by a course of law" but the train of thought and imagery (*Sear'd, torture*) indicates "racked" or "stretched out (in body and in *life*, i.e. death-pangs)" as more probable (cf. *R 2*, III. ii. 198 ff). It would also be possible (keeping F punctuation after *worst*) to take *extended* as indicating the relationship between *worst* and *worse*: i.e. "no other kind of torture (or, perhaps, name-searing) can extend the worst to make it still worse". Cf. "but one resource / The last—the worst—if torture were not worse" (Byron, *The Corsair*, III, 280–1).

173. *vildest torture*] Painter says, "let me be burnt".

175. *organ weak*] Shakespeare seems to have associated *organ* with shrill piping noises. Cf. *Tw. N.*, I. iv. 32, and perhaps *Ham.*, III. ii. 359. Such seems to have been the sound of many early organs.

176–7. *what . . . way*] "There's sense in what you say, but it is not *common* sense" (Brigstocke).

178–9. *for all . . . estimate*] You must be reckoned to be enriched by all the qualities that are believed to make life precious.

181. *prime*] "the 'springtime' of human life" (*O.E.D. sb.*[1] 8).

183. *desperate*] does not qualify *skill*, but the idea of disposition inherent in *skill.*

186–7. *in property Of*] *property* is "An attribute or quality belonging to a thing or person" (as in *Lr.*, I. i. 113 and below, II. iii. 130). I take this phrase to mean "in respect of the particulars belonging to".

Hel.   But will you make it even?   190
King. Ay, by my sceptre and my hopes of heaven.
Hel. Then shalt thou give me with thy kingly hand
    What husband in thy power I will command:
    Exempted be from me the arrogance
    To choose from forth the royal blood of France   195
    My low and humble name to propagate
    With any branch or image of thy state;
    But such a one, thy vassal, whom I know
    Is free for me to ask, thee to bestow.
King. Here is my hand; the premises observ'd,   200
    Thy will by my performance shall be serv'd;
    So make the choice of thy own time, for I,
    Thy resolv'd patient, on thee still rely.
    More should I question thee, and more I must,
    Though more to know could not be more to trust: 205
    From whence thou cam'st, how tended on; but
       rest,
    Unquestion'd, welcome, and undoubted bless'd.
    Give me some help here, ho! If thou proceed
    As high as word, my deed shall match thy deed.
                    Flourish. Exeunt.

191. heaven] *Theobald¹, conj. Thirlby;* helpe *F.*   209. S.D. *Exeunt.*] *Exit. F.*

190. *make it even*] balance my request with your fulfilment.

191. *heaven*] The original "helpe" may be right; it makes sense and the break in the rhyme may have been designed, as Thiselton thinks.

194–7.] Cf. Painter: "without presumption to any of your children or other of your bloud".

197. *branch or image*] Presumably the basic idea uniting these two words is that of a genealogical tree, from whose branches hang coats of arms or portraits of the members of the family. Illustrations of the tree of Jesse are often of this kind, as is the title-page of Hall's Chronicles.

203. *still*] always.

[SCENE II.—*Rossillion. The Count's palace.*]

Enter COUNTESS *and* CLOWN.

Count. Come on, sir; I shall now put you to the height of
your breeding.

Clo. I will show myself highly fed and lowly taught. I
know my business is but to the court.

Count. To the court! Why, what place make you special,   5
when you put off that with such contempt? But to
the court!

Clo. Truly, madam, if God have lent a man any manners
he may easily put it off at court: he that cannot make
a leg, put off's cap, kiss his hand, and say nothing,   10
has neither leg, hands, lip, nor cap; and indeed such
a fellow, to say precisely, were not for the court; but
for me, I have an answer will serve all men.

Count. Marry, that's a bountiful answer that fits all
questions.   15

Clo. It is like a barber's chair that fits all buttocks:
the pin-buttock, the quatch-buttock, the brawn-
buttock, or any buttock.

Scene II

Scene II] *Capell; not in* F.   *Rossillion.*] *Rousillon.* Pope; *not in* F.   *The Count's
palace*] *A Room in the Count's Palace. Capell; not in* F.   1. *Count.*] *Lady.* F (*Lady or
La. throughout scene*).

3. *highly . . . taught*] a variation
(prompted by the *height* in the preceding line) on the proverbial "better fed
than taught", which, says Kelly (*Complete Collection*, 1721), is "spoken to
children of wealthy parents, who are
commonly saucy, insolent, and ill-
natured". We have therefore a parody
of the distinction between physical
nurture and moral discipline so important in the play.

9. *put it off*] In view of the *lent* above,
I assume this is *O.E.D.* put off. *j.* (to
sell) rather than *k.* (to palm off or
foist upon some one). The clown
catches up the Countess's *put off* above
(= brush aside) and repeats it in yet
another meaning in *put off's cap* below.

9–10. *make a leg*] make obeisance.

10. *and say nothing*] Again Shakespeare emphasizes the contrast between the physical skill of the courtier
and his mental incapacity.

16. *like a barber's chair*] proverbial.
Steevens quotes Roger Sharpe, *More
Fooles Yet* (1610):
     . . . a Barbor's chayre;
As fit for every Iacke and
     Iourneyman,
As for a knight, or worthy
     Gentleman.
Notice the extent to which the clown's
similes serve to degrade satirically
what he is talking about.

17. *quatch*] No other instance of this
word seems to be recorded; it must

Count. Will your answer serve fit to all questions?

Clo. As fit as ten groats is for the hand of an attorney, as   20
your French crown for your taffety punk, as Tib's
rush for Tom's forefinger, as a pancake for Shrove
Tuesday, a morris for May-day, as the nail to his
hole, the cuckold to his horn, as a scolding quean to
a wrangling knave, as the nun's lip to the friar's   25
mouth; nay, as the pudding to his skin.

Count. Have you, I say, an answer of such fitness for all
questions?

Clo. From below your duke to beneath your constable, it
will fit any question.   30

Count. It must be an answer of most monstrous size that
must fit all demands.

Clo. But a trifle neither, in good faith, if the learned
should speak truth of it. Here it is, and all that
belongs to't: ask me if I am a courtier; it shall do you   35
no harm to learn.

Count. To be young again, if we could, I will be a fool in
question, hoping to be the wiser by your answer.
I pray you, sir, are you a courtier?

Clo. O Lord, sir! There's a simple putting off. More,   40
more, a hundred of them.

Count. Sir, I am a poor friend of yours that loves you.

---

37. could,] *Knight*[1]; could: *F*; could! *Case.*   39. I pray] *F3*; *La.* I pray *F.*

---

mean something like plump. Cf. the
dialectical "quat" (*O.E.D.* a.2) meaning "low and squat".

20. *ten groats*] an attorney's fee.

21. *French crown*] the punk's fee, and
the punk's disease.

taffety] expensively (and showily)
dressed (cf. below, IV. v. 1).

21-2. *as Tib's . . . forefinger*] Rings
made of rushes were formerly ex-
changed in rustic mock-marriages.
Brigstocke refers to Brand's *Popular
Antiquities*, Bohn edn, II. 107.

25-6. *as the nun's . . . skin*] Cf. the
proverb "as fit as a pudding for a
friar's mouth" (Tilley P 620).

33. *neither*] used to strengthen

the implied negative (*O.E.D.* s.v
A.3).

39. *I pray you . . .*] F gives a second
speech-prefix to the Countess at this
point. As this occurs at the beginning of a new F page some difficulty
in the printing-house seems to be implied.

40. *O Lord, sir!*] "a fashionable
stopgap when conversation flagged or
when an awkward question called for
a reply" (Herford and Simpson, *Jonson*, n. on *E.M.O.*, III. i. 25). Cf. *LLL.*,
v. ii. 485, 496, 499, and Marston,
Dutch Curtezan, II. i. 197 f: "*Hol.* O
Lord sir. *Cocl.* Well spoken, good
english."

Clo. O Lord, sir! Thick, thick; spare not me.

Count. I think, sir, you can eat none of this homely meat.

Clo. O Lord, sir! Nay, put me to't, I warrant you.   45

Count. You were lately whipp'd, sir, as I think.

Clo. O Lord, sir! Spare not me.

Count. Do you cry "O Lord, sir!" at your whipping, and
  "spare not me"? Indeed your "O Lord, sir!" is very
  sequent to your whipping; you would answer very   50
  well to a whipping, if you were but bound to't.

Clo. I ne'er had worse luck in my life in my "O Lord, sir!"
  I see things may serve long, but not serve ever.

Count. I play the noble housewife with the time,
  To entertain it so merrily with a fool.   55

Clo. O Lord, sir! Why, there't serves well again.

Count. An end, sir! To your business: give Helen this,
  And urge her to a present answer back.
  Commend me to my kinsmen and my son.
  This is not much.   60

Clo. Not much commendation to them?

Count. Not much employment for you. You understand
  me?

Clo. Most fruitfully. I am there before my legs.

Count. Haste you again.   *Exeunt.*   65

54–5.] *As Knight*[1]*; prose F.*   57. An end, sir! To] An end, Sir; to *Rowe*[3]*; And
end sir to F; And end; sir to F3.*   63. me?] *Capell; me. F.*

43. *Thick*] quickly; "to talk thick" is
to talk quickly.

49–50. *Indeed . . . whipping*] Your
O Lord, sir! (i.e. have pity on me)
would follow very closely on your
being whipped.

50. *answer*] (1) repay; (2) reply
(*O Lord, sir!*).

51. *bound to't*] (1) bound by oath to

answer; (2) tied to a whipping-post.

64. *fruitfully*] probably connected
with an obscene pun on *understand*.

there] probably "in Paris (by imagination)", but perhaps "I can understand you better than *my* legs can
stand under *you*" (cf. *Tw. N.,* III. i. 76–
7).

65. *again*] back again.

[SCENE III.—*Paris. The King's palace.*]

Enter BERTRAM, LAFEW, *and* PAROLLES.

Laf. They say miracles are past; and we have our philo-
sophical persons to make modern and familiar, things
supernatural and causeless. Hence is it that we make
trifles of terrors, ensconcing ourselves into seeming
knowledge when we should submit ourselves to an   5
unknown fear.

Par. Why, 'tis the rarest argument of wonder that hath
shot out in our latter times.

Ber. And so 'tis.

Laf. To be relinquish'd of the artists—   10

Par. So I say—both of Galen and Paracelsus.

Scene III

Scene III] *Capell; not in F.*   *Paris. The King's palace.*] *Paris. A Room in the King's
Palace. Capell; not in F.*   *Enter Bertram, Lafew*] *Enter Count, Lafew F; Enter
Lafeu | Sisson.*   1. *Laf.*] *Ol. Laf. F (so to 184; except 38, 59, 93 Old Laf., 99 Ol.
Lord).*   7–9. *Par.* Why . . . times. *Ber.* And so 'tis.] *F;* Why . . . times. *Par.* And
so 'tis. *Sisson.*   11–12.] *As F; Par.* So I say. *Laf.* Both . . . Paracelsus. *Par.* So I
say. *Laf.* Of all . . . *Globe, conj. Camb.*   11. say—both] say, both *Rowe¹;* say
both *F.*

S.D. Enter Bertram] Sisson's omission of Bertram from the entry might
seem to be justified in view of the little
that Bertram has to say, but this very
silence seems to me the point. Lafew's
remarks, ll. 1–61, show an attempt to
proceed to a coherent discourse in
spite of Parolles' continual intrusions.
To whom should this discourse be delivered but to Parolles' master? Bertram manages to squeeze his tongue
in only once, and then only as an
echo of Parolles. The rearrangements
of the speeches in Globe and Sisson, by
which Parolles is reduced to an echo,
have an obvious theatrical point, but
it is dangerous to assume that Shakespeare's clowning is making only
obvious points. I keep F's arrangement and assume that the gradual
retreat of Lafew before the flood of
Parolles' verbosity is intentional. Dis-
illusion with Bertram and his follower
here would explain the tone of Lafew's

remarks in ll. 45, 99–101, 184 ff.

1. *miracles are past*] Cf. *H 5,* I. i. 67.

2. *modern*] everyday, commonplace;
the only meaning in Shakespeare.

3. *causeless*] here must mean something like "whose cause is hidden",
i.e. inexplicable.

4–6. *ensconcing . . . fear*] seeking
refuge in presumed knowledge when
we should be admitting humbly
that the world is fearfully unknown.
A sconce is a fort; *fear* (= *terrors* above)
is metonymy of effect (the feeling) for
cause (the object).

7. *argument*] subject.

8. *shot out*] The rather curious verb
suggests that Parolles is thinking of a
more traditional cause of wonder and
piety—a comet.

10. *artists*] graduates in arts;
scholars.

11. *both . . . Paracelsus*] physicians of
both schools of medicine then current.
Bucknill points out that ". . . in Shake-

Laf. Of all the learned and authentic Fellows—
Par. Right; so I say.
Laf. That gave him out incurable—
Par. Why, there 'tis; so say I too.   15
Laf. Not to be help'd.
Par. Right; as 'twere a man assur'd of a—
Laf. Uncertain life and sure death.
Par. Just. You say well. So would I have said.
Laf. I may truly say it is a novelty to the world.   20
Par. It is indeed; if you will have it in showing, you shall
     read it in what-do-ye-call there.
Laf. [*Reading*] *A showing of a heavenly effect in an earthly*
     actor.
Par. That's it; I would have said the very same.   25
Laf. Why, your dolphin is not lustier; fore me, I speak in
     respect—
Par. Nay, 'tis strange, 'tis very strange; that is the brief

13. Right; so] Right, so *F3;* Right so *F.*   21. indeed; if] indeed, if *Rowe*[1]*;*
indeede if *F.*   22. what-do-ye-call there] *Case, conj. Glover;* what do ye call
there *F;* what-do-ye-call't there *N.S.;* what-do-ye-/call't here *Alexander;*
what do you call these *Harrison.*   23. S.D. *Reading*] *Reading the ballad title. Alex-*
ander; not in F.   23–4. *A . . . actor.*] *italic Warburton; roman F.*   25. it; I . . . said
the] it, I . . . said the *F4;* it, I . . . said, the *F.*

speare's time . . . those physicians who would be spoken of as 'our most learned doctors' of 'the congregated college' . . . would not be the disciples 'both of Galen and Paracelsus', but of the former only" (*Medical Knowledge*, p. 102). It is possible that Parolles is, in consequence, being ridiculed for his fake erudition.

12. *authentic Fellows*] those accredited, legally qualified or licensed. This has been seen as another reference to the Royal College of Physicians. Cf. Jonson, *E.M.O.*, IV. iii. 24: "by the iudgement of the autenticall physicians".

21. *in showing*] visible to the eyes: in print.

22. *what-do-ye-call*] Cf. Jonson, *S.N.*, I. v. 32: "How do you call him there?" The emendation "call't" seems unnecessary; cf. *Wint.*, v. iii. 100: "Strike all that look upon with

marvel". H. F. Brooks compares from Milton's Sonnet "On the New Forcers of Conscience": "By shallow *Edwards* and Scotch what d' ye call" (where the rhyme precludes misprint).

23–4. A showing . . . actor] Shakespeare assumes that the recovery of the King has been greeted, as in England it probably would have been, by the printing of broadsheet ballads.

26. *dolphin*] This may refer to the Dauphin (anglicized Dolphin by the Elizabethans), i.e. the King is as lusty as his heir, but the parallel of *Ant.*, v. ii. 88–9: "his delights / Were dolphin-like" makes it probable that Shakespeare was thinking (primarily at least) of the fish, which (according to Valerianus' *Hieroglyphica*) was a symbol of youthful love.

fore me] See below, II. iv. 29.

28–9. *brief and the tedious*] Parolles'

and the tedious of it; and he's of a most facinerious
spirit that will not acknowledge it to be the—   30
Laf. Very hand of heaven.
Par. Ay, so I say.
Laf. In a most weak—
Par. And debile minister; great power, great transcen-
dence, which should indeed give us a further use to   35
be made than alone the recov'ry of the king, as to
be—
Laf. Generally thankful.

Enter KING, HELENA, *and Attendants.*

Par. I would have said it; you say well. Here comes the
king.   40
Laf. Lustique, as the Dutchman says. I'll like a maid the
better whilst I have a tooth in my head. Why, he's
able to lead her a coranto.
Par. Mor du vinager! Is not this Helen?
Laf. Fore God, I think so.   45

33–8.] *As F; Laf.* In . . . weak— *Par.* Ay, so I say. *Laf.* And debile . . . king, as to
be [*after a pause*] generally thankful. *Globe, conj. Camb.; Laf.* In . . . weak and
debile. . . King, as to be generally thankful. *Sisson.*   38. S.D. *Enter King,
Helena, and Attendants] As F (Hellen); Capell (after 40).*   44. *Mor du vinager] F;
Mort du vinaigre Rowe³; Mort du vainqueur Collier²; Mort d'une vierge conj. Thiselton.*

affected version of "the short and the
long"; cf. *MND.*, v. i. 56, *R 3*, I. iv. 89,
and Shirley, *Love in a Maze*, III. i: "I
can be as brief as you, and tedious
too."

29. *facinerious*] "The usual form is
'facinorous' (= wicked), and edd.
suppose that either Parolles or the
printer blundered. But N.E.D. gives it
as a true form, cites 'facinorious' from
Heywood and traces it to O.F.
'facinereux'." (*N.S.*).

41. *Lustique*] Steevens' quotation
"all lustick, all frolicksome" from a
play of 1634 gives sufficient idea of its
Elizabethan use. For the relation of
the word here to *The Weakest Goeth to
the Wall* see Intro., p. xxii.

42. *a tooth*] a "sweet tooth" or a
taste for the delights of the senses.

43. *coranto*] a lively dance.

44. Mor du vinager] This pseudo-
French is meaningless; so are the Galli-
cisms supplied by edd. It ought to
be noted, however, that euphemistic
weakenings of oaths (e.g. "by cock and
pie") are often meaningless. Case, in
Yale edn, says that "Mort du vinaigre"
means "by the Crucifixion" but gives
no authority.

45.] Lafew cannot be surprised that
Helen has been the means of the King's
recovery, for he himself introduced
her. It is to be presumed, therefore,
that the phrase is ironical, at Parolles'
expense: "if it's not Helena I don't
know who it is." The Clarkes' suggestion that Lafew is merely following up
his own line of thought from l. 43 is
plausible and attractive.

King. Go, call before me all the lords in court.

                              [Exit Attendant.]

    Sit, my preserver, by thy patient's side,
    And with this healthful hand, whose banish'd sense
    Thou hast repeal'd, a second time receive
    The confirmation of my promis'd gift,   50
    Which but attends thy naming.

Enter three or four lords.

    Fair maid, send forth thine eye. This youthful parcel
    Of noble bachelors stand at my bestowing,
    O'er whom both sovereign power and father's voice
    I have to use. Thy frank election make;   55
    Thou hast power to choose, and they none to forsake.
Hel. To each of you one fair and virtuous mistress
    Fall, when love please! Marry, to each but one!
Laf. I'd give bay curtal and his furniture
    My mouth no more were broken than these boys',   60
    And writ as little beard.
King.   Peruse them well.
    Not one of those but had a noble father.

She addresses her to a lord.

46. S.D. *Exit Attendant*] *Exeunt some Attendants Capell; not in* F.   51. S.D. *Enter three or four lords.*] F; *Enter four Lords and Bertram. Sisson.*   62. S.D. *She addresses her to a lord.*] F; N.S. *(after* stream 76) *; coming from her Seat, and addressing herself to the Lords. Capell (after* 57) *; om. Var.* '78.

49. *repeal'd*] called back from exile; cf. *R 2*, II. ii. 49.

52. *parcel*] small party; cf. *Mer. V.*, I. ii. 97.

53. *at my bestowing*] The institution of wardship entitled the King to bestow his wards in marriage only with the proviso he did not commit "disparagement", i.e. marry them to a commoner (see *Shak. Eng.*, I, 387). The whole tenor of the play, however, seems to indicate that Shakespeare did not intend Bertram to have this good ground for his refusal of Helena.

55. *frank election make*] choose without restraint.

56. *forsake*] deny.

58. *Marry . . . but one*] There is only one to whom I cannot wish a fair and virtuous mistress—the one I choose, for he will have to be content with me.

59. *bay curtal and his furniture*] my bay horse with the docked tail and his trappings.

60. *mouth . . . broken*] usually glossed "I still had all my teeth" (cf. II. iii. 42 above), i.e. were as fit to be her husband; there may also be a reference to the mouth (furnished with a bit) of a horse which is "broken". In *Shak. Eng.*, II, 33 Onions suggests a reference to the "breaking" of a boy's voice.

61. *writ*] claimed for myself.

62. S.D.] Curious, and deleted by

Hel. Gentlemen,
    Heaven hath through me restor'd the king to
      health.
All. We understand it, and thank heaven for you.   65
Hel. I am a simple maid, and therein wealthiest
    That I protest I simply am a maid.
    Please it your majesty, I have done already.
    The blushes in my cheeks thus whisper me:
    "We blush that thou should'st choose; but, be
      refused,   70
    Let the white death sit on thy cheek for ever,
    We'll ne'er come there again."
King.   Make choice, and see,
    Who shuns thy love shuns all his love in me.
Hel. Now, Dian, from thy altar do I fly,
    And to imperial Love, that god most high   75
    Do my sighs stream. [*To First Lord*] Sir, will you hear
      my suit?
First Lord. And grant it.
Hel.   Thanks, sir; all the rest is mute.
Laf. I had rather be in this choice than throw ames-ace
    for my life.

63–4.] *As Capell; prose F.*   70. choose; but, be refused,] *Rann;* choose, but be
refused; *F.*   75. imperial Love] imperiall loue *F;* imperiall Ioue *F2;* impar-
tiall *Ioue F3.*   78–9.] *As Pope; . . .* throw / Ames-ace . . . life. / *F (verse).*

19th-century edd. but it may mean no
more than that she squares up to the
first candidate while speaking to them
all. The Capell arrangement of the
lines following allows a significant
pause after *Gentlemen* for Helena to
gather her resources.

    70. *choose . . . refused*] The F punctua-
tion, if understood as involving a syntactical break after *refused*, makes
Helena imply that she expects to be
refused, which cannot be true; it also
deprives the following lines of any
connected meaning. It is probable,
however, that the F semicolon is only
a rhetorical pause, to give force to the
curse which follows.

    77. *the rest is mute*] "i.e. I have no
more to say to you. So, Hamlet:—the

rest is silence." (Steevens). *N.S.* remarks that Helena "asks 1 Lord
whether he will *hear* her suit, though
when he eagerly replies that he will
'grant it' she sees she has gone a little
too far and passes quickly from
him."

    78. *ames-ace*] two aces, the lowest
throw at dice; *throw ames-ace for my life*
must mean "put my life in grave
hazard" and the whole sentence must
be spoken ironically, for what Lafew
actually means is "I'd very much like
to be in this". P. A. Daniel compares
"I would rather have it than a poke
in the eye with a birch rod" (*apud*
Henry Irving Shakespeare); such
ironical comparisons are common in
colloquial speech.

Hel. [*To Second Lord*] The honour, sir, that flames in your
    fair eyes   80
    Before I speak, too threat'ningly replies.
    Love make your fortunes twenty times above
    Her that so wishes, and her humble love!
Second Lord. No better, if you please.
Hel.   My wish receive,
    Which great Love grant; and so I take my leave.   85
Laf. Do all they deny her? And they were sons of mine I'd
    have them whipp'd, or I would send them to th'
    Turk to make eunuchs of.
Hel. [*To Third Lord*] Be not afraid that I your hand
    should take;
    I'll never do you wrong, for your own sake.   90
    Blessing upon your vows, and in your bed
    Find fairer fortune if you ever wed!
Laf. These boys are boys of ice; they'll none have her.
    Sure they are bastards to the English; the French
    ne'er got 'em.   95
Hel. [*To Fourth Lord*] You are too young, too happy, and
    too good,
    To make yourself a son out of my blood.
Fourth Lord. Fair one, I think not so.
Laf. There's one grape yet. I am sure thy father drunk

85. Love] loue *F*; Jove *F3*.   86. And] *F*; An *Capell*.   96. *Hel.*] *F3*; *La. F.*

80. *honour*] what *flames* is, as *N.S.*
points out, actually admiration, but
this may, in the oblique language of
courtship here adopted, be termed
honour, for admiration means consent
and marriage, and this is the *honour*
which threatens her here.

84. *No . . . please*] I don't wish for any
better fortune than you and your
humble love.

My wish receive] *wish* is the emphatic
word, picking up the *wishes* of l. 83 and
emphasizing, by the stress on *great Love*,
the absence of Helena's *humble love*.

86–8.] As Johnson pointed out,
Lafew, here and below, misunder-
stands the meaning of the exchange
between Helena and the lords, taking
in that she is being refused, not refus-
ing. The whole structure of this scene
with its use of commentary to establish the moral values involved (e.g.
the impropriety of Bertram's refusal)
is in the manner of Jonson's comedy;
cf. also *Troil.*, v. ii.

99–101. *There's one . . . already*]
There's one fruit of noble stock left
yet; I am sure your father put good
blood into your veins ("good drinke
makes good bloud"—Lyly's *Campaspe*,
v. iii. 11 f [cf. Tilley W 461]), but for
all that you are too foolish to do the
right thing; the contrast is the usual
one in the play between inheritance
and achievement. Cf. Byron, *Don
Juan*, xv, vii: "But Adeline was of the
purest vintage, / The unmingled
essence of the grape."

wine; but if thou be'st not an ass, I am a youth of   100
        fourteen; I have known thee already.

Hel. [*To Bertram*] I dare not say I take you, but I give
        Me and my service, ever whilst I live,
        Into your guiding power. This is the man.

King. Why, then, young Bertram, take her; she's thy wife.   105

Ber. My wife, my liege! I shall beseech your highness,
        In such a business give me leave to use
        The help of mine own eyes.

King.   Know'st thou not, Bertram,
        What she has done for me?

Ber.   Yes, my good lord,
        But never hope to know why I should marry her.   110

King. Thou know'st she has rais'd me from my sickly bed.

Ber. But follows it, my lord, to bring me down
        Must answer for your raising? I know her well:
        She had her breeding at my father's charge—
        A poor physician's daughter my wife! Disdain   115
        Rather corrupt me ever!

King. 'Tis only title thou disdain'st in her, the which
        I can build up. Strange is it that our bloods,
        Of colour, weight, and heat, pour'd all together,
        Would quite confound distinction, yet stands off   120

108-10. Know'st ... her] *As Pope; prose F.*

101. *known*] probably = "seen
through you"; cf. *Troil.*, II. iii. 45, *Lr.*,
II. ii. 11, 96, *1 H 4*, III. iii. 63, and
Deloney, *The Gentle Craft* (ed. Mann,
p. 128): "Go too, go too (said Florence) you are like to Penelopes
puppy, that doth bite and whine, I
know you well enough."

113. *I know her well*] Cf. Painter:
"The Countie knew her well."

115-16. *Disdain . . . ever*] I choose
that my disdain of her should ruin my
favour in your sight rather than that I
should be "brought down" by marriage to one beneath me. Brigstocke
took *Disdain* to mean "your disdain of
me", which, though possible, seems to
multiply the number of disdains without necessity. It is Bertram's disdain
that is referred to in the following line.

117. *only title*] "only lack of title. Cf.
'I almost die for food' (*AYL.*, II. vii.
104)" (Brigstocke).

118-21. *Strange . . . mighty*] *Of* frequently means "as regards" in Shakespeare (Abbott §173), and "to distinguish of" is a normal Shakespearian
expression (see *Ham.*, III. ii. 62, *2 H 6*,
II. i. 128, etc.). The passage, which is
based (as Tilley [D 335] points out) on
the proverbial "there is no difference
of bloods in a basin", may be para-
phrased: "it is strange that no one
would be able to distinguish noble
blood from base blood, in respect
of colour, weight, or heat, if these
bloods were poured together, and
yet you think your blood (pedigree)
separated by such a difference from
hers."

In differences so mighty. If she be
All that is virtuous, save what thou dislik'st—
A poor physician's daughter—thou dislik'st
Of virtue for the name. But do not so.
From lowest place when virtuous things proceed,   125
The place is dignified by th' doer's deed.
Where great additions swell's and virtue none,
It is a dropsied honour. Good alone
Is good, without a name; vileness is so:
The property by what it is should go,   130
Not by the title. She is young, wise, fair;
In these to nature she's immediate heir,
And these breed honour; that is honour's scorn
Which challenges itself as honour's born
And is not like the sire. Honours thrive   135
When rather from our acts we them derive

---

124. the name] *F;* a name *N.S., conj. Collier.*   125. place when] *Theobald[1],
conj. Thirlby;* place, whence *F.*   129. good, without a name; vileness] *Capell;*
good without a name? Vilenesse *F;* good, without a name vileness *Johnson.*

---

124. *name*] i.e. lack of title; same construction as l. 117.

127. *additions*] titles.

128-9. *Good . . . so*] Brigstocke kept F question mark after *name* and construed the first clause: "Is only goodness good when it has no title?", but this is not plausible. The Elizabethans used question-marks very loosely by modern standards, often only to give emphasis, and a rhetorical question is out of place in didactic couplets of this kind. *Good alone* probably means "good isolated (from the *additions*), by itself"; the F punctuation "Good a lone," would seem to show the "isolating function" of the Elizabethan comma, and could only be modernized unambiguously by some periphrasis such as "good in itself". We may paraphrase the passage: "goodness is not any less good for being itself without a title; similarly, vileness is not altered by the possession of a title, however complimentary."

130-1. *The property . . . title*] a particular quality (such as goodness or

vileness) should pass by virtue of its intrinsic nature, not because of what people call it. The combination of *property* and *title* suggests that Shakespeare may have had the idea of "title-deed" (i.e. "legality" as against "justice") in his mind as well.

130. *go*] *O.E.D.* "go" vb. I.12: "of coin, etc. To circulate, to pass current at a certain value."

132. *immediate heir*] "To be *immediate heir* is to inherit without any intervening transmitter: thus she inherits beauty *immediately* from *nature*, but honour is transmitted by ancestors" (Johnson).

133-5. *that is . . . sire*] True honour is scornful of any claim to honour derived from forebears which does not justify itself by honourable conduct.

135. *Honours thrive*] The widely-accepted correction of F2: "Honours best thriue" is obviously a sophistication, introduced to complete the metre, not observing the *sire* is disyllabic (see Abbott §480).

Than our foregoers. The mere word's a slave,
Debosh'd on every tomb, on every grave
A lying trophy, and as oft is dumb,
Where dust and damn'd oblivion is the tomb   140
Of honour'd bones indeed. What should be said?
If thou canst like this creature as a maid,
I can create the rest. Virtue and she
Is her own dower; honour and wealth from me.

Ber. I cannot love her nor will strive to do't.   145

King. Thou wrong'st thyself if thou should'st strive to choose.

Hel. That you are well restor'd, my lord, I'm glad.
    Let the rest go.

King. My honour's at the stake, which to defeat,
    I must produce my power. Here, take her hand,   150
    Proud, scornful boy, unworthy this good gift,
    That dost in vile misprision shackle up
    My love and her desert; that canst not dream
    We, poising us in her defective scale,
    Shall weigh thee to the beam; that wilt not know   155
    It is in us to plant thine honour where

---

138. grave] grave, *Var. '73;* graue: *F.*   140–1. tomb / Of . . . indeed. What]
Theobald[1]; Tombe. / Of . . . indeed, what *F.*

---

138. *Debosh'd*] mod. "debauched".

140–1. *Where . . . said*] F punctuation has been defended by Thiselton, but the point that the tomb is a tomb or truly honourable bones must be made if the wrongness of its being dumb is to be stressed, and if an effective antithesis to *every tomb* is to be provided. Admittedly *What should be said* is strangely isolated by this emendation (though cf. *1 H 6,* I. i. 15: "what should I say?"), but we may take it that the King is pausing to think out a practical course of action which will embody his general precepts. The tomb image is a commonplace one to illustrate the divergent paths of virtue and fortune; see Juvenal, x, 140 ff.

143. *and she*] and her intrinsic qualities. Cf. *Lr.,* I. i. 241: "she is herself a dowry".

145–6.] Notice the repetition of *strive.* Bertram says, "I will not even strive. Bertram says, "I will not even

attempt to love her"; and the King replies, "your place (as a ward) is not to attempt (either way) but to obey." Perhaps *choose* here (as in *Mer. V.,* I. ii. 42) means "have it your own way."

149. *at the stake*] image from bearbaiting: my honour is "shackled up" to the post and is baited by the dogs of your disobedience.

which to defeat] The antecedent of *which* is the whole clause preceding; in modern English we might express it, "which danger to defeat". See Abbott §271, Franz §347. Cf. *R 2,* I. i. 145.

152. *misprision*] Rushton has noticed a quibble here: (1) false imprisonment; (2) disdain.

156. *in us*] F "in Vs"; as *N.S.* remarks, "The capital denotes an emphatic word". Notice the return of the royal "we" in this magnificent speech of lofty chastisement, though the King has referred to himself as "I" above.

We please to have it grow. Check thy contempt;
Obey our will which travails in thy good;
Believe not thy disdain, but presently
Do thine own fortunes that obedient right   160
Which both thy duty owes and our power claims;
Or I will throw thee from my care for ever
Into the staggers and the careless lapse
Of youth and ignorance; both my revenge and hate
Loosing upon thee in the name of justice,   165
Without all terms of pity. Speak. Thine answer.

Ber. Pardon, my gracious lord; for I submit
My fancy to your eyes. When I consider
What great creation and what dole of honour
Flies where you bid it, I find that she, which late   170
Was in my nobler thoughts most base, is now
The praised of the king; who, so ennobled,
Is as 'twere born so.

King.   Take her by the hand
And tell her she is thine; to whom I promise
A counterpoise, if not to thy estate,   175
A balance more replete.

163. careless] *F;* cureless *Dyce², conj. W. S. Walker.*   166. Speak. Thine]
Speake, thine *F;* Speak thine *F3.*   168. eyes. When] *Rowe¹;* eies, when *F.*
170. it,] *Capell;* it: *F.*

160. *obedient right*] right of obedience.

163. *staggers*] a disease of horses;
irresponsible giddiness of conduct.

careless] Dyce quotes reasons from
W. W. Williams for his emendation to
"cureless": (1) the unwanted correspondence with *care* in the preceding
line; (2) ease of *a/u* misprints; (3) the
strong parallel of *Mer. V.*, IV. i. 141–2
("Repair thy wit, good youth, or it
will fall To cureless ruin"). "cureless",
however, does not fit with *youth and
ignorance* here, whereas *careless* (=
reckless, irresponsible) fits well, and,
besides, provides a better parallel to
staggers.

lapse] fall (Lat. *lapsus*).

166. *Without . . . pity*] "without pity
in any form" (On.).

168. *fancy*] It is worth noting that it

is his *fancy* not his "judgment" that
Bertram submits.

eyes. When] F punctuation leaves the
temporal clause equally attached to
the preceding verb *submit* and to the
following one *find.*

169.] *N.S.* states that the *great
creation* and the *dole of honour* are anti-
thetical, as "great titles" against
"petty dignities". I find no evidence,
however, that *dole* means a *petty* portion (see "large doles of death"
quoted in *O.E.D.*). It seems best to
take *dole of honour* as parallel to *great
creation.*

175–6. *if not . . . replete*] There are
two possible meanings here: (1) "my
counterpoise, even if it does not equal
your estate, will make the balance
more perfect" (see *O.E.D.* s.v. Replete.
*a.*4); (2) "If my counterpoise errs on

Ber.   I take her hand.
King. Good fortune and the favour of the king
        Smile upon this contract; whose ceremony
        Shall seem expedient on the now-born brief,
        And be perform'd tonight. The solemn feast   180
        Shall more attend upon the coming space,
        Expecting absent friends. As thou lov'st her
        Thy love's to me religious; else, does err.   *Exeunt.*

        PAROLLES *and* LAFEW *stay behind, commenting of
                        this wedding.*

Laf. Do you hear, monsieur? A word with you.
Par. Your pleasure, sir.   185
Laf. Your lord and master did well to make his recan-
        tation.

either side it will be because the *balance* (= counterweight) I give Helena will be too replete (= abundant)." Cf. *Tim.*, I. i. 148–9.

176. *I . . . hand*] Note that Bertram does not complete the King's command, but the reference to *this contract* seems to indicate that the King understands consent.

177–8. *and the favour . . . contract*] Brigstocke remarks that it is "curious that the King should speak thus of himself", but it is only curious if we take *smile* to be an imperative rather than an indicative.

178–9. *whose . . . brief*] *shall seem* may mean "shall be proper" (*O.E.D.* v.² 1), in which case *expedient*, as nearly always in Shakespeare, means "expeditious"; *now-born brief* has given rise to a variety of interpretations: Monk Mason, taking *expedient* = "proper" (as in *Ado*, v. ii. 72), supposes *brief* to be an adj. and paraphrases "the ceremony of which it seems expedient to abridge for the present"; Thiselton, defending F "now borne", takes it to mean "which I am sending forth". *N.S.* paraphrases "shall swiftly follow on the signing of the legal papers, which are already prepared", but there is no word of "signing" in the

text, and *now-born* is not very obviously the same as "already prepared". Below (v. iii. 137) and elsewhere in Shakespeare *brief* means "summary"; and the same meaning seems probable here. In the text three stages of the marriage are distinguished: of these the "contract" which we have just witnessed—the assumed consent of both parties and the consent of the King (both sovereign and guardian)—is the most summary (see D. P. Harding in *J.E.G.P.* xlix) and might well be called a *now-born brief*; the *ceremony* to follow will be, I assume, the religious rite (see below, l. 265) which made the marriage more proper, though not more legal; thirdly will follow the social celebration or *feast*. The "royal edict" meaning of *brief* (*O.E.D.* sb. 1) may, however, be the correct one here, in which case see the Clarkes' paraphrase: ". . . follow immediately on this our now given command".

181–2. *Shall more . . . friends*] will await the arrival of friends now absent, using the interval to prepare for them; *attend* seems to be used in two of its many meanings: (1) to wait for; (2) to apply oneself to.

183. S.D.] See Intro., p. xiii.

Par. Recantation! My lord! My master!

Laf. Ay. Is it not a language I speak?

Par. A most harsh one, and not to be understood without 190
bloody succeeding. My master!

Laf. Are you companion to the Count Rossillion?

Par. To any Count; to all Counts; to what is man.

Laf. To what is Count's man; Count's master is of
another style. 195

Par. You are too old, sir; let it satisfy you, you are too old.

Laf. I must tell thee, sirrah, I write man; to which title
age cannot bring thee.

Par. What I dare too well do, I dare not do.

Laf. I did think thee for two ordinaries to be a pretty wise 200
fellow; thou didst make tolerable vent of thy travel;
it might pass. Yet the scarfs and the bannerets about
thee did manifoldly dissuade me from believing thee
a vessel of too great a burthen. I have now found thee;

200. ordinaries to] *F3;* ordinaries: to *F.*

191. *bloody succeeding*] subsequent shedding of blood (Brigstocke).

192. *companion*] fellow, rascal; the usual sense in Shakespeare. Parolles, however, seems to understand the word in its modern sense of "associate" with its implication of equality.

193.] Shakespeare may be remembering the etymology of *count* here (i.e. *comes* = companion); the progression: one, all, the genus, is repeated in *Cym.,* III. v. 73: "Than lady, ladies, woman".

193–4. *man . . . man*] Parolles means "to what is manly". Lafew uses the word to mean "servant". *N.S.* paraphrases Lafew's answer: "You may be familiar with a count's servants, I am familiar with a count's master, viz. the King."

197. *write man*] lay claim to manhood.

199.] To punish you would be easy physically, but is impossible morally, or in terms of the social code.

200. *two ordinaries*] two meal-times.

201. *vent of thy travel*] Parolles had entertained the company at dinner with travellers' tales; Shakespeare gives to Parolles as to most of his fops the characteristics of an affected traveller. Cf. below, II. v. 27–30.

202. *the scarfs and the bannerets*] The *scarf* was the mark of the military man (see Dekker, *1 Honest Whore,* I. ii. 101–8, and Hall's *Satires,* IV, 6); it was a sash worn over the shoulder or round the waist and sometimes tied round the hat or arm as a memento (see Rowlands, *More Knaves yet* (1613), sig. A4ᵛ, and *First Part of Jeronimo,* III. ii. 163 S.D.), which may explain ll. 245 f below. *Shak. Eng.* (I, 20) says that it was a new fashion in this period. Parolles is said, hyperbolically, to wear so many scarfs that they look like the scarfs or pennants used to adorn a ship (the "scarfed bark" of *Mer. V.,* II. vi. 15).

204–5. *I have . . . care not*] *found* is the modern "found out", and *lose* is the modern "get rid of", with a play on the proverb "better lost than found".

when I lose thee again I care not. Yet art thou good 205
for nothing but taking up, and that thou'rt scarce
worth.

Par. Hadst thou not the privilege of antiquity upon
thee—

Laf. Do not plunge thyself too far in anger, lest thou 210
hasten thy trial; which if—Lord have mercy on thee
for a hen! So, my good window of lattice, fare thee
well; thy casement I need not open, for I look
through thee. Give me thy hand.

Par. My lord, you give me most egregious indignity.   215

Laf. Ay, with all my heart; and thou art worthy of it.

Par. I have not, my lord, deserv'd it.

Laf. Yes, good faith, ev'ry dram of it; and I will not bate
thee a scruple.

Par. Well, I shall be wiser.   220

Laf. Ev'n as soon as thou canst; for thou hast to pull at a
smack a' th' contrary. If ever thou be'st bound in thy
scarf and beaten thou shall find what it is to be proud
of thy bondage. I have a desire to hold my acquaintance with thee, or rather my knowledge, that I may 225
say, in the default, "He is a man I know".

206. *taking up*] There is almost certainly a quibble here, and one of the
senses is, almost certainly, "picking
up" (as from the ground) for the *Yet*
shows an antithesis to *lose*. Johnson
supposed that the other meaning was
"contradicting, calling to account";
N.S. "enlisting"; it is also possible that
it means "arresting" (*O.E.D.* s.v.
"take-up" l).

212. *window of lattice*] Lafew implies
that Parolles is (1) as common as an
ale-house (of which a red-lattice was a
sign); (2) as transparent as an open
window (see K. Tillotson in G. Tillotson's *Essays in Criticism and Research*,
pp. 204–7, on the Shakespearian association of (wooden) windows with
opaqueness). J. C. Adams supposes
that there was such a *lattice* in one of
the stage-doors of the Elizabethan
playhouse and remarks: "The presence of [this] . . . helps to explain,

therefore, the frequency with which. . .
tavern-lattice allusions occur in the
plays of the period" (*The Globe Playhouse*, p. 162). Cf. the similar insult in
Jonson *C's R*, v. iv. 109–10.

215. *egregious*] probably thought to
be a ridiculous word. It is used elsewhere in Shakespeare only by Pistol
and by Posthumus in rant. For further
examples see King.

221–2. *to pull . . . contrary*] You will
have to swallow a fair taste of your
own folly before you have sufficient
self-knowledge to be called wise. The
imagery is taken up from *dram* and
scruple above.

223–4. *proud of thy bondage*] because
he is proud of his scarfs and these will
become the instruments of his bondage. See *O.E.D.* s.v. Bondage sb. 2.c:
"that which binds".

226. *in the default*] There is no evidence, as *N.S.* points out, to support

Par. My lord, you do me most insupportable vexation.

Laf. I would it were hell-pains for thy sake, and my poor
doing eternal; for doing I am past, as I will by thee,
in what motion age will give me leave.   *Exit.* 230

Par. Well, thou hast a son shall take this disgrace off me;
scurvy, old, filthy, scurvy lord! Well, I must be
patient; there is no fettering of authority. I'll beat
him, by my life, if I can meet him with any convenience, and he were double and double a lord. I'll have 235
no more pity of his age than I would have of—I'll
beat him and if I could but meet him again.

[*Re-*]*enter* LAFEW.

Laf. Sirrah, your lord and master's married; there's news
for you; you have a new mistress.

Par. I most unfeignedly beseech your lordship to make 240
some reservation of your wrongs. He is my good lord;
whom I serve above is my master.

Laf. Who? God?

Par. Ay, sir.

Laf. The devil it is that's thy master. Why dost thou 245
garter up thy arms a' this fashion? Dost make hose of
thy sleeves? Do other servants so? Thou wert best
set thy lower part where thy nose stands. By mine
honour, if I were but two hours younger I'd beat
thee. Methink'st thou art a general offence and 250

235, 237. and] *F;* an *Pope.*   250. Methink'st] *F;* methinks *Rowe³;* methinks't
Dyce¹, conj. W. S. Walker.

Johnson's gloss "at a need"; *N.S.* interpretation "when you fail in battle" has
no stronger support. Perhaps it simply
means "when you fail" (without
reference to the kind of failure; cf.
below, II. v. 44–5, III. vi. 13–15), but
the Clarkes may be right in seeing an
allusion to the legal meaning "non-
appearance in court at a day
assigned".

229. *doing*] presumably in the obscene sense (*O.E.D.* vbl. sb. 1b).

past, as . . . by thee] The sense of *past*
is carried into the next clause: "as

I will (pass) by thee", and Lafew
illustrates his meaning by his quick
exit.

236. *would have of—*] Parolles seems
to be unable to think of anything to
which he could be pitiless.

241. *my good lord*] " 'To be a good
lord' was an idiomatic phrase for
affording patronage or protection, for
being favourable towards a person"
(the Clarkes).

250. *Methink'st*] Shakespeare treats
the impersonal verb as if it were personal.

every man should beat thee. I think thou wast
created for men to breathe themselves upon thee.
Par. This is hard and undeserved measure, my lord.
Laf. Go to, sir. You were beaten in Italy for picking a
kernel out of a pomegranate. You are a vagabond   255
and no true traveller. You are more saucy with lords
and honourable personages than the commission of
your birth and virtue gives you heraldry. You are not
worth another word, else I'd call you knave. I leave
you.   *Exit.* 260

[*Re-*]*enter* BERTRAM.

Par. Good, very good; it is so then. Good, very good; let
it be conceal'd awhile.
Ber. Undone and forfeited to cares for ever!
Par. What's the matter, sweetheart?
Ber. Although before the solemn priest I have sworn,   265
I will not bed her.
Par. What, what, sweetheart?
Ber. O my Parolles, they have married me!
I'll to the Tuscan wars and never bed her.
Par. France is a dog-hole and it no more merits   270
The tread of a man's foot; to th' wars!
Ber. There's letters from my mother; what th' import is
I know not yet.
Par. Ay, that would be known. To th' wars, my boy, to th'
wars!

He wears his honour in a box unseen   275

257–8. commission . . . heraldry] *F*; heraldry . . . commission *Hanmer*.   260.
S.D. *Re-enter Bertram.*] *Enter Count Rossillion. F; Capell (after 262).*   265–6.] *As
Rowe*³; *prose F.*

252. *breathe themselves upon*] take
exercise on.

254. *in Italy*] perhaps with the sense
"even among the degenerate Italians"
(see above, II. i. 13, 14).

254–5. *for picking . . . pomegranate*]
"for so trivial an offence" (the
Clarkes). Presumably *a kernel* means
"one seed" here, as in the passage of
Golding's Ovid that may have led to
it: "She gathering . . . a ripe Powne-
garnet, tooke / Seuen kernels out"

(Bk v—story of Ascalaphus and
Proserpine).

255–6. *vagabond . . . traveller*] not one
who travels (as Elizabethans were
required to) with official licence, but a
mere tramp.

257–8. *commission of your birth and
virtue*] by neither birth nor virtue are
you "commissioned" as a gentleman,
so you have no *heraldry* or coat-of-arms.

275. *box*] Partridge sees a sexual
image here.

That hugs his kicky-wicky here at home,
Spending his manly marrow in her arms,
Which should sustain the bound and high curvet
Of Mars's fiery steed. To other regions!
France is a stable; we that dwell in't jades.   280
Therefore to th' war!

Ber. It shall be so. I'll send her to my house,
Acquaint my mother with my hate to her
And wherefore I am fled, write to the king
That which I durst not speak. His present gift   285
Shall furnish me to those Italian fields
Where noble fellows strike. Wars is no strife
To the dark house and the detested wife.

Par. Will this capriccio hold in thee, art sure?

Ber. Go with me to my chamber and advise me.   290
I'll send her straight away. Tomorrow
I'll to the wars, she to her single sorrow.

Par. Why, these balls bound; there's noise in it. 'Tis
      hard:
   A young man married is a man that's marr'd.

276. kicky-wicky] *F;* kicksie-wicksie *F2.*   279. regions!] *Capell;* Regions, *F;*
regions *Pope.*   288. detested] *Rowe[1];* detected *F.*

276. *kicky-wicky*] a term not recorded
elsewhere (though F2 "kicksy-wicksy"
has parallels) but presumably intended to represent the dotage of a uxorious
husband. Partridge suggests a deri-
vation from *quelquechose.* H. F. Brooks
aptly compares similar dotages in
Otway's *Venice Preserved* ("Acky-
Nacky" and "Nicky-Nacky" in III. i)
and in the scenes between Fondlewife
and Laetitia in Congreve's *The Old
Bachelor* ("Nykin" and "Cocky").

278. *curvet*] "a leap of a horse in
which the fore-legs are raised together and equally advanced, and the
hind-legs raised with a spring before
the fore-legs reach the ground"
(*O.E.D.*)—accented on the second
syllable. Notice that the horse imagery
is carried through *steed . . . stable . . .
jades.*

288. *the dark house*] either "the
gloomy house" or "the madhouse" (as

Thiselton suggests) since madmen
were confined in darkness in this
period. Cf. *Tw. N.,* v. i. 329, *Err.,* IV.
iv. 91, and *Westward Ho,* I. i. 156:
"dark as a room in Bedlam".

289. *capriccio*] an affected word. In
Dekker's *Patient Grissil* (1600), II. i.
58, "Caprichious" is included in a list
of "raise velvet tearmes"; *The Court
and Times of James I* (1616) speaks of
"Some of the capriccios of the Court"
(I, 441). Cf. Jonson, *Case is Altered,* II.
vii. 47.

293. *these balls bound*] Now you are
playing the game properly.

hard] refers both to the *balls* (which
have to be hard before they will
bounce), and to the situation of
Bertram (= unfortunate).

294.] The phrase "marrying is
marring" is proverbial (Tilley M 701).
The context in Shakespeare is extraordinarily close to that in Puttenham,

Therefore away, and leave her bravely; go.   295
The king has done you wrong; but hush 'tis so.   *Exeunt.*

[SCENE IV.—*Paris. The King's palace.*]

Enter HELENA *and* CLOWN.

Hel. My mother greets me kindly; is she well?

Clo. She is not well, but yet she has her health; she's very
merry, but yet she is not well. But thanks be given
she's very well and wants nothing i' th' world; but
yet she is not well.   5

Hel. If she be very well what does she ail that she's not
very well?

Clo. Truly, she's very well indeed, but for two things.

Hel. What two things?

Clo. One, that she's not in heaven, whither God send her   10
quickly! The other, that she's in earth, from whence
God send her quickly!

Enter PAROLLES.

Par. Bless you, my fortunate lady.

Hel. I hope, sir, I have your good will to have mine own
good fortune.   15

Par. You had my prayers to lead them on, and to keep

296. hush 'tis] *F*; hush, 'tis *Rowe*[1].   S.D. *Exeunt.*] *Exit F.*

Scene IV

Scene IV] *Capell; not in F.   Paris. The King's palace.*] *The same. Another Room in
the same. Capell; not in F.*

Arte of English Poesie (1589): of the
figure *Antanaclasis* Puttenham writes:
"Ye haue another figure which by his
nature we may call the *Rebound*,
alluding to the tennis ball which being
smitten with the racket rebounds
backe againe . . . this playeth with one
word written all alike but carrying
diuers sences as thus.

   The maide that soone married is,
   soone marred is."

Scene IV

2-5.] The clown seems to be playing
on two senses of *well*: (1) the physical
sense = "healthy", (2) the theological
sense = "delivered from the burden of
the flesh". H. F. Brooks aptly compares *Ant.*, II. v. 31 ff: *Mess. . . .
Madam, he is well. | Cleo. . . . But,
sirrah, mark, we use | To say the dead
are well. Cf. also *Mac.*, IV. iii. 176 ff
Tw. N., I. v. 60 ff.

them on have them still. O, my knave! How does my
old lady?

Clo. So that you had her wrinkles and I her money, I
would she did as you say.   20

Par. Why, I say nothing.

Clo. Marry, you are the wiser man; for many a man's
tongue shakes out his master's undoing. To say
nothing, to do nothing, to know nothing, and to have
nothing, is to be a great part of your title, which is   25
within a very little of nothing.

Par. Away! Th'art a knave.

Clo. You should have said, sir, "Before a knave th'art a
knave"; that's "Before me, th'art a knave". This had
been truth, sir.   30

Par. Go to, thou art a witty fool; I have found thee.

Clo. Did you find me in your self, sir, or were you taught
to find me? . . . The search, sir, was profitable; and
much fool may you find in you, even to the world's
pleasure and the increase of laughter.   35

Par. A good knave i'faith, and well fed.
Madam, my lord will go away tonight;
A very serious business calls on him.

---

26. little] *F;* tittle *conj. this edn.*   33. find me? . . . The] *This edn;* finde me?
Clo. The *F;* find me? The *Rowe¹;* find me? *Par.* In myself. *Clo.* The *N.S.*, *conj.*
Nicholson; find me? [*Parolles shakes his head*] The *Sisson.*

20. *did as you say*] The point of the
clown's answer is not obvious, unless
we assume that *did* was pronounced in
a way which suggested the sound of
"died". There is no clear evidence
that the two sounds were ever completely identical, but Elizabethan
phonetic spellers write both "did" and
"died" as *ded* (C. Davies, *English Pronunciation*).

22–3. *Marry . . . undoing*] The clown
quibbles on *man* as (1) human being; (2) servant. There is dramatic
irony in this, in view of II. iii. 193–5
above.

25. *title*] claim to possessions or
status (as a servant). *N.S.* suggests a
quibble on Parolles' name.

25–6. *which . . . nothing*] perhaps

quibbling on *title* above as "tittle".
Cf. *R 2*, II. iii. 75.

29. *Before me*] "A form of assevera-
tion, meaning 'upon my soul' " (*N.S.*).
Cf. "fore me" above (II. iii. 26).

31. *found thee*] found thee out. Cf. II.
iii. 204.

32. *in*] modern "by".

33. *me? . . . The search*] F follows *me*
with another "*Clo.*" speech-prefix. A
reply by Parolles (perhaps containing
the idea of *search*) may have been lost,
but it is possible to keep F text assuming only that the clown pauses and,
presuming Parolles' answer, replies to
that.

36. *well fed*] referring again to the
proverb "better fed than taught" as
above, II. ii. 3.

The great prerogative and rite of love,
Which as your due time claims, he does acknowledge, 40
But puts it off to a compell'd restraint;
Whose want and whose delay is strew'd with sweets,
Which they distil now in the curbed time,
To make the coming hour o'erflow with joy
And pleasure drown the brim.
Hel.   What's his will else?   45
Par. That you will take your instant leave a' th' king,
And make this haste as your own good proceeding,
Strength'ned with what apology you think
May make it probable need.
Hel.   What more commands he?
Par. That, having this obtain'd, you presently   50
Attend his further pleasure.
Hel. In everything I wait upon his will.
Par. I shall report it so.   *Exit.*
Hel. I pray you. Come, sirrah.   *Exeunt.*

---

39. rite] *F;* right *Capell.*   54. you. Come] *Theobald[1]; you come F.*   S.D.
Exeunt.] Exit F.

39. *rite*] F spelling 'rite' no doubt
covers "right" as well.
41. *to*] probably "in accordance
with", "in answer to".
42–5. *whose want . . . brim*] l. 39 provides the antecedent for *whose.* The
delay in consummating the marriage
is conceived of as imposing a process of
restraint and pressure which distils the
joys of this so that they will eventually
drown the brim (the idea of quantity
[*o'erflow*] being substituted for that of
quality, inherent in distillation). The
they in l. 43 seems to be used vaguely:
it may refer back to *want* and *delay,* but

as subject of *distil* it can mean little
more than "people". The whole
image is taken from perfume-making
(then a household occupation): the
sweets or flowers strewn across this
delay will not wither but be *curbed* in
a still (Latin *cucurbita*), and so by the
pressure of *restraint* distilled into per-
fume.
49. *probable need*] Helena's departure
is a *need* anyway; but she can make it a
probable need, i.e. a plausible one, by
her excuse to the King. Johnson
glosses: "a specious appearance of
necessity".

[SCENE V.—*Paris. The King's palace.*]

Enter LAFEW *and* BERTRAM.

Laf. But I hope your lordship thinks not him a soldier.

Ber. Yes, my lord, and of very valiant approof.

Laf. You have it from his own deliverance.

Ber. And by other warranted testimony.

Laf. Then my dial goes not true; I took this lark for a   5
bunting.

Ber. I do assure you, my lord, he is very great in knowledge, and accordingly valiant.

Laf. I have then sinn'd against his experience and transgress'd against his valour; and my state that way is   10
dangerous, since I cannot yet find in my heart to
repent. Here he comes. I pray you make us friends;
I will pursue the amity.

Enter PAROLLES.

Par. [*To Bertram*] These things shall be done, sir.

Laf. Pray you, "sir", who's his tailor?   15

Par. Sir!

Laf. O, I know him well. Ay, "sir", he, sir, 's a good work-
man, a very good tailor.

Ber. [*Aside to Parolles*] Is she gone to the king?

Par. She is.   20

Ber. Will she away tonight?

Scene v

Scene v] *Capell; not in F.*   *Paris. The King's palace.*] *The same. Another Room in the same. Capell; not in F.*   14. S.D. *To Bertram*] *Capell; not in F.*   15, 17. "sir"] *This edn; sir F.*   19. S.D. *Aside to Parolles*] *Rowe[1]; not in F.*

---

2. *approof*] (1) proved so; or (2) in approbation (so the Clarkes).

5–6. *I took . . . bunting*] I under-estimated him; a reversal of the usual form of the proverb "to take a bunting for a lark", i.e. to overrate the unworthy.

8. *accordingly*] correspondingly.

9–12. *sinn'd . . . transgress'd . . . dangerous . . . repent*] all words with a religious implication.

15.] The Clarkes' suggestion that Lafew is pretending to take Parolles for a lackey come from a tailor (perhaps his clothes make him like a walking advertisement for a tailor) is supported by the emphasis on *sir*. On the other hand the parallel of *Lr.*, II. ii. 50–1, where Kent pretends to believe that a tailor made Oswald, and the use of the same insult below, ll. 43 f, suggest that this is the point here.

Par. As you'll have her.

Ber. I have writ my letters, casketed my treasure,
 Given order for our horses; and tonight,
 When I should take possession of the bride,   25
 End ere I do begin.

Laf. [*Aside*] A good traveller is something at the latter
 end of a dinner, but one that lies three thirds and
 uses a known truth to pass a thousand nothings with,
 should be once heard and thrice beaten. [*Aloud*] God 30
 save you, captain!

Ber. Is there any unkindness between my lord and you,
 monsieur?

Par. I know not how I have deserved to run into my lord's
 displeasure.   35

Laf. You have made shift to run into't, boots and spurs
 and all, like him that leap'd into the custard; and out
 of it you'll run again rather than suffer question for
 your residence.

Ber. It may be you have mistaken him, my lord.   40

Laf. And shall do so ever, though I took him at's prayers.
 Fare you well, my lord, and believe this of me: there
 can be no kernel in this light nut; the soul of this man
 is his clothes. Trust him not in matter of heavy
 consequence; I have kept of them tame, and know 45
 their natures. Farewell, monsieur; I have spoken
 better of you than you have or will to deserve at my
 hand; but we must do good against evil.   [*Exit.*]

---

26. End] *Collier*[1]; And *F.* 48. S.D. *Exit.*] *Rowe*[1]; *not in F.*

27–8. *A good . . . dinner*] to tell tall
stories. Cf. "What art thou? / A
traveller. / . . . thou wouldst do well
To . . . tell me lies at dinner time."
Marlowe, *Ed. 2*, ll. 28–31.

37. *that leap'd into the custard*] The
jester's leaping into an enormous custard was a famous feature of Lord
Mayor's Feasts in London. Cf. Jonson,
The Devil is an Asse, I. i. 95 ff.

38–9. *for your residence*] why you happen to be there.

40–1. *mistaken him . . . took him*] Even
if I *took* him at his prayers I would still

mis-take him, i.e. take his action
amiss, in a bad sense. Cf. *R 2*, III. iii.
15 ff and Jonson, *B.F.*, II. ii. 101 f.

45. *kept of them tame*] I have kept
creatures like this for domestic amuse-
ment—so Lafew accepts Parolles at
the end of the play. *O.E.D.* quotes "a
tame fool" from 1711; cf. the remark
of Charles II quoted in Hotson, *Shakespeare's Motley*, p. 98. *of them* is a parti-
tive genitive; cf. French *des* = some
of.

48. *we must . . . evil*] Cf. 1 Thessa-
lonians v. 15.

Par. An idle lord, I swear.
Ber. I think not so.   50
Par. Why, do you not know him?
Ber. Yes, I do know him well; and common speech
  Gives him a worthy pass. Here comes my clog.

Enter HELENA.

Hel. I have, sir, as I was commanded from you,
  Spoke with the king, and have procur'd his leave   55
  For present parting; only he desires
  Some private speech with you.
Ber.   I shall obey his will.
  You must not marvel, Helen, at my course,
  Which holds not colour with the time, nor does
  The ministration and required office   60
  On my particular. Prepar'd I was not
  For such a business; therefore am I found
  So much unsettled. This drives me to entreat you
  That presently you take your way for home,
  And rather muse than ask why I entreat you;   65
  For my respects are better than they seem,
  And my appointments have in them a need
  Greater than shows itself at the first view
  To you that know them not. This to my mother.
          [Giving a letter.]
  'Twill be two days ere I shall see you, so   70
  I leave you to your wisdom.

50. not so] *Singer*[2]*; so F.*   51. not know] *F; know Singer*[2], *conj. W. S. Walker.*
69. S.D. *Giving a letter] Rowe*[1]*; not in F.*

49. *idle*] "foolish, silly" (On.); perhaps even "mad" (cf. *1 Honest Whore*,
v. ii. 119, 306).

50.] F "I thinke so" is hard to justify
as an antithesis to *I swear*, however
much under Parolles' influence Bertram may be supposed to be; it directly
contradicts what Bertram says, ll. 52–
3. I suppose that Bertram says "I dis-
agree with you"; Parolles answers
"What! Haven't you seen through
him yet?" (cf. *known* at II. iii. 101).
Bertram in reply takes up the common

sense of "know": "I am well acquainted with him, and besides, his general
reputation is high".

53. *clog*] a weight tied to an animal
to restrict its activity. Cf. *Wint.*, IV. iv.
669.

59. *holds . . . time*] is not very appropriate to a wedding-day.

59–61. *nor does . . . particular*] My
course involves the omission of my
particular duties as a husband.

66. *my respects*] the considerations
prompting me.

Hel.   Sir, I can nothing say
But that I am your most obedient servant.
Ber. Come, come; no more of that.
Hel.   And ever shall
With true observance seek to eke out that
Wherein toward me my homely stars have fail'd   75
To equal my great fortune.
Ber.   Let that go.
My haste is very great. Farewell. Hie home.
Hel. Pray sir, your pardon.
Ber.   Well, what would you say?
Hel. I am not worthy of the wealth I owe,
Nor dare I say 'tis mine—and yet it is;   80
But, like a timorous thief, most fain would steal
What law does vouch mine own.
Ber.   What would you have?
Hel. Something, and scarce so much; nothing indeed.
I would not tell you what I would, my lord.
Faith, yes: 85
Strangers and foes do sunder and not kiss.
Ber. I pray you, stay not, but in haste to horse.
Hel. I shall not break your bidding, good my lord.
Where are my other men? Monsieur, farewell.   *Exit.*
Ber. Go thou toward home, where I will never come   90
Whilst I can shake my sword or hear the drum.
Away, and for our flight.
Par.   Bravely. Coragio!   [*Exeunt.*]

76–7.] *As Pope;* . . . Farwell: / Hie home. / *F.*   84–6.] *As Dyce*[2]*;* I . . . yes, /
. . . kisse. / *F.*   89. Where . . . men? Monsieur, farewell.] *F; Ber.* Where . . .
men, Monsieur?—farewel. *Theobald*[2]*; Ber.* Where . . . men? *Hel.* Monsieur,
farewell. *Keightley.*   92. Exeunt.] *Rowe*[1]*; not in F.*

74. *observance*] dutiful service, rever-
ence (On.).
75. *my homely stars*] the fate which
gave me humble parents.
79. *owe*] own.
89.] I follow F in giving this line to
Helena. To end her words at *lord*
muffles the effect of her exit, and
makes her slip out feebly. Dignity
and resource characterize her actions

elsewhere and there is no dramatic
reason why they should not be preserved here. As the favourite of the
King and the wife of a count she cannot be without a retinue for her journey to Rossillion. Cf. Hermione's exit
in *Wint.*, II. i. 124 f.
92. *Coragio*] Popular slang Italian.
Cf. Stephano in *Temp.*, v. i. 258, and
Jonson, *The Case is Altered*, I. v. 6.

ACT III

[SCENE I.—*Florence. The Duke's palace.*]

Flourish. Enter the Duke of Florence, the two French Lords, with a
troop of soldiers.

Duke. So that from point to point now have you heard
    The fundamental reasons of this war,
    Whose great decision hath much blood let forth,
    And more thirsts after.
First Lord.   Holy seems the quarrel
    Upon your Grace's part; black and fearful   5
    On the opposer.
Duke. Therefore we marvel much our cousin France
    Would in so just a business shut his bosom
    Against our borrowing prayers.
Second Lord.   Good my lord,
    The reasons of our state I cannot yield,   10
    But like a common and an outward man
    That the great figure of a council frames
    By self-unable motion; therefore dare not
    Say what I think of it, since I have found
    Myself in my incertain grounds to fail   15
    As often as I guess'd.

ACT III

Scene i

Act III Scene i] *Rowe*[1]*; Actus Tertius F.*   *Florence. The Duke's palace.] Florence.*
A Room in the Duke's Palace. Capell; not in F.   *the two French Lords]* two French
Lords *Rowe*[1]*; the two Frenchmen F.*   9. Second Lord.] *Rowe*[1]*; French E. | F; First*
Lord. Dyce[1].

3–4. *Whose . . . after*] The process of
deciding the issue of the war has
already caused much bloodshed and is
likely to cause more.

  7. *cousin*] fellow-sovereign.

  10–13. *The reasons . . . motion*] I cannot speak of state reasons except as a
commoner who stands outside the
council-chamber, and can only imagine what goes on inside by the analogy
of individual, and hence insufficient,
motives.

Duke.   Be it his pleasure.
First Lord. But I am sure the younger of our nature
  That surfeit on their ease will day by day
  Come here for physic.
Duke.   Welcome shall they be,
  And all the honours that can fly from us   20
  Shall on them settle. You know your places well;
  When better fall, for your avails they fell.
  Tomorrow to the field.   *Flourish.* [*Exeunt.*]

[SCENE II.—*Rossillion. The Count's palace.*]

Enter COUNTESS *and* CLOWN.

Count. It hath happen'd all as I would have had it, save
  that he comes not along with her.
Clo. By my troth, I take my young lord to be a very
  melancholy man.
Count. By what observance, I pray you?   5
Clo. Why, he will look upon his boot and sing; mend the
  ruff and sing; ask questions and sing; pick his teeth
  and sing. I know a man that had this trick of melancholy sold a goodly manor for a song.

17. *First Lord.*] *Camb.; Fren. G. | F; 2 Lord. Rowe*[1]. nature] *F;* Nation *Rowe*[1].
23. to the] to'th the *F.* S.D. *Flourish. Exeunt.*] *Flourish. F; Exeunt. Rowe*[1].

Scene II

Scene II] *Pope; not in F.* *Rossillion. The Count's palace.*] *Rossillion. A Room in the Count's Palace. Capell; not in F.* 9. sold] *F3;* hold *F.*

17. *nature*] temperament, outlook.
H. F. Brooks, supporting Rowe's
emendation, points out the ease of a
mis-reading *nature* for "nation": if the
compositor set *nat* from copy, it would
be quite easy for him to assimilate the
ending to *sure* or *pleasure* just preceding.
If "nation" is correct the second
speech (17–19) would follow the first
(9–16) more logically, since both
would then (as truth and excuse),
refer directly to the French. *nature*
however, makes sense and should be
preserved.

18. *surfeit . . . ease*] The ease of a life

of peace upsets them; only the active
life of war will restore them to health.

22. *When better . . . fell*] "when better
places fall vacant, they will have fallen
vacant for you to fill" (*N.S.*); *fell* is
past for future perfect.

Scene II

7. *ruff*] Editors assume here that *ruff*
must refer to *boot* and so interpret it as
a variant of "ruffle" (*O.E.D.* sb.[1]
II.6): "The loose turned-over portion
or flap of a top-boot".

8–9. *I know . . . song*] The Folio text
seems to be impossible; emendation of

Count. Let me see what he writes, and when he means to   10
    come.   [*Reads the letter.*]

Clo. I have no mind to Isbel since I was at court. Our old
    lings and our Isbels a' th' country are nothing like
    your old ling and your Isbels a' th' court. The brains
    of my Cupid's knock'd out, and I begin to love as an   15
    old man loves money, with no stomach.

Count. What have we here?

Clo. E'en that you have there.   *Exit.*

Count.[*Reads*] *I have sent you a daughter-in-law; she hath*
    recovered the king and undone me. I have wedded her, not   20
    bedded her, and sworn to make the "not" eternal. You shall
    hear I am run away; know it before the report come. If there
    be breadth enough in the world I will hold a long distance.
    My duty to you.

                          Your unfortunate son,   25
                          BERTRAM

This is not well, rash and unbridled boy,
To fly the favours of so good a king,
To pluck his indignation on thy head
By the misprizing of a maid too virtuous   30
For the contempt of empire.

            [*Re-*]*enter* CLOWN.

10, 17. *Count.*] *Lad. F (La. throughout scene, except 64, Old La.*).   11. S.D. *Reads
the letter.*] *Theobald[1]; Opening the Letter. Capell; not in F.*   12–14. old lings . . .
old ling] *F*; old Ling . . . old Ling *F2*; oldings . . . oldings *conj. Hudson;* codlings
. . . codlings *Brigstocke, conj. Kinnear.*   18. E'en] *Theobald[1]*; In *F.*   19. S.D.
Count. Reads] *A Letter F.*   31. S.D. *Re-enter Clown*] *Enter Clowne F.*

either *know* or *hold* will restore the
grammatical concords; the change of
know to *knew* is graphically easier, but
the existence of the proverb "sold for a
song" in Shakespeare's day (Tilley
S 636) makes the text as emended here
more probable.

12–13. *old lings*] " 'old ling' is salted
cod, and when it is remembered that
'salt' = lecherous, and that 'cod' also
has a second meaning of which 'cod-
piece' is a familiar illustration, it becomes clear that the text is correct"
(*N.S.*).

16. *stomach*] probably contains the
idea of "carnal appetite" as well as
that of "zest". Notice the comic
equation of *brains* and *stomach*.

18. *E'en*] The Folio *In* can be made
to yield sense, but the fact that in some
Shakespearian texts *In* appears to be
merely a variant spelling of *E'en* in-
clines one to accept the latter reading.

21. "*not*"] *N.S.* and Kökeritz suggest a pun on the "knot", then as now
symbolic of marriage.

31. *For . . . empire*] for even an
emperor to despise her.

Clo. O madam, yonder is heavy news within, between
      two soldiers and my young lady.

Count. What is the matter?

Clo. Nay, there is some comfort in the news, some com-   35
      fort; your son will not be kill'd so soon as I thought
      he would.

Count. Why should he be kill'd?

Clo. So say I, madam—if he run away, as I hear he does;
      the danger is in standing to't; that's the loss of men,   40
      though it be the getting of children. Here they come
      will tell you more. For my part, I only hear your son
      was run away.   [*Exit.*]

             Enter HELENA *and the two French Lords.*

First Lord. Save you, good madam.

Hel. Madam, my lord is gone, for ever gone.   45

Second Lord. Do not say so.

Count. Think upon patience. Pray you, gentlemen—
        I have felt so many quirks of joy and grief
        That the first face of neither on the start
        Can woman me unto't. Where is my son, I pray you? 50

Second Lord. Madam, he's gone to serve the Duke of
        Florence;
        We met him thitherward, for thence we came,
        And, after some dispatch in hand at court,
        Thither we bend again.

Hel. Look on his letter, madam; here's my passport: 55

---

43. S.D. *Exit.*] *Exit Clown. Capell; not in F.*   S.D. *Enter Helena and the two French Lords.*] *Neilson; Enter Hellen and two Gentlemen. F.*   44. *First Lord.*] *Neilson; French E. | F; 1 Gen. Rowe¹; 2 Lord. Kittredge; 2 Gent. Alexander. So throughout scene, except 62 (q.v.).*   46. *Second Lord.*] *Neilson; French G. | F; 2 Gen. Rowe¹; 1 Lord. Kittredge; 1 Gent. Alexander. So throughout scene.*

40. *danger . . . men*] The joke depends
on the usual obscene quibbles on "die"
(implied in *danger*) and *stand.*

43. S.D. Exit] The Folio does not
give the Clown a separate exit and it
may be that he remains in attendance
till the general exit at l. 98. It seems
more convenient, however, to remove
him at this point.

49. *on the start*] Onions glosses this

phrase "when it suddenly appears".

50. *Can woman me unto't*] can make
me behave (i.e. weep) as women are
supposed to. Schmidt glosses *woman* as
"subdue". Cf. *Wint.*, II. i. 107–10.

55. *passport*] licence to wander
abroad as a beggar (see Spenser,
Mother Hubberds Tale, 189–98). Helena
has been licensed to wander from
home by Bertram's letter.

[*Reads*] *When thou canst get the ring upon my finger, which*
never shall come off, and show me a child begotten of thy
body that I am father to, then call me husband; but in such
a "then" I write a "never".

This is a dreadful sentence.   60

Count. Brought you this letter, gentlemen?

First Lord. Ay, madam; and for the contents' sake are
    sorry for our pains.

Count. I prithee, lady, have a better cheer.
    If thou engrossest all the griefs are thine   65
    Thou robb'st me of a moiety. He was my son,
    But I do wash his name out of my blood
    And thou art all my child. Towards Florence is
      he?

Second Lord. Ay, madam.

Count.   And to be a soldier?

Second Lord. Such is his noble purpose; and, believe't,   70
    The duke will lay upon him all the honour
    That good convenience claims.

Count.   Return you thither?

First Lord. Ay, madam, with the swiftest wing of speed.

Hel. [*Reads*]   *Till I have no wife I have nothing in France.*
    'Tis bitter.

Count.   Find you that there?

Hel.   Ay, madam.   75

First Lord. 'Tis but the boldness of his hand, haply, which
    his heart was not consenting to.

Count. Nothing in France until he have no wife!
    There's nothing here that is too good for him
    But only she, and she deserves a lord   80
    That twenty such rude boys might tend upon
    And call her, hourly, mistress. Who was with him?

---

56. S.D. *Reads*] Capell; *not in* F.   62. *First Lord*] *Neilson;* 1. G. | F; 1. Gen. F4.
65. engrossest all] *F4;* engrossest, all *F.*   74. S.D. *Reads*] Reading. Rowe[1]; *not
in F.*

65. *engrossest*] monopolize. Both *en-*
grossest and *moiety* are technical finan-
cial terms.

   68. *all*] only, exclusively (On.).

   72. *That...claims*] that Bertram can
claim as fit and proper for himself.

O.E.D. illustrates this meaning by "the
convenience of both their ages and
estates" from Grafton's Chronicle.

   74.] Until Helena has ceased to
exist Bertram cannot possess anything
in France.

First Lord. A servant only, and a gentleman which I have
    sometime known.
Count. Parolles, was it not?   85
First Lord. Ay, my good lady, he.
Count. A very tainted fellow, and full of wickedness;
    My son corrupts a well-derived nature
    With his inducement.
First Lord.   Indeed, good lady,
    The fellow has a deal of that too much,   90
    Which holds him much to have.
Count.   Y'are welcome, gentlemen.
    I will entreat you, when you see my son,
    To tell him that his sword can never win
    The honour that he loses; more I'll entreat you
    Written to bear along.
Second Lord.   We serve you, madam,   95
    In that and all your worthiest affairs.
Count. Not so, but as we change our courtesies.
    Will you draw near?   *Exeunt [Countess and Lords.]*
Hel. "Till I have no wife I have nothing in France."
    Nothing in France until he has no wife!   100
    Thou shalt have none, Rossillion, none in France;
    Then hast thou all again. Poor lord, is't I
    That chase thee from thy country, and expose
    Those tender limbs of thine to the event
    Of the none-sparing war? And is it I   105
    That drive thee from the sportive court, where
      thou
    Wast shot at with fair eyes, to be the mark

89-96. Indeed ... affairs.] *As Capell; prose F.*   90. that too] *Rowe*[3]*;* that, too *F.*
91. holds] *F;* soils *conj. Theobald;* hurts *Keightley.*   97. courtesies.] *Rowe*[3]*;*
courtesies, *F.*   98. S.D. *Exeunt Countess and Lords.*] *Exit. F.*

90-1. *The fellow . . . to have*] he has
too much of that power of inducement
which stands him in such good stead
with Bertram; *holds* would seem to be
O.E.D. v. 25: "avail, profit, be of
use", though the examples there all
belong to interrogative negative sen-
tences. The Clarkes' view that it is an
aphetic form of "upholds" is also
possible.

97. *Not so*] "The gentlemen declare
that they are servants to the Countess;
she replies,—No otherwise than as she
returns the same offices of civility"
(Johnson).

101, 120. *Rossillion*] Presumably
Bertram is referred to by his title in
this speech, in order to strengthen the
point that France is his natural home.
    104. *event*] consequence.

Of smoky muskets? O you leaden messengers,
That ride upon the violent speed of fire,
Fly with false aim; move the still-piecing air   110
That sings with piercing; do not touch my lord.
Whoever shoots at him, I set him there;
Whoever charges on his forward breast,
I am the caitiff that do hold him to't;
And though I kill him not, I am the cause   115
His death was so effected. Better 'twere
I met the ravin lion when he roar'd
With sharp constraint of hunger; better 'twere
That all the miseries which nature owes
Were mine at once. No; come thou home,
    Rossillion,   120
Whence honour but of danger wins a scar,
As oft it loses all; I will be gone;
My being here it is that holds thee hence.
Shall I stay here to do't? No, no, although

---

110. still-piecing] *Var. '78, conj. Anon; still-peering F; still-piercing F2; still-'pearing Delius⁴, conj. (withdrawn) Grant White; still-pairing Case, conj. Dowden.*

108. *smoky*] in antithesis to "fair" above.

110. *still*] always.

still-piecing] The Folio reading can be defended, most plausibly as an aphetic form of "still-appearing", or one may follow Sisson in believing that the basic image is that of the wind-cherubs who "peer" down from the corners of old maps; the most generally accepted emendation, *still-piecing* (peecing), however, gives a clearer and seemingly more poetic form to the sense which must be present: move the air which is unaffected by bullets because it closes up again when the bullet has passed through it. Lord Chedworth (in a work printed to prove his sanity—see *D.N.B.*—[*Notes*, 1805]) first pointed out the Biblical parallel in *Wisdom of Soloman*, v 12: "Or like as when an arrow is shot at a mark, it parteth the air, which immediately cometh together again, so that a man cannot tell where it went through." Cf. "woundless air" in *Ham.*, iv. i. 44, and

> Wound the loud winds, or with
>   bemock'd-at stabs
> Kill the still-closing waters
>   (*Tp.*, iii. iii. 63–4).

111. *sings with piercing*] The *sings* refers primarily to the whine of the bullet, but there may be a secondary connotation: the air is so little affected by piercing that it sings. Cf. "He . . . cut the winds, / Who nothing hurt withal, hiss'd him in scorn" (*Rom.*, i. i. 109–10).

113. *forward*] "facing the enemy" and/or "in the van of the fight".

117. *ravin*] ravenous.

119. *owes*] owns.

121–2. *Whence . . . all*] from the wars, where honour only wins a scar for all the danger it undergoes, and where it may lose life.

The air of paradise did fan the house   125
And angels offic'd all. I will be gone,
That pitiful rumour may report my flight
To consolate thine ear. Come, night; end, day;
For with the dark, poor thief, I'll steal away.   *Exit.*

[SCENE III.—*Florencc.*]

Flourish. Enter the DUKE OF FLORENCE, BERTRAM, *Drum and Trumpets, Soldiers,* PAROLLES.

Duke. The general of our horse thou art, and we,
          Great in our hope, lay our best love and credence
          Upon thy promising fortune.
Ber.   Sir, it is
          A charge too heavy for my strength; but yet
          We'll strive to bear it for your worthy sake   5
          To th'extreme edge of hazard.
Duke.   Then go thou forth;

Scene III

Scene III] *Capell; not in F.   Florence.*] *Florence. Before the Duke's Palace. Capell; not in F.   Bertram, Drum and Trumpets, Soldiers, Parolles.*] *Rossillion, drum and trumpets, soldiers, Parrolles. F; Bertram, Lords, Officers, Soldiers, and Others. Capell; Bertram, Parolles, Lords, Officers, Soldiers, and others. Collier*[1].

126. *angels offic'd all*] Since "offices" are domestic quarters, it seems probable that this means, "angels acted as domestic servants".

127. *pitiful*] She calls rumour *pitiful* because she thinks of it as taking pity on Bertram.

129. *thief*]*thief* is appropriate because of *dark* and *steal*; we should also remember that Helena sees herself as one who has stolen the title of wife. Effectively, with this speech and invocation of darkness, the first half of the play ends; the second half will be found to take up these ideas and to use darkness as a main means of concluding the plot.

Scene III

S.D. Enter . . .] Modern editors usually regularize the F entry to a descending order of social rank. This is dangerous, for the postponement of Parolles' entry to the end of the list may well be deliberate, to facilitate some stage-business, as in the Q2 entry for *Ham.*, I. ii.

2. *Great in our hope*] Images of pregnancy and hope begin the second half of the play, as images of disease and death began the first half.

2–3. *lay . . . fortune*] wager the sign of our love and trust (this high position) upon your promise of future fortune.

And fortune play upon thy prosperous helm
As thy auspicious mistress!
Ber.   This very day,
Great Mars, I put myself into thy file;
Make me but like my thoughts and I shall prove   10
A lover of thy drum, hater of love.   *Exeunt omnes.*

[SCENE IV.—*Rossillion. The Count's palace.*]

Enter COUNTESS *and* STEWARD.

Count. Alas! and would you take the letter of her?
Might you not know she would do as she has done
By sending me a letter? Read it again.
Stew. [*Reads*] *I am Saint Jaques' pilgrim, thither gone.*
Ambitious love hath so in me offended   5
That barefoot plod I the cold ground upon,
With sainted vow my faults to have amended.
Write, write, that from the bloody course of war

Scene IV

Scene IV] *Capell; not in* F.   *Rossillion. The Count's palace.*] *Rossillion. A Room in the Count's Palace. Capell; not in* F.   4. S.D. *Stew. Reads*] *Letter.* F.

7–8. *And fortune . . . mistress*] "By using the word 'play' here, Shakespeare ingeniously conveys the image of favouring sunshine" (the Clarkes). Cf. ". . . conjuring the moon / To stand's auspicious mistress" (*Lr.*, II. i. 39–40).

11. *drum*] Mars is given a drum (instead of the usual trumpet) also in *Ven.*, 107 and *Two Noble Kinsmen*, I. i. 202.

Scene IV

4. Saint Jaques] The obvious shrine of Saint Jaques (called *Great* and *le Grand* below—i.e. Saint James the Greater) for an Elizabethan audience would be that at Compostella. It is true that Florence is (as Johnson re-

marked) "somewhat out of the road from Rousillon to Compostella" but it is more probable that Shakespeare would make this mistake than refer to other shrines of merely local celebrity. *Jaques* must be pronounced here, as often in Shakespeare, as a disyllable; Shakespeare, however, uses the monosyllabic form more commonly (see Kökeritz, p. 118).

7. *sainted vow*] a vow to a saint.

to have amended] probably = to cause to be amended; Abbott (§360) cites this as an example of the "Complete Present Infinitive" (i.e. the present infinitive with "have").

8. course of war] according to Kökeritz, *course* seems to have had a pronunciation similar to that of

My dearest master, your dear son, may hie.
Bless him at home in peace, whilst I from far   10
His name with zealous fervour sanctify.
His taken labours bid him me forgive;
I, his despiteful Juno, sent him forth
From courtly friends, with camping foes to live
Where death and danger dogs the heels of worth.   15
He is too good and fair for death and me;
Whom I myself embrace to set him free.

Count. Ah, what sharp stings are in her mildest words!
    Rynaldo, you did never lack advice so much
    As letting her pass so; had I spoke with her,   20
    I could have well diverted her intents,
    Which thus she hath prevented.

Stew.   Pardon me, madam;
    If I had given you this at overnight
    She might have been o'erta'en; and yet she writes
    Pursuit would be but vain.

Count.   What angel shall   25
    Bless this unworthy husband? He cannot thrive,
    Unless her prayers, whom heaven delights to hear
    And loves to grant, reprieve him from the wrath
    Of greatest justice. Write, write, Rynaldo,

9–10. *hie. Bless . . . peace,*] *hie; Bless . . . Peace, Rowe*[1]*; hie, Blesse . . . peace. F.*
18. *Count.*] *Cou. Capell; not in F.*

"curse", so that the presence of the latter idea in the phrase should not be overlooked.

11. His name . . . sanctify] This may mean "make his name holy by repeating it in my prayers" or "by living in a saintly way make his name (which I bear) that of a saint".

12. taken] undertaken. Cf. Jonson, *C's R.,* v. xi. 45: "your ta'ne toil", and Peele's *Arraignment* (M.S.R.), l. 79.

labours] referring to the labours of Hercules imposed on him by the enmity of Juno.

17. Whom . . . free] the *whom* refers to *death,* the *him* to Bertram.

19. *advice*] "*Advice* is discretion or thought" (Johnson).

22. *prevented*] forestalled.

23. *at overnight*] "on the previous evening" (*O.E.D.* 1).

25–9. *What angel . . . justice*] J. D. Rea (*Philological Quarterly* VIII) takes this to refer to the plea of the Blessed Virgin Mary in the *Processus Belial*; but there is no need to foist in this esoteric doctrine; even a straightforward reference to the Virgin as intercessor is too Popish to be probable. The word *husband* points to Helena; since heaven has already granted her prayers for the King's recovery, and since she has signified her intention, just above, to sanctify Bertram's name, it is most probable that it is she who is referred to.

29. *Write, write*] catching up the actual words of Helena's letter (l. 8).

To this unworthy husband of his wife;   30
Let every word weigh heavy of her worth
That he does weigh too light; my greatest grief,
Though little he do feel it, set down sharply.
Dispatch the most convenient messenger.
When haply he shall hear that she is gone,   35
He will return; and hope I may that she,
Hearing so much, will speed her foot again,
Led hither by pure love. Which of them both
Is dearest to me I have no skill in sense
To make distinction. Provide this messenger.   40
My heart is heavy and mine age is weak;
Grief would have tears and sorrow bids me speak.

Exeunt.

[SCENE V.—*Outside Florence.*]

A tucket afar off. Enter old WIDOW *of Florence, her daughter* [DIANA],
VIOLENTA, *and* MARIANA, *with other citizens.*

Wid. Nay, come; for if they do approach the city, we shall
    lose all the sight.

Scene v
Scene v] *Capell; not in* F.   *Outside Florence.*] *Without the Walls of Florence.*
Capell; not in F.   1-15.] *As Pope;* ... come, / ... Citty, / ... sight. / ... done /
... seruice. / ... reported, / ... Commander, / ... slew / ... labour, / ... harke, /
... Trumpets. / ... againe, / ... it. / ... Earle, / ... name, / ... rich / ... honestie. /
... neighbour / ... Gentleman / ... Companion. / F (*verse*).

30. *unworthy . . . wife*] husband unworthy of his wife.

Scene v
    Violenta] This name cannot be
justified as representing even a mute,
for by ll. 96 f there are only four persons present; presumably it indicates
an idea abandoned in the course o.
composition, but not erased from the
"foul papers". The name appears in
37th and 42nd novels of Painter, and
is printed, in mistake for Viola, in the
F text of the next play printed—
Twelfth Night (I. v. 157 S.D.). We may
regard the comma preceding the

name as a misprint or, at least, as not
disjunctive and suppose that Violenta
represents a first idea for Diana's name
—an explanation reinforced by the
wording of the entry for IV. ii.
    1-15.] The curious pseudo-verse
lines in which this passage is printed in
F occur at the end of a page. *N.S.* suggests that the arrangement is due "to
the compositor's necessity of filling out
the tail-end of his stint with insufficient matter", and this is strengthened
by Hinman's discovery of the way in
which F pages were composed (*Sh. Q.*,
VI (1955)). III. v. entry is spaced very
widely, probably for the same reason.

Dia. They say the French count has done most honourable service.

Wid. It is reported that he has taken their great'st com-   5
   mander, and that with his own hand he slew the
   duke's brother. [*Tucket*] We have lost our labour;
   they are gone a contrary way. Hark! You may know
   by their trumpets.

Mar. Come, let's return again and suffice ourselves with   10
   the report of it. Well, Diana, take heed of this French
   earl; the honour of a maid is her name, and no legacy
   is so rich as honesty.

Wid. I have told my neighbour how you have been
   solicited by a gentleman his companion.   15

Mar. I know that knave, hang him! one Parolles; a filthy
   officer he is in those suggestions for the young earl.
   Beware of them, Diana: their promises, entice-
   ments, oaths, tokens, and all these engines of lust, are
   not the things they go under; many a maid hath been   20
   seduced by them; and the misery is, example, that so
   terrible shows in the wrack of maidenhood, cannot
   for all that dissuade succession, but that they are
   limed with the twigs that threatens them. I hope I
   need not to advise you further; but I hope your own   25
   grace will keep you where you are, though there
   were no further danger known but the modesty
   which is so lost.

Dia. You shall not need to fear me.

Enter HELENA.

Wid. I hope so. Look, here comes a pilgrim. I know she   30
   will lie at my house; thither they send one another.

3. *Dia.*] *Diana. F; Violenta. conj. Camb.*   7. S.D. *Tucket*] *Capell; not in F.*
22. wrack] *F;* wreck *Rowe[1]+.*   29. S.D. *Enter Helena.*] *Enter Hellen. F; Enter
Helena disguised like a Pilgrim. Rowe[1].*

16–17. *a filthy . . . earl*] He is a foul
agent to tempt you on behalf of the
earl. The modern sense of *officer* may be
glanced at as well.

20. *not the things they go under*] not all
they appear to be.

23. *dissuade succession*] prevent others
from following in her footsteps.

but that] See Abbott §122 on "But"
signifying prevention.

24. *limed . . . them*] caught with bird-
lime, in spite of having fair warning.

I'll question her: God save you, pilgrim! Whither
are bound?

Hel. To Saint Jaques le Grand.

Where do the palmers lodge, I do beseech you?   35

Wid. At the Saint Francis here beside the port.

Hel. Is this the way?   *A march afar.*

Wid. Ay, marry, is't. Hark you, they come this way.
If you will tarry, holy pilgrim
But till the troops come by   40
I will conduct you where you shall be lodg'd;
The rather for I think I know your hostess
As ample as myself.

Hel.   Is it yourself?

Wid. If you shall please so, pilgrim.

Hel. I thank you and will stay upon your leisure.   45

Wid. You came, I think, from France?

Hel.   I did so.

Wid. Here you shall see a countryman of yours
That has done worthy service.

Hel.   His name, I pray you.

Dia. The Count Rossillion. Know you such a one?

Hel. But by the ear, that hears most nobly of him;   50
His face I know not.

Dia.   Whatsome'er he is,
He's bravely taken here. He stole from France,
As 'tis reported, for the king had married him
Against his liking. Think you it is so?

Hel. Ay, surely, mere the truth; I know his lady.   55

Dia. There is a gentleman that serves the count
Reports but coarsely of her.

34. le] *F3; la F.*   37. S.D. *A march afar.] F; Malone (after* you *38); Dyce*[1] *(after* way *38); Camb. (after* is't *38).*   37–40.] *As F; prose Pope; . . .* Hark you! / *. . .* pilgrim, / *. . .* by, / *Capell (verse); . . .* Hark you! / *. . .* way. / *. . .* pilgrim, / *. . .* by, / *Brigstocke (verse); . . .* Hark you! / *. . .* tarry / *. . .* by, / *conj. this edn (verse).*

36. *At the Saint Francis*] at the inn
with the sign of St Francis.

port] gate of the city.

37–40.] The short verse-lines printed in F may represent a compositor's
effort to regularize confused copy, but
the verse-speaking is obviously broken-
up by pauses and by noises off, and the

line-division may have been intended
to allow for this.

43. *ample*] well.

51. *Whatsome'er*] Shakespearian form
of "whatever".

52. *bravely taken*] made a fine impression.

55. *mere the truth*] absolutely true.

Hel.   What's his name?

Dia. Monsieur Parolles.

Hel.   O, I believe with him,
In argument of praise or to the worth
Of the great count himself, she is too mean   60
To have her name repeated; all her deserving
Is a reserved honesty, and that
I have not heard examin'd.

Dia.   Alas, poor lady!
'Tis a hard bondage to become the wife
Of a detesting lord.   65

Wid. I warrant, good creature, wheresoe'er she is,
Her heart weighs sadly. This young maid might do her
A shrewd turn if she pleas'd.

Hel.   How do you mean?
Maybe the amorous count solicits her
In the unlawful purpose?

Wid.   He does indeed,   70
And brokes with all that can in such a suit
Corrupt the tender honour of a maid;
But she is arm'd for him and keeps her guard
In honestest defence.

Drum and colours. Enter BERTRAM, PAROLLES, *and the
whole army.*

Mar.   The gods forbid else!

Wid. So, now they come.   75

66. I warrant,] *Globe;* I write *F;* I right *F2;* Ah! right *Rowe¹;* A right *Var.* '*78;*
I weet, *Alexander,* conj. *Steevens.*

59. *In argument . . . worth*] if we are
going to talk in her praise, or compare
her worth (with that of the count).

61–2. *all . . . honesty*] Cf. Dekker, etc.
Patient Grissil, i. ii. 48–9: "all thy portion / Is but an honest name."

62. *reserved honesty*] strictly preserved
chastity. Brigstocke compares *Cym.,*
i. iv. 125–6: "I will bring from thence
that honour of hers which you imagine
so reserv'd". Notice the jingle on
deserving and *reserved.*

66. *I warrant*] F "I write" seems to be

inadmissible, since all the other examples of "write" in the sense of
"lay claim" are used reflexively (as
above, ii. iii. 197). The Globe emendation "warrant" seems the most
plausible, since Shakespeare's "warrant" (probably abbreviated "wrt")
is misprinted elsewhere—e.g. as "wit"
in Q2 text of *Ham.,* ii. i. 38.

68. *shrewd*] mischievous (On.).

71. *brokes*] trades; Malone notes,
"A *broker,* in our author's time, meant
a bawd or pimp."

That is Antonio, the duke's eldest son;
That Escalus.

Hel.   Which is the Frenchman?

Dia.   He—

That with the plume; 'tis a most gallant fellow.
I would he lov'd his wife; if he were honester
He were much goodlier. Is't not a handsome gentleman?

Hel. I like him well.   81

Dia. 'Tis pity he is not honest. Yond's that same knave
That leads him to these places. Were I his lady
I would poison that vile rascal.

Hel.   Which is he?

Dia. That jackanapes with scarfs. Why is he melancholy?   85

Hel. Perchance he's hurt i' th' battle.

Par. Lose our drum! Well!

Mar. He's shrewdly vex'd at something. Look, he has
spied us.

Wid. Marry, hang you!   90

Mar. And your curtsy, for a ring-carrier!

Exeunt [Bertram, Parolles and the army.]

83. places] *F;* Paces *Theobald¹;* passes *Dyce²,* conj. *Lettsom.*   91. S.D.] *Exeunt
Ber. and Par. c&. Rowe¹ (after 90); Exit. F.*

82. *Yond's*] a demonstrative pro-
noun (like Scottish "yon"), not an
adverb (like modern poetical "yonder"); see Franz §319.

83. *places*] Cf. Peacham's *Compleat
Gentleman* ". . . buy their acquaintance
at over deare a rate, by being drawne
either into base Actions and Places of
which they are ashamed for ever after"
(ed. Gordon, p. 223) and *Lr.,* v. iii.
172 f.

87. *drum*] "the loss of drums in those
days was a matter of great importance, because they were decorated
with the colours of the regiment. The
loss was therefore equivalent to the
loss of the colours" (Brigstocke). Bertram, below (III. VI. 62), calls it an
"instrument of honour". T. W. Baldwin adds: "this appears to be a symbolic drum, since Bertram had sworn
to follow the drum to the exclusion of
love [III. iii. 10 f], but through the

instigation of Parolles is now following
love. Parolles has thus allegorically
lost Bertram's drum" (*Five-Act Structure,* p. 732).

91. *curtsy*] the bow or salute which
Bertram has given them. The Elizabethans did not distinguish in spelling
between "curtsy" and "courtesy" so
that either (or both) may be meant
here.

ring-carrier] probably means a bawd,
though from some contexts the simple
sense of "deceiver" seems to be indicated (e.g. Nashe, III, 366). What is
presumably the full form of the phrase,
i.e. "to carry a ring in ones mouth" is
found in a gloss to Fenton's *Bandello:*
"The she baud of London caryeth a
basket in her hande, the he baude a
ring in his mouth" (*Tudor Translations,*
II, 151). The ring that is carried is presumably the promise of marriage, with
which he allures young maids like

Wid. The troop is past. Come, pilgrim, I will bring you
  Where you shall host; of enjoin'd penitents
  There's four or five, to Great Saint Jaques bound,
  Already at my house.
Hel.   I humbly thank you. 95
  Please it this matron and this gentle maid
  To eat with us tonight; the charge and thanking
  Shall be for me; and, to requite you further,
  I will bestow some precepts of this virgin, 99
  Worthy the note.
Both.   We'll take your offer kindly. *Exeunt.*

[SCENE VI.—*The Florentine camp.*]

Enter BERTRAM *and the two French Lords.*

First Lord. Nay, good my lord, put him to't; let him have
  his way.
Second Lord. If your lordship find him not a hilding, hold
  me no more in your respect.
First Lord. On my life, my lord, a bubble. 5

92–3. bring you / Where] *Rowe*[3]; bring / you, Where *F.*

Scene VI

Scene VI] *Capell; not in F.* *The Florentine camp.*] *Camp under Florence. Capell; not
in F.* *Enter ... Lords.*] *Rowe*[1]; *Enter Count Rossillion and the Frenchmen, as at first. F.*
1. *First Lord.*] *Rowe*[1]; *Cap. E. | F;* 2 *Lord. Camb. So to 105.* 3. *Second Lord.*]
Rowe[1]; *Cap. G. | F; First Lord. Camb. So to 105.*

Diana. Cf. *Love and Fortune* (M.S.R.), 1110 and 1372 and Dekker, *2 Honest Whore,* III. i. 79 ff. For another possibility see Greene, *Quip for an Upstart Courtier,* sig. D1: "had upon his fingers as many gold Rings as would . . . beseeme a Pandar of long profession to weare".

93. *host*] lodge.

 enjoin'd penitents] persons bound by oath to undertake a pilgrimage, in penance for sin; so Helena regards herself.

97–8. *the charge . . . me*] I shall pay, and thank you all for coming.

99. *of*] probably = "on" (Abbott §175); *N.S.* supposes it to belong to *worthy the note.*

Scene VI

S.D.] See Intro., p. xvi.

3. *hilding*] coward.

5. *a bubble*] a glittering and ephemeral cheat; cf. *R 3,* IV. iv. 88 ff: "A dream . . . a garish flag. . . A sign of dignity, a breath, a bubble". Hamlet calls Osric a bubble (v. ii. 188).

Ber. Do you think I am so far deceived in him?

First Lord. Believe it, my lord, in mine own direct knowledge, without any malice, but to speak of him as my
kinsman, he's a most notable coward, an infinite and
endless liar, an hourly promise-breaker, the owner   10
of no one good quality worthy your lordship's entertainment.

Second Lord. It were fit you knew him; lest, reposing too
far in his virtue, which he hath not, he might at some
great and trusty business in a main danger fail you.   15

Ber. I would I knew in what particular action to try him.

Second Lord. None better than to let him fetch off his
drum, which you hear him so confidently undertake
to do.

First Lord. I, with a troop of Florentines, will suddenly   20
surprise him; such I will have whom I am sure he
knows not from the enemy. We will bind and hoodwink him so, that he shall suppose no other but that
he is carried into the leaguer of the adversaries when
we bring him to our own tents. Be but your lordship   25
present at his examination; if he do not for the promise of his life, and in the highest compulsion of base
fear, offer to betray you and deliver all the intelligence in his power against you, and that with the
divine forfeit of his soul upon oath, never trust my   30
judgment in anything.

Second Lord. O, for the love of laughter, let him fetch his
drum; he says he has a stratagem for't. When your
lordship sees the bottom of his success in't, and to
what metal this counterfeit lump of ore will be   35
melted, if you give him not John Drum's entertain-

6.] *As Pope;* . . . farre / . . . him. / *F (verse).*   34. his] *Rowe[1]*; this *F.*   35. ore]
Theobald[1]; ours F.

8–9. *as my kinsman*] with the same
partiality I would use if he were my
kinsman.

24. *leaguer*] the Dutch word for
camp—a piece of military jargon.

35. *ore*] The F reading is just possible, but Theobald's emendation
(graphically plausible since "oure" is

listed by *O.E.D.* as a variant spelling)
has been universally accepted; if it
is correct, perhaps *ore* here (as in
Ham., IV. i. 25—the only other appearance of the word in Shakespeare)
means "gold"—by a confusion with
the heraldic "or".

36–7. *John Drum's entertainment*]

ment your inclining cannot be removed. Here he
comes.

Enter PAROLLES.

First Lord. O, for the love of laughter, hinder not the
honour of his design; let him fetch off his drum in   40
any hand.

Ber. How now, monsieur! This drum sticks sorely in your
disposition.

Second Lord. A pox on't! let it go; 'tis but a drum.

Par. But a drum! Is't but a drum? A drum so lost! There   45
was excellent command: to charge in with our horse
upon our own wings and to rend our own soldiers!

Second Lord. That was not to be blam'd in the command
of the service; it was a disaster of war that Caesar
himself could not have prevented if he had been   50
there to command.

Ber. Well, we cannot greatly condemn our success; some
dishonour we had in the loss of that drum, but it is
not to be recovered.

Par. It might have been recovered.   55

Ber. It might; but it is not now.

Par. It is to be recovered. But that the merit of service is
seldom attributed to the true and exact performer,
I would have that drum or another, or *hic jacet*.

Ber. Why, if you have a stomach, to't, monsieur! If you   60
think your mystery in stratagem can bring this
instrument of honour again into his native quarter,
be magnanimious in the enterprise and go on; I will
grace the attempt for a worthy exploit; if you speed

60. stomach, to't, monsieur. If] stomacke, too't Monsieur: if *F;* stomack to't,
Monsieur: if *F3;* stomack to't, monsieur, if *Capell.*

Tilley (J 12) quotes, ". . . they maye
have Iacke Drummes entertainment,
and fair and orderly be turned out of
doores".

40–1. *in any hand*] in any case.

48–9. *the command of the service*] the
orders given for the action.

52, 76. *success*] result, fortune.

60–7.] The elaborate circumlocu-
tions used here by Bertram must
either parody or imitate those of Parolles.

61. *mystery*] art or craft (as in "mystery plays").

63. *magnanimious*] alternative spelling of "magnanimous", used by
Shakespeare in its basic sense of
"great-hearted".

    well in it the duke shall both speak of it and extend to   65
    you what further becomes his greatness, even to the
    utmost syllable of your worthiness.

Par. By the hand of a soldier, I will undertake it.

Ber. But you must not now slumber in it.

Par. I'll about it this evening; and I will presently pen   70
    down my dilemmas, encourage myself in my cer-
    tainty, put myself into my mortal preparation; and
    by midnight look to hear further from me.

Ber. May I be bold to acquaint his grace you are gone
    about it?   75

Par. I know not what the success will be, my lord, but the
    attempt I vow.

Ber. I know th'art valiant; and to the possibility of thy
    soldiership will subscribe for thee. Farewell.

Par. I love not many words.   *Exit.*   80

First Lord. No more than a fish loves water. Is not this a
    strange fellow, my lord, that so confidently seems to
    undertake this business, which he knows is not to be
    done; damns himself to do, and dares better be
    damn'd than to do't.   85

Second Lord. You do not know him, my lord, as we do;
    certain it is that he will steal himself into a man's
    favour and for a week escape a great deal of dis-
    coveries, but when you find him out you have him
    ever after.   90

78-9.] *As Pope;* . . . valiant, / . . . souldiership, / . . . Farewell. / *F (verse).*

---

67. *syllable*] referring again, perhaps, to the name Parolles.

68. *By the hand of a soldier*] Such
affected oaths are part of the stock in
trade of the Elizabethan *miles gloriosus*.

71. *dilemmas*] Warburton notes: "By
this word Parolles is made to insinuate
that he had several ways, all equally
certain, of recovering his drum. For a
dilemma is an argument that concludes
both ways"; Halliwell strengthens this
by citing "*Dilemma*, an argument
whiche on euery parte conuinceth
hym to whome it is spoken" from
Elyot's *Dictionary* (1548). It seems

more likely, however, that the dilemmas belong to the course in moral
encouragement that Parolles is pro-
posing, as in the "dilemma of deaths"
that the Clarkes quote from Fuller.

72. *mortal preparation*] This might
mean "preparation for my death"
(e.g. by taking the last sacrament) or
"preparation for the deaths of others"
(girding himself with weapons etc.);
mortal could bear both these constructions in Elizabethan English.

78. *possibility*] capacity.

80.] denying the name Parolles; cf.
however Jonson, *E.M.I.*, III. i. 84.

Ber. Why, do you think he will make no deed at all of this
that so seriously he does address himself unto?

First Lord. None in the world; but return with an invention, and clap upon you two or three probable lies;
but we have almost emboss'd him; you shall see his   95
fall tonight; for indeed he is not for your lordship's
respect.

Second Lord. We'll make you some sport with the fox ere
we case him; he was first smok'd by the old Lord
Lafew; when his disguise and he is parted tell me   100
what a sprat you shall find him; which you shall see
this very night.

First Lord. I must go look my twigs. He shall be caught.

Ber. Your brother, he shall go along with me.   104

First Lord. As't please your lordship. I'll leave you.   [*Exit.*]

Ber. Now will I lead you to the house and show you
The lass I spoke of.

Second Lord.   But you say she's honest.

Ber. That's all the fault. I spoke with her but once
And found her wondrous cold, but I sent to
        her
By this same coxcomb that we have i' th' wind   110
Tokens and letters which she did re-send

103.] *As Pope;* ... twigges, / ... caught. / F (*verse*).   105. *First Lord.* As't ...
lordship. I'll ... you.] *Malone; Cap.* G. As't ... Lordship, Ile ... you. *F; 2 Ld.*
As't ... Lordship, I'll ... you. *Rowe[1]; Fr. Gent.* As't ... lordship. *Fr. Env.* I'll
... you. *Collier[1].*   S.D. *Exit*] *Theobald[1]; not in* F.   107, 113. *Second Lord.*]
Malone; Cap. E. / F; 1. Ld. Rowe[3].

94. *probable lies*] "lies wearing an
appearance of probability" (the
Clarkes).

95. *emboss'd*] (1) ult. identical with
"imbosk" says *O.E.D.* = driven to
extremity, most often used of a deer,
when (as Lyly glosses it) "he fomde at
the mouth with running" (*Midas*, IV.
iii. 30). (2) It appears from Cot-
grave that embossed can also mean
"shut up, as within a box", so that
Furnivall takes the word here to be
equivalent to "emboxed". The hunting images which follow make it
probable that the first meaning is intended, though the connection of

"box" and "case" should also be
noted.

99. *case*] flay, skin; hence "unmask".

smok'd] (1) forced into the open like
a fox smoked out of its earth; (2)
scented, suspected.

103. *twigs*] twigs smeared with bird-
lime, used to catch birds.

105, 107, 113.] For the confusion of
speech-prefixes here, see Intro., pp.
xvi f. Collier's neat emendation, split-
ting l. 105 between the two speakers, is
not dependent, of course, on his interpretation of "E" and "G" as "Envoy"
and "Gentleman".

And this is all I have done. She's a fair creature;
Will you go see her?
Second Lord.   With all my heart, my lord.   *Exeunt.*

[SCENE VII.—*Florence. The Widow's house.*]

Enter HELENA *and* WIDOW.

Hel. If you misdoubt me that I am not she,
    I know not how I shall assure you further
    But I shall lose the grounds I work upon.
Wid. Though my estate be fall'n, I was well born,
    Nothing acquainted with these businesses,   5
    And would not put my reputation now
    In any staining act.
Hel.   Nor would I wish you.
    First give me trust the count he is my husband,
    And what to your sworn counsel I have spoken
    Is so from word to word; and then you cannot,   10
    By the good aid that I of you shall borrow,
    Err in bestowing it.
Wid.   I should believe you,
    For you have show'd me that which well approves
    Y'are great in fortune.
Hel.   Take this purse of gold,
    And let me buy your friendly help thus far,   15
    Which I will over-pay, and pay again
    When I have found it. The count he woos your daughter,
    Lays down his wanton siege before her beauty,
    Resolv'd to carry her; let her in fine consent

Scene VII

Scene VII] *Capell; not in F.   Florence. The Widow's house.] Florence. A Room in the Widow's House. Capell; not in F.   Enter Helena and Widow] Enter Hellen, and Widdow F.   19. Resolv'd] Resolved Collier[1]; Resolue F; Resolves F2.*

3. *But I . . . upon*] "i.e. except by dis-
covering myself to the count" (Warburton).

9. *sworn counsel*] "To your private
knowledge, after having required from
you an oath of secrecy" (Johnson).

11. *By*] *O.E.D.* A. IV. 26: "with respect to, in regard to".

19. *carry her*] as a fortress is "carried"
by assault, after the *siege*.

in fine] finally (On.); or possibly "to
sum up".

As we'll direct her how 'tis best to bear it.   20
Now his important blood will naught deny
That she'll demand; a ring the county wears
That downward hath succeeded in his house
From son to son some four or five descents
Since the first father wore it. This ring he holds   25
In most rich choice; yet, in his idle fire,
To buy his will it would not seem too dear,
Howe'er repented after.
Wid.   Now I see
The bottom of your purpose.
Hel. You see it lawful then; it is no more   30
But that your daughter, ere she seems as won,
Desires this ring; appoints him an encounter;
In fine, delivers me to fill the time,
Herself most chastely absent. After,
To marry her I'll add three thousand crowns   35
To what is pass'd already.
Wid.   I have yielded.
Instruct my daughter how she shall persever
That time and place with this deceit so lawful
May prove coherent. Every night he comes
With musics of all sorts, and songs compos'd   40
To her unworthiness; it nothing steads us
To chide him from our eaves, for he persists
As if his life lay on't.
Hel.   Why then tonight
Let us assay our plot; which, if it speed,

28–9. Now . . . purpose.] *As Capell; one line F.*   34. After,] *This edn; after F;* after this *F2+.*

21. *important*] importunate.
26. *choice*] "special estimation" (On.).
idle] careless or worthless.
27. *will*] "carnal appetite, lust" (On.).
34. *After*] Editors usually piece out the metre here by adding "this" at the end of the line, but a pause (before *After*) may be left deliberately, to indicate a delicacy or hesitancy in the speaker.

37. *persever*] accent on the second syllable.
41. *unworthiness*] It is often supposed that the *unworthiness* of Diana is brought about by public scandal at the Count's serenading, in which case *to* must have the sense of "leading to"; the widow, however, may merely be speaking with polite humility about her daughter—she is not a fit subject for all this attention.
steads] avails.

Is wicked meaning in a lawful deed,   45
And lawful meaning in a lawful act,
Where both not sin, and yet a sinful fact.
But let's about it.   [*Exeunt.*]

48. S.D. *Exeunt.*] *Rowe*[1] *; not in F.*

45. *meaning*] intention.

45–7. *Is wicked...fact*] Malone justifies the text by explaining that the deed is "*lawful*, as being the duty of marriage . . . but his [sc. Bertram's] *meaning* was *wicked* because he intended to commit adultery. The second line relates to Helena; whose *meaning* was *lawful*, in as much as she intended to reclaim her husband, and demanded only the rights of a wife. The *act* or *deed* was *lawful* for the reason already given. The subsequent line relates to them both. The *fact* was *sinful*, as far as Bertram was concerned, because he intended to commit adultery; yet neither he nor Helena *actually* sinned . . ." Compare the similar riddling at the end of Act III of *Meas.* Cf. also Jasper Mayne, *The Amorous Warre* (1648), v. viii: "They've turn'd what I thought *Fornication* / Into the acts of *wedlocke*. How I love / Such projects, where men are betray'd unto / Their lawful pleasure, and tempted to commit / *Adultery* with Innocence, and no sinne follow". Cf. Intro., p. xl on appearance and reality.

ACT IV

[SCENE I.—*Outside the Florentine camp.*]

Enter First French Lord, with five or six other soldiers in ambush.

First Lord. He can come no other way but by this hedge-corner. When you sally upon him speak what terrible language you will; though you understand it not yourselves, no matter; for we must not seem to understand him, unless some one among us, whom 5 we must produce for an interpreter.

First Sold. Good captain, let me be th' interpreter.

First Lord. Art not acquainted with him? Knows he not thy voice?

First Sold. No sir, I warrant you. 10

First Lord. But what linsey-woolsey hast thou to speak to us again?

First Sold. E'en such as you speak to me.

First Lord. He must think us some band of strangers i' th' adversary's entertainment. Now he hath a smack of 15

ACT IV

Scene I

Act IV Scene I] *Rowe*[1]; *Actus Quartus F.*   *Outside the Florentine camp.*] *Without the Florentine Camp. Capell; not in F.*   *Enter First French Lord] Enter first Lord | Capell; Enter one of the Frenchmen | F; Enter Second French Lord | Camb.*   I. *First Lord.*] *Capell;* I. *Lord E. | F; Second Lord. Camb.* So (*Lor. E., Lo. E., L. E. | F*) *throughout scene.*

1–2. *this hedge-corner*] J. C. Adams (*The Globe Playhouse* 165–6) supposes that the "posts placed a little out from the wall on either side of the platform doorways" provided the usual setting for scenes of ambush such as this. See J. W. Saunders in *Shakespeare Survey* VII (1954), however, for objections to Adams' theory, and the alternative

suggestion that the projecting wings of the tiring-house façade provided a more adequate concealment.

11. *linsey-woolsey*] a mixture of flax and wool; hence here a medley of words.

14–15. *strangers . . . entertainment*] "foreign troops in the enemy's pay" (Johnson).

all neighbouring languages; therefore we must every
one be a man of his own fancy, not to know what we
speak one to another; so we seem to know is to know
straight our purpose—choughs' language: gabble
enough and good enough. As for you, interpreter,   20
you must seem very politic. But couch, ho! Here he
comes to beguile two hours in a sleep, and then to
return and swear the lies he forges.

Enter PAROLLES.

Par. Ten a'clock. Within these three hours 'twill be time
enough to go home. What shall I say I have done? It   25
must be a very plausive invention that carries it.
They begin to smoke me, and disgraces have of late
knock'd too often at my door. I find my tongue is too
foolhardy, but my heart hath the fear of Mars before
it and of his creatures, not daring the reports of my   30
tongue.

First Lord. This is the first truth that e'er thine own
tongue was guilty of.

Par. What the devil should move me to undertake the
recovery of this drum, being not ignorant of the   35
impossibility, and knowing I had no such purpose?
I must give myself some hurts, and say I got them
in exploit; yet slight ones will not carry it. They
will say, "Came you off with so little?" And great

17–18. fancy, . . . another;] *F;* fancy; . . . another, *Neilson, conj. Perring.*

17–19. *a man . . . purpose*] "We must
each fancy a jargon for himself, without [aiming to] be understood by one
another, for provided we appear [sc.
to Parolles] to understand, that will be
sufficient for the success of our project." (Henley). The punctuation
given in the text (equivalent to that of
the Folio) is plausible if we take *not
to know* to mean either (as in Henley's paraphrase) "not seeking to
know" or "not knowing" (see Abbott
§356). The punctuation, . . . *fancy;
. . . another, so . . .* gives a more obvious
sense.

19. *choughs' language*] "jackdaws'
gabble" (Brigstocke). Cf. *Temp.*, II. i.
257.

19–20. *gabble . . . good enough*] Probably a proverbial turn of phrase; cf.
Day, *Ile of Guls*, sig. G2ᵛ: "Ridiculous
enough, and good enough"; Wilkins,
Miseries of Enforced Marriage, sig.
A2: "impudent enough and good
enough"; Jonson, *Poet.*, IV. i. 31–2:
"impudently enough . . . and well
enough".

24. *three hours*] See above, III. vi.
73.

26. *plausive*] plausible.

ones I dare not give; wherefore, what's the instance?   40
Tongue, I must put you into a butter-woman's
mouth, and buy myself another of Bajazeth's mule if
you prattle me into these perils.

First Lord. Is it possible he should know what he is, and be
that he is?   45

Par. I would the cutting of my garments would serve the
turn, or the breaking of my Spanish sword.

First Lord. We cannot afford you so.

Par. Or the baring of my beard, and to say it was in
stratagem.   50

First Lord. 'Twould not do.

Par. Or to drown my clothes and say I was stripp'd.

First Lord. Hardly serve.

Par. Though I swore I leap'd from the window of the
citadel—   55

First Lord. How deep?

Par. Thirty fadom.

First Lord. Three great oaths would scarce make that be
believed.

Par. I would I had any drum of the enemy's; I would   60
swear I recover'd it.

First Lord. You shall hear one anon.

42. Bajazeth's mule] *F;* Bajazet's mute *Hanmer, conj. Warburton;* Balaam's mule
conj. Addis (N. & Q. 1866); Bajazet's mate *N.S.*

40. *instance*] usually glossed as
"proof", or "motive", but better
seems the explanation of the Clarkes:
"that which is to be instanced, or
brought forward in evidence".

42. *Bajazeth's mule*] Lowes ('Tudor'
edn 1912) thinks that Parolles is really
referring to Balaam's ass (Numbers
xxii)—cf. collation; this would be appropriate, for the ass only spoke when
the Lord opened his mouth, but the
allusion (though in Parolles' vein)
seems too well hidden to be dramatic-
ally effective. *N.S.* emends to "mate",
supposing a reference to Marlowe's
Zabina, said to scold like a butter-
woman; but the whole sense demands
an antithesis, not a parallel, to *butter-
woman,* for Parolles wishes to exchange

his tongue for one less compromising.
Of emendations, "mute" gives the
most obvious sense, but seems too
obvious for the particularity of the
context, while in *H 5,* I. ii. 232, we find
a "Turkish mute" described as having
a "tongueless mouth". Shakespeare
associates "mules" and "silence"
again in *Cor.,* II. i. 237; the origin of the
association may lie in Psalm xxxii,
verse 9: "Be ye not as the horse, or as
the mule, which have no understanding: whose mouth must be held in with
bit and bridle, lest they come near
unto thee", but this would leave *Bajazeth,* of course, totally unexplained.

48. *afford you so*] give you that much.

49. *baring*] shaving—a use found
also in *Meas.,* IV. ii. 168.

Par. A drum now of the enemy's—

Alarum within.

First Lord. *Throca movousus, cargo, cargo, cargo.*

All. *Cargo, cargo, cargo, villianda par corbo, cargo.*   65
[*They seize him.*]

Par. O, ransom, ransom! [*They blindfold him.*] Do not
hide mine eyes.

First Sold. *Boskos thromuldo boskos.*

Par. I know you are the Muskos' regiment,
And I shall lose my life for want of language.   70
If there be here German, or Dane, Low Dutch,
Italian, or French, let him speak to me,
I'll discover that which shall undo the Florentine.

First Sold. *Boskos vauvado.* I understand thee, and can
speak thy tongue. *Kerelybonto.* Sir, betake thee to thy   75
faith, for seventeen poniards are at thy bosom.

Par. O!

First Sold. O, pray, pray, pray! *Manka revania dulche.*

First Lord. *Oscorbidulchos volivorco.*

First Sold. The general is content to spare thee yet,   80
And, hoodwink'd as thou art, will lead thee on
To gather from thee. Haply thou may'st inform
Something to save thy life.

66-7.] *As Pope;* . . . ransome / Do . . . eyes. / *F (verse).*   65, 66. S.D. *They seize
him* . . . *They blindfold him.*] *This edn; They seize him and blindfold him. Rowe*[1] *(after
eyes); not in F.*   68. *First Sold.*] *1. S. Capell; Inter. F. So (74, 80, Int. F) throughout
scene.*   69. Muskos'] *Capell; Muskos F.*   72-3.] *As F;* . . . me; I'll / . . . Florentine. *Capell.*   78.] *As Staunton;* . . . pray, / *Manka* . . . *dulche. F.*

63. *A drum* . . . *enemy's*] Alexander
places the S.D. before this statement,
so that Parolles seems to be describing
the sound he has heard, but the
comedy of the scene is better preserved
by keeping the Folio order, so that
Parolles' meditation on some stratagem is answered by the alarum.

65. Cargo] This word (taken presumably from the Spanish) is used as
an exclamation elsewhere. See Wilkins' *Miseries of Enforced Marriage,* sig.
F4: "But *Cargo,* my fiddlestick cannot
play".

66-7.] The two short lines in F may
indicate space left clear for business.

69. *Muskos'*] presumably = Musco-
vites'. In *Edward III* a Polonian captain brings troops from "great Musco,
fearefull to the Turke, / And lofty
Poland . . ." (III. i. 43-4).

70. *lose* . . . *language*] The situation is
particularly galling for one whose significant name is Parolles.

72. *me,*] The comma of the Folio
should not be raised to a semicolon;
the *let* . . . *me* clause relates forward as
well as backward.

Par.   O, let me live,
  And all the secrets of our camp I'll show,
  Their force, their purposes; nay, I'll speak that   85
  Which you will wonder at.
First Sold.   But wilt thou faithfully?
Par. If I do not, damn me.
First Sold.   *Acordo linta.*
  Come on; thou art granted space.
                              Exit [with Parolles guarded].

                    A short alarum within.

First Lord. Go tell the Count Rossillion and my brother   89
  We have caught the woodcock and will keep him muffled
  Till we do hear from them.
Second Sold.   Captain, I will.
First Lord. 'A will betray us all unto ourselves:
  Inform on that.
Second Sold. So I will, sir.
First Lord. Till then I'll keep him dark and safely lock'd.   95
                                                      Exeunt.

          [SCENE II.—*Florence. The Widow's house.*]

        Enter BERTRAM *and the maid called* DIANA.

Ber. They told me that your name was Fontybell.

88. art] *F3+ ; are F.*   S.D. *Exit . . . guarded.] Capell; Exit F.*   91, 94. *Second Sold.] 2. S. Capell; Sol. F.*   93. Inform on] *F;* Inform 'em *Rowe[1].*   95. S.D. *Exeunt.] Exit. F.*

Scene II
Scene II] *Pope; not in F.   Florence. The Widow's house.] Florence. A Room in the Widow's House. Capell; not in F.*

87. *damn me*] Parolles would seem to be damned, either way, for he only speaks *faithfully* when the faith is, in fact, treason.

88. S.D.] *N.S.* comments: "No one seems to have asked the meaning of this 'short alarum'; I take it to be the drum once more giving a comic 'burden' to the whole episode."

90. *woodcock*] proverbially stupid bird.

Scene II
S.D. the maid called Diana] see Intro., p. xiii and III. v headnote.
1. *Fontybell*] Thiselton thinks this may refer to a fountain with a statue of Diana, and there was such a fountain,

Dia. No, my good lord, Diana.
Ber.   Titled goddess;
  And worth it, with addition! But, fair soul,
  In your fine frame hath love no quality?
  If the quick fire of youth light not your mind   5
  You are no maiden but a monument.
  When you are dead you should be such a one
  As you are now; for you are cold and stern,
  And now you should be as your mother was
  When your sweet self was got.   10
Dia. She then was honest.
Ber.   So should you be.
Dia.   No.
  My mother did but duty; such, my lord,
  As you owe to your wife.
Ber.   No more a' that!
  I prithee do not strive against my vows;
  I was compell'd to her, but I love thee   15
  By love's own sweet constraint, and will for ever
  Do thee all rights of service.
Dia.   Ay, so you serve us
  Till we serve you; but when you have our roses,
  You barely leave our thorns to prick ourselves,
  And mock us with our bareness.
Ber.   How have I sworn!   20
Dia. 'Tis not the many oaths that makes the truth,

8. now; . . . stern,] *F;* now, . . . stern; *Rowe*[1].

erected at Cheapside in 1596, and perhaps glanced at in *AYL.*, IV. i. 137; but
there is no evidence that this was ever
called *Fontybell* or *font bel*. Even if it had
been, why should Bertram be told that
his beloved had the name of a fountain?

2–3. *Titled . . . addition*] You have
already the name of a goddess, and
you deserve that, with further distinctions.

9–10. *And now . . . got*] This recalls
the arguments of Parolles at I. i. 126–7.
See the note there.

14. *vows*] his vow never to be a husband to Helena.

19. *barely . . . thorns*] leave the thorns
(? of remorse) *bare* or exposed.

21–31.] Diana's argument falls into
two sections as if to answer two asser-
tions by Bertram, that he had sworn
(1) frequently, (2) deeply. She states
(1) that sincerity in making one single
vow is a surer sign of truth than multi-
plicity of oaths; (2) that we swear inevitably by the highest thing we know;
but even then people's oaths to God
cannot make us trust courses of action
directed against godly living for there
is no congruence in such an oath. Cf.
Troil., v. iii. 23 f, *2 H 6*, v. i. 181–9, and
John, III. i. 279–89:

But the plain single vow that is vow'd true.
What is not holy, that we swear not by,
But take the high'st to witness; then, pray you, tell me:
If I should swear by Jove's great attributes   25
I lov'd you dearly, would you believe my oaths
When I did love you ill? This has no holding,
To swear by Him whom I protest to love
That I will work against Him. Therefore your oaths
Are words, and poor conditions but unseal'd—   30
At least in my opinion.

Ber.   Change it, change it.
Be not so holy-cruel; love is holy;
And my integrity ne'er knew the crafts
That you do charge men with. Stand no more off,
But give thyself unto my sick desires,   35
Who then recovers. Say thou art mine, and ever
My love as it begins shall so persever.

†*Dia.* I see that men make rope's in such a scarre,†

25. Jove's] Ioues *F;* love's *Grant White, conj. Johnson;* God's *Globe, conj. Camb.*
28, 29. Him] *Neilson;* him *F.*   30. words, and poor conditions] *This edn;*
words and poore conditions, *F;* words and poor, conditions *N.S.*   38. make
rope's . . . scarre] *F;* make Hopes . . . Affairs *Rowe¹;* make hopes . . . scene
Malone; make rapes . . . scour *conj. N.S.;* may grope's . . . scarre *conj. Tucker
Brooke;* may cope's . . . stir *conj. Tannenbaum;* may rope's . . . snare *Sisson, conj.
Daniel.*

It is religion that doth make vows
kept;
But thou hast sworn against religion
By what thou swear'st against the
thing thou swear'st,
And mak'st an oath the surety for
thy truth
Against an oath, etc.

25. *Jove's*] It is obvious that the
amorous Zeus is an inappropriate
deity to invoke as a defender of chastity; the attributes involved are plainly
those of the Christian God; but it is not
necessary to suppose that the text ever
contained the reading "God's".
Shakespeare's contemporaries regu-
larly applied Christian attributes to
pagan deities.

27. *ill*] used here in a vaguely priva-
tive sense (cf. *O.E.D.* A. adj. 7, and

compounds like "ill-contented" (=
discontented)), in antithesis to the
vague intensive *dearly* above. The
sense "morally evil" is also brought
out by the context.

30. *poor conditions but unseal'd*] The
but cannot be disjunctive; it may be an
adverb modifying *unseal'd*, with the
sense of "merely": the *conditions* (contract) are *poor* because they are *unseal'd* (without legal force) just as the
oaths are mere words when sworn to a
God whose will we do not obey. Alternatively the *but* may be displaced (see
Abbott §129) so that the sense would
be, "but poor conditions unsealed".

32. *holy-cruel*] cruel by being holy
(chaste).

35. *sick desires*] It is now for Bertram
that Helena has to act the physician.

38.] Editors have only succeeded in

That we'll forsake ourselves. Give me that ring.
Ber. I'll lend it thee, my dear, but have no power   40
    To give it from me.
Dia.   Will you not, my lord?
Ber. It is an honour 'longing to our house,
    Bequeathed down from many ancestors,
    Which were the greatest obloquy i' th' world
    In me to lose.
Dia.   Mine honour's such a ring;   45
    My chastity's the jewel of our house,
    Bequeathed down from many ancestors,
    Which were the greatest obloquy i' th' world
    In me to lose. Thus your own proper wisdom
    Brings in the champion Honour on my part   50
    Against your vain assault.
Ber.   Here, take my ring;
    My house, mine honour, yea, my life be thine,
    And I'll be bid by thee.
Dia. When midnight comes, knock at my chamber window;
    I'll order take my mother shall not hear.   55
    Now will I charge you in the band of truth,
    When you have conquer'd my yet maiden bed,
    Remain there but an hour, nor speak to me.
    My reasons are most strong and you shall know them
    When back again this ring shall be deliver'd;   60
    And on your finger in the night I'll put
    Another ring, that what in time proceeds

sophisticating the nonsense of this prime crux in the Folio text, and therefore I leave the original reading untouched. The line must be intended to explain or justify the demand which follows, and may well, in consequence, have been spoken aside.

42.] Cf. Marlowe, *Edward 2*, 1440: "And all the honors longing to my crowne".

honour] This sense of *honour* does not seem to be recorded in *O.E.D.* but must be parallel to that in "the honours of Scotland", i.e. the Scottish regalia, and may be regarded as an extension of *O.E.D.* sb. 6 "a source or

cause of honour". Cf. *2 H 4*, IV. v. 96. Cf. also "and before the pall was the Bairns honours borne" from the description of Charles I's christening in Nichol's *Progresses of Elizabeth* (Year 1594, p. 23).

44–5. *Which . . . lose*] Cf. *Nennio*, tr. Jones (1595), fol. 31ᵛ where we learn that the son of Scipio had the ring with his father's picture engraven in it taken from him, because he was thought unworthy.

45. *honour*] chastity.
49. *proper*] personal.
56. *band*] bond, obligation.
62. *Another ring*] The exchange of

May token to the future our past deeds
Adieu till then; then, fail not. You have won
A wife of me, though there my hope be done.   65
Ber. A heaven on earth I have won by wooing thee.   [*Exit.*]
Dia. For which live long to thank both Heaven and me!
    You may so in the end.
    My mother told me just how he would woo
    As if she sat in's heart. She says all men   70
    Have the like oaths. He had sworn to marry me
    When his wife's dead; therefore I'll lie with him
    When I am buried. Since Frenchmen are so braid,
    Marry that will, I live and die a maid.
    Only, in this disguise, I think't no sin   75
    To cozen him that would unjustly win.   *Exit.*

[SCENE III.—*The Florentine camp.*]

Enter the two French Lords, and some two or three soldiers.

First Lord. You have not given him his mother's letter?

66. *Exit.*] *Ex. F2; not in F.*   71. had] *F; has Grant White.*

Scene III

Scene III] *Pope; not in F.   The Florentine camp.] Capell; not in F.   Enter . . .
Lords] Rowe¹; Enter . . . Captaines F.   1. First Lord.] Rowe¹; Cap. G. | F; Second
Lord. Neilson, N.S. (up to 71; 77 ff 1 Lord).*

rings was part of the ceremony of
betrothal (see *Gent.*, II. ii. 5–7); since
Diana claims Bertram as her husband
in v. iii perhaps the exchange is
thought of as having a similar force
here; but cf. l. 71. Chaucer's Troilus
and Criseyde similarly exchange rings
in bed (III. 1368), as in the *Filocolo*. So
also in *Decameron*, x. viii.

65. *though there my hope be done*]
though through this deed my hope of
being a wife is destroyed.

67. *Heaven*] I have distinguished by
capitalization the false heaven which
Bertram seeks and the true Heaven
which prevents him.

71. *had*] presumably = "would have

if I had given him a chance". But in
v. iii she acts as if he has promised.
Cf. also IV. iii. 93 f.

73. *braid*] variously interpreted; the
idea of plaited (cf. *Lr.*, I. i. 280),
woven-up, hence deceitful, seems primary. See Dr Hulme in *R.E.S.* VI
(1955), 135 f.

75. *in this disguise*] pretending to
agree to Bertram's proposals. Cf. the
similar riddle about the bed-trick in
Meas., "So disguise shall by th' disguised, / Pay with falsehood false
exacting" (III. ii. 262–3).

76.] Cf. Terence, *Eunuch*, 385: Nunc
referam gratiam atque eas itidem
fallam, ut ab illis fallimur.

Second Lord. I have deliv'red it an hour since; there is
    something in't that stings his nature, for on the
    reading it he chang'd almost into another man.

First Lord. He has much worthy blame laid upon him for   5
    shaking off so good a wife and so sweet a lady.

Second Lord. Especially he hath incurred the everlasting
    displeasure of the king, who had even tun'd his
    bounty to sing happiness to him. I will tell you a
    thing, but you shall let it dwell darkly with you.   10

First Lord. When you have spoken it 'tis dead, and I am
    the grave of it.

Second Lord. He hath perverted a young gentlewoman
    here in Florence, of a most chaste renown, and this
    night he fleshes his will in the spoil of her honour; he   15
    hath given her his monumental ring, and thinks
    himself made in the unchaste composition.

First Lord. Now, God delay our rebellion! As we are
    ourselves, what things are we!

2. *Second Lord.*] *Rowe*[1]; *Cap E.* | *F* (*304, 306 Lo. E.*); *First Lord. Neilson, N.S.* (*up
to 71; 77ff 2 Lord*).   18. delay] *F*; allay *Hanmer;* lay *N.S.*

4. *another man*] Brigstocke takes this
to mean "grew pale", citing Marlowe's *Jew of Malta*: "at the reading of
the letter he look'd like a man of
another world" (ll. 1721-2), but "a
man of another world" is not the same
thing as *another man*; *nature* in the line
above would seem to mean "moral
nature" rather than "complexion".
N.S. remarks that the phrase can
hardly refer to a moral change in view
of the censures which follow. It is difficult, however, to be sure about the
moral movements of a nature as
strange to us as that of Bertram. It may
be that all that is implied is the capacity for moral change.

15. *fleshes*] To "flesh a hound with
the spoil" was to give it some of the
flesh of the hunted animal to eat, to
stimulate its hunting instincts. So,
Bertram's *will* (lust) is to be *fleshed*
(rewarded and stimulated) with the
honour of the girl it has hunted down.

16. *monumental*] *O.E.D.* provides a
definition: "serving as a memento",

but the other illustration given for this
sense: "I exposed her with these monumental toyes" from Thornley's *Longus*
(translating γνωρίσματα—elsewhere
translated "monitory ornaments")
seems to give a meaning better expressed by, "serving as a token of
identity and worth". This meaning
would also seem more appropriate
here.

16-17. *thinks . . . composition*] thinks
he's a made man as a result of his dis-
honourable agreement; there is also
a play on *composition* (= "make") with
made.

18. *delay*] perhaps in the modern
sense, in which case Brigstocke's paraphrase: "may God make us slow to
rebel" seems admirable; to Williams'
objection that "no advantage could
arise from mere postponement" one
can only reply that the speech seems to
take humble cognizance of Original
Sin. It is more probable, however, that
delay here has the sense "quench"
(*O.E.D.* v[2]) as often in Spenser, e.g.

Second Lord. Merely our own traitors. And as in the com-   20
        mon course of all treasons we still see them reveal
        themselves till they attain to their abhorr'd ends; so
        he that in this action contrives against his own
        nobility, in his proper stream o'erflows himself.

First Lord. Is it not meant damnable in us to be trum-   25
        peters of our unlawful intents? We shall not then
        have his company tonight?

Second Lord. Not till after midnight, for he is dieted to his
        hour.

First Lord. That approaches apace. I would gladly have   30
        him see his company anatomiz'd, that he might take
        a measure of his own judgments wherein so curi-
        ously he had set this counterfeit.

Second Lord. We will not meddle with him till he come,

---

24. nobility, . . . stream] *Theobald*[1]; Nobility . . . streame, *F.*

"Those dreadfull flames she also found
delayd, / And quenched quite, like a
consumed torch" (*Faerie Queene*, III.
xii. 42).

19. *ourselves*] "unaided by God"
(Brigstocke).

20. *Merely*] entirely.

21. *still*] always.

21–4. *reveal . . . o'erflows himself*]
abhorr'd ends is usually taken to refer to
the final (judicial) punishment of the
traitors when they have sufficiently
revealed themselves; likewise *in his proper
stream o'erflows himself* is usually glossed
in Johnson's words as, "betray his own
secrets in his own talk", so that the
general sense runs: "as traitors cannot
conceal their natures and so are
detected and punished, so Bertram's
talk betrays him to be corrupt, not
noble". This interpretation, however,
ignores the rhetorical structure of the
comparison, in which *o'erflows himself*
is parallel to the *abhorr'd ends*, *proper
streams* to *common course*, and *contrives*
equivalent to *reveal themselves*; its sense
is also deficient, for the self-traitor in
Bertram has achieved success, not
punishment. The other possibility is to
use Steevens' gloss ("the mischief they

intend to do") for *abhorr'd ends*, to
interpret *reveal themselves* as "reveal
themselves to be themselves"—i.e.
the traitors maintain their essential
nature, single actions being part of a
consistent course—and so to paraphrase *in his proper stream o'erflows himself* as "undoes himself by means of the
very powers which make him noble".
As the reply in ll. 25 f indicates, the
punishment is not execution but
damnation.

24. *proper stream*] probably "the
course of life native to him"; cf. *Meas.*,
III. ii. 132, *2 H 4*, v. ii. 34.

25. *Is . . . damnable*] Is it not designed
as a mortal sin? For the omission of
"as" cf. above I. ii. 15 f and *Rom.*, III. v.
148: ". . . hate that is meant love."

28–9. *dieted to his hour*] restricted in
his "date". See above, IV. ii. 58.

31. *company*] companion.

anatomiz'd] dissected, opened up for
inspection.

32–3. *wherein . . . counterfeit*] in which
he has given this sham jewel such an
elaborate setting.

34. *We . . . come*] *him* (and *the other* in
the next line) refers to Parolles; *he* is
Bertram.

for his presence must be the whip of the other.   35

First Lord. In the meantime, what hear you of these wars?

Second Lord. I hear there is an overture of peace.

First Lord. Nay, I assure you, a peace concluded.

Second Lord. What will Count Rossillion do then? Will he travel higher, or return again into France?   40

First Lord. I perceive by this demand you are not altogether of his council.

Second Lord. Let it be forbid, sir! So should I be a great deal of his act.

First Lord. Sir, his wife some two months since fled from   45 his house. Her pretence is a pilgrimage to Saint Jaques le Grand; which holy undertaking with most austere sanctimony she accomplish'd; and there residing, the tenderness of her nature became as a prey to her grief; in fine, made a groan of her last   50 breath, and now she sings in heaven.

Second Lord. How is this justified?

First Lord. The stronger part of it by her own letters, which makes her story true even to the point of her death. Her death itself, which could not be her office   55 to say is come, was faithfully confirm'd by the rector of the place.

Second Lord. Hath the count all this intelligence?

First Lord. Ay, and the particular confirmations, point from point, to the full arming of the verity.   60

Second Lord. I am heartily sorry that he'll be glad of this.

First Lord. How mightily sometimes we make us comforts of our losses!

---

42. council] *Rowe*[3]*;* councell *F;* counsel *Rowe*[1]*, Alexander.*

---

40. *higher*] See note on II. i. 12.

42. *council*] A modernized text must choose between "counsel" and "council"; an Elizabethan spelling (such as F "councell") conveyed either idea indifferently. The pun on *act* in the line following (as in "Acts of the Council") seems to make *council* the better modernization.

46. *pretence*] means "intention", not "false pretext".

55–7. *Her ... place*] Some commentators find here a grave flaw in Helena's character—in that she corrupted an official to make a false statement. Notice, however, that the emphasis of the context is on Bertram, and how the matter affects him, not on Helena.

56. *rector*] The commentators gloss this as "ruler", but the ordinary sense of "priest" is more appropriate for a death-bed witness, and is pointed to by *office*.

Second Lord. And how mightily some other times we
    drown our gain in tears! The great dignity that his   65
    valour hath here acquir'd for him shall at home be
    encount'red with a shame as ample.

First Lord. The web of our life is of a mingled yarn, good
    and ill together; our virtues would be proud if our
    faults whipp'd them not, and our crimes would   70
    despair if they were not cherish'd by our virtues.

Enter a Messenger.

How now? Where's your master?

Mess. He met the duke in the street, sir, of whom he hath
    taken a solemn leave: his lordship will next morning
    for France. The duke hath offered him letters of   75
    commendations to the king.

Second Lord. They shall be no more than needful there if
    they were more than they can commend.

Enter BERTRAM.

First Lord. They cannot be too sweet for the king's tart-
    ness. Here's his lordship now. How now, my lord?   80
    Is't not after midnight?

Ber. I have tonight dispatch'd sixteen businesses a
    month's length apiece. By an abstract of success: I
    have congied with the duke, done my adieu with his
    nearest, buried a wife, mourn'd for her, writ to my   85
    lady mother I am returning, entertain'd my convoy,

78. S.D. *Enter Bertram.*] *Enter Count Rossillion. F.*   79. *First Lord.*] *Cap. G. | F3;
Ber. F.*

65. *drown . . . tears*] This seems to
have a double reference, connecting
both back and forward: (1) when Bertram "gained" Helena he "wept" (i.e.
was unhappy); (2) though Bertram
has gained honour in Florence, this is
drowned by the dishonour he has left
in France, which makes his friends
weep.

77–8. *They shall . . . commend*] the
recommendations cannot be more
powerful than what is required to re-

concile the King to Bertram, even if
they said more than any commendation could.

83. *By an abstract of success*] "to give
an abstract of my successes. His summary follows" (*N.S.*) or else "to give
a successive abstract—one item after
another".

84. *congied*] taken my leave (French
congé).

86. *entertain'd my convoy*] hired my
transport.

and between these main parcels of dispatch effected
many nicer needs; the last was the greatest, but that
I have not ended yet.

Second Lord. If the business be of any difficulty, and this   90
morning your departure hence, it requires haste of
your lordship.

Ber. I mean, the business is not ended, as fearing to hear
of it hereafter. But shall we have this dialogue between the Fool and the Soldier? Come, bring forth   95
this counterfeit module has deceiv'd me like a
double-meaning prophesier.

Second Lord. Bring him forth.   [*Exeunt Soldiers.*]
Has sat i' th' stocks all night, poor gallant knave.

Ber. No matter. His heels have deserv'd it in usurping his   100
spurs so long. How does he carry himself?

Second Lord. I have told your lordship already: the stocks
carry him. But to answer you as you would be understood: he weeps like a wench that had shed her milk;
he hath confess'd himself to Morgan, whom he   105
supposes to be a friar, from the time of his remembrance to this very instant disaster of his setting i' th'
stocks. And what think you he hath confess'd?

Ber. Nothing of me, has 'a?

Second Lord. His confession is taken, and it shall be read to   110
his face; if your lordship be in't, as I believe you are,
you must have the patience to hear it.

[*Re-*]*enter* [*Soldiers and*] PAROLLES, *with* [*First Soldier as*] *his
Interpreter.*

87. effected] *F3;* affected *F.*   96. has] *F2;* ha s *F;* 'has *F3;* h'as *Rowe*[3]*;* he has
Var. '73.   98. S.D. *Exeunt Soldiers.*] *Capell; not in F.*   99. Has] ha's *F;* h'as
F4; he has *Var. '73.*   112. S.D. *Re-enter Soldiers and Parolles, with First
Soldier as his Interpreter.*] *Enter Parolles with his Interpreter. F.*

87. *parcels of dispatch*] items to be
settled.

93–4. *I . . . hereafter*] Diana may
claim him as her husband.

96. *counterfeit module*] false pattern of
soldiership.

97. *double-meaning prophesier*] Cf.

"And be these juggling fiends no
more believ'd / That palter with us
in a double sense" (*Mac.*, v. viii. 19–
20).

99. *gallant*] *O.E.D.* A.1, "Showy in
appearance, finely dressed".

104. *shed*] spilled.

Ber. A plague upon him! muffled! He can say nothing of
  me.

First Lord. [*aside to Bertram*] Hush, hush! Hoodman comes.   115
  [*aloud*] *Portotartarossa.*

First Sold. He calls for the tortures. What will you say
  without 'em?

Par. I will confess what I know without constraint. If ye
  pinch me like a pasty I can say no more.   120

First Sold. Bosko chimurcho.

First Lord. Boblibindo chicurmurco.

First Sold. You are a merciful general. Our general bids
  you answer to what I shall ask you out of a note.

Par. And truly, as I hope to live.   125

First Sold. [*Reads*] *First, demand of him, how many horse the
  duke is strong.* What say you to that?

Par. Five or six thousand; but very weak and unservice-
  able: the troops are all scattered and the com-
  manders very poor rogues, upon my reputation and 130
  credit—and as I hope to live.

First Sold. Shall I set down your answer so?

Par. Do. I'll take the sacrament on't, how and which way
  you will.

Ber. All's one to him. What a past-saving slave is this!   135

114–15. me. | *First Lord.* Hush, hush! Hoodman] *Dyce*², *conj. W. S. Walker;*
me: hush, hush. | *Cap. G.* Hoodman *F.*   115–16. S.D. *aside to Bertram . . .
aloud*] *This edn; not in F.*   117. *First Sold.*] *Inter. F. So* (*Int.,* Interp.) *throughout
scene.*   126, 154, 170, 203. S.D. *Reads*] *Camb.; not in F.*   126–7, 154–5,
170–5.] *italic Capell; roman F.*   134–5. will. | *Ber.* All's . . . him. What] *Capell;*
will: all's . . . him. | *Ber.* What *F.*

113. *muffled*] blindfolded.

115. *Hush . . . comes*] The Folio
assigns *Hush, hush!* to Bertram, but
this cannot be right. The contrast between the enjoyment of the two lords
in the unmasking and the confusion of
Bertram would be blurred by any such
division. The four words presumably
belong together as the warning signal
in the game of "hoodman-blind" or
"blind-man's-buff".

124. *note*] abstract or memorandum.

130–1. *upon . . . live*] I suppose that
the second, more realistic oath follows
after a short pause, in which Parolles

realizes the irrelevance of his usual
magniloquent style.

133–4. *how . . . will*] The obvious
reference is to the *kinds* in which the
sacrament was delivered (bread only
or bread and wine) but there may also
be a further reference to the disputed
matter whether it should be received
sitting or kneeling.

135. *All's . . . him*] This cannot belong to Parolles, though the Folio
gives it to him; the simplest solution is
to join it on to Bertram's remarks
which follow, but it may be spoken by
one of the lords.

First Lord. Y'are deceiv'd, my lord; this is Monsieur
Parolles, the gallant militarist—that was his own
phrase—that had the whole theoric of war in the
knot of his scarf, and the practice in the chape of his
dagger.   140

Second Lord. I will never trust a man again for keeping his
sword clean, nor believe he can have everything in
him by wearing his apparel neatly.

First Sold. Well, that's set down.

Par. "Five or six thousand horse" I said—I will say true 145
—"or thereabouts" set down, for I'll speak truth.

First Lord. He's very near the truth in this.

Ber. But I con him no thanks for't, in the nature he
delivers it.

Par. "Poor rogues" I pray you say.   150

First Sold. Well, that's set down.

Par. I humbly thank you, sir; a truth's a truth; the
rogues are marvellous poor.

First Sold. [*Reads*] *Demand of him of what strength they are
a-foot.* What say you to that?   155

Par. By my troth, sir, if I were to live this present hour, I

141. *Second Lord.*] *Cap. E. | F; Ber. conj. W. S. Walker.*   156. live] *F;* die *Dyce²*,
conj. W. S. Walker; leave *N.S.*   this] *F;* but this *Hanmer.*

138-9. *theoric . . . practice . . .*] These
two words seem to be the technical
terms for the divisions of military as of
other science. They appear in two
titles of the period: (1) Hoby's
Theorique and Practice of Warre (1597)
(a translation of Barnardino Men-
doza's *Theorica y practica de guerra*);
(2) Barret's *The Theorike and Practice of
Modern Warres* (1598). Cf. *Oth.*, I. i. 24,
H 5, I. i. 52.

139. *knot of his scarf*] We learn in
The First Part of Jeronimo, II. vi. 15 ff,
that the "amorous knot" in the scarf was
tied by the lady who gave the favour.

chape] "metal plate or mounting of a
scabbard, esp. that which covers the
point" (On.).

141-4.] This speech would have
more obvious point if spoken by Bertram, and W. S. Walker's conjecture

that it should be assigned to him is
attractive.

148-9. *But . . . it*] But I acknowledge
no gratitude, considering the kind of
truth (i.e. treasonable) that it is.

156. *live*] The sense seems to demand
some word of opposite meaning, such
as "die" or "leave". Tollet tried to
defend *live* by supposing that Parolles
made a mistake through fear, but this
seems to impose an excessive amount
on the actor. Tolerable meaning can
be derived from the words as they
stand if we understand "live this present hour (and no more)". Thiselton
paraphrases: "if my living this present
hour depended on it". Mrs 'Espinasse
suggests to me a possible connection
with the Middle English "live and
die" (= die) as in *Havelok*, 256 f, 1405,
2210.

will tell true. Let me see: Spurio, a hundred and
fifty; Sebastian, so many; Corambus, so many;
Jaques, so many; Guiltian, Cosmo, Lodowick, and
Gratii, two hundred fifty each; mine own company, 160
Chitopher, Vaumond, Bentii, two hundred fifty
each; so that the muster-file, rotten and sound, upon
my life, amounts not to fifteen thousand poll; half of
the which dare not shake the snow from off their
cassocks lest they shake themselves to pieces.   165

Ber. What shall be done to him?

First Lord. Nothing but let him have thanks. Demand of
him my condition, and what credit I have with the
duke.

First Sold. Well, that's set down. [*Reads*] *You shall demand* 170
of him whether one Captain Dumaine be i' th' camp, a
Frenchman; what his reputation is with the duke, what his
valour, honesty and expertness in wars; or whether he thinks
it were not possible with well-weighing sums of gold to
corrupt him to a revolt. What say you to this? What do 175
you know of it?

Par. I beseech you, let me answer to the particular of the
inter'gatories. Demand them singly.

First Sold. Do you know this Captain Dumaine?

Par. I know him: 'a was a botcher's prentice in Paris, 180
from whence he was whipp'd for getting the shrieve's

157–61.] This is a very curious list of
names. *Spurio* we have met already
(II. i. 41); *Sebastian, Jaques, Cosmo,
Lodowick*, and *Vaumond* are plausible
'Continental' forms; *Corambus* is virtually the same name as that given to
Polonius in the First Quarto of *Hamlet*; *Guiltian* and *Chitopher* are perhaps
corruptions (as *N.S.* suggests) of
Guilliam and Christopher; *Gratii* and
Bentii look like plurals (cf. *Spinii*
above, II. i. 41) but are not used as
plurals in the text—Mario Praz
(*Shakespeare Survey* VII) suggests that
they may be "peculiar spellings of the
Florentine family names, *Grazzi,
Benci*". There is always the possibility
that Shakespeare may have deliberately invented strange names in order
to suggest an international force—if
one side has *Muskos*, the other may
have equally strange allies.

163. *poll*] heads; cf. "head of cattle".

165. *cassocks*] military cloaks.

171, 179, 239, 274. Dumaine] so
spelled in F in first three instances
(274, "Dumain"), but usually modernized "Dumain". The analogy of
LLL. (Dumaine, Dumane) supports
the fuller form as representing the
intended English pronunciation.

174. well-weighing] with a double
meaning, as Brigstocke pointed out:
(1) heavy, (2) powerful to influence.

180. *botcher*] a tailor or cobbler who
makes his living by patching.

181–2. *shrieve's fool*] an idiot without
large means. The persons and proper-

fool with child, a dumb innocent that could not say
him nay.

Ber. Nay, by your leave, hold your hands—though I
know his brains are forfeit to the next tile that falls.   185

First Sold. Well, is this captain in the Duke of Florence's
camp?

Par. Upon my knowledge he is, and lousy.

First Lord. Nay, look not so upon me; we shall hear of
your lordship anon.   190

First Sold. What is his reputation with the duke?

Par. The duke knows him for no other but a poor officer
of mine, and writ to me this other day to turn him
out a' th' band. I think I have his letter in my pocket.

First Sold. Marry, we'll search.   195

Par. In good sadness, I do not know; either it is there or it
is upon a file, with the duke's other letters, in my
tent.

First Sold. Here 'tis; here's a paper; shall I read it to you?

Par. I do not know if it be it or no.   200

Ber. Our interpreter does it well.

First Lord. Excellently.

First Sold. [*Reads*] *Dian, the count's a fool, and full of gold.*

Par. That is not the duke's letter, sir; that is an advertisement to a proper maid in Florence, one Diana, to   205
take heed of the allurement of one Count Rossillion,
a foolish idle boy, but for all that very ruttish. I pray
you, sir, put it up again.

---

190. lordship] *Pope;* Lord *F.*

ties of *innocents* (idiots) belonged in the
first place to the crown, but it dele-
gated its authority to the sheriff or
shrieve in cases where there was no
estate worth plundering.

185. *the next tile*] "a trite metaphor
for a sudden death" (Brigstocke). Cf.
Rowlands, *More Knaves Yet* (1613),
sig. E1, and Witney's *Choice of Emblems* (ed. Green), p. 176.

196. *In good sadness*] in perfect
seriousness.

201.] This approval of the Interpreter is placed, for comic effect, immediately before the example of his zeal that

Bertram would rather do without.

203.] Johnson, noticing that there is
no line in the rest of the poem to
rhyme with *gold*, assumed a line to be
lost, and other critics have emended
the line to procure a rhyme with *score*.
There is no reason, however, why the
poem should be found complete when
detached from its context. No audience (and few readers) notice the lack
of rhyme in lines thirteen lines apart.

204–5. *advertisement*] advice.

205. *proper*] honest, respectable.

207. *ruttish*] lustful. Deer are said to
be "in rut" in the mating season.

First Sold. Nay, I'll read it first by your favour.

Par. My meaning in't, I protest, was very honest in the 210
behalf of the maid; for I knew the young count to be
a dangerous and lascivious boy, who is a whale to
virginity, and devours up all the fry it finds.

Ber. Damnable both-sides rogue!

First Sold. [*Reads*] *When he swears oaths, bid him drop gold,
    and take it;*   215
After he scores he never pays the score.
Half-won is match well made; match, and well make it;
He ne'er pays after-debts; take it before.
And say a soldier, Dian, told thee this:
Men are to mell with, boys are not to kiss;   220
For count of this, the count's a fool, I know it,
Who pays before, but not when he does owe it.
    Thine, as he vow'd to thee in thine ear,

                                        PAROLLES.

Ber. He shall be whipp'd through the army, with this 225
rhyme in's forehead.

Second Lord. This is your devoted friend, sir, the manifold
linguist, and the armipotent soldier.

Ber. I could endure anything before but a cat, and now
he's a cat to me.   230

First Sold. I perceive, sir, by the general's looks, we shall
be fain to hang you.

Par. My life, sir, in any case! Not that I am afraid to die,
but that, my offences being many, I would repent

---

215. S.D. *First Sold. Reads*] *Int. Let. F.*   231. the] *F3;* your *F;* our *Capell.*

212. *whale*] The image is that of a
whale devouring whole shoals of *fry* or
small fish. Cf. *Per.,* II. i. 29–32. See *Sh.
Q.* v, 211–13 for a general commentary on the whale as a symbol of lust.

216.] he won't pay the price *after*
he's hit the mark.

217.] The assumption of Henley
and Malone that Parolles is advising
Diana to ask for half the cash down
does not seem to be well-founded. I
paraphrase: make your bargain well
and you are half-way to success; so,

make your bargain first and all will
turn out well.

218. *after-debts*] debts still owed
after the goods are delivered.

220. Men (like Parolles) are the people to have intercourse with; boys (like
Bertram) are not even worth kissing.

227–8. *manifold . . . armipotent . . .*]
relics of Parolles' grandiloquence.

229.] Cf. *Mer. V.,* IV. i. 48: "Some
that are mad if they behold a cat".

231.] F "your" may be defended as
the vague possessive (*O.E.D.* 5 and 6).

out the remainder of nature. Let me live, sir, in a 235
dungeon, i' th' stocks, or anywhere, so I may live.

First Sold. We'll see what may be done, so you confess
freely. Therefore once more to this Captain
Dumaine: you have answer'd to his reputation with
the duke and to his valour; what is his honesty?   240

Par. He will steal, sir, an egg out of a cloister; for rapes
and ravishments he parallels Nessus. He professes
not keeping of oaths; in breaking 'em he is stronger
than Hercules. He will lie, sir, with such volubility
that you would think truth were a fool; drunkenness 245
is his best virtue, for he will be swine-drunk, and in
his sleep he does little harm, save to his bedclothes
about him; but they know his conditions and lay him
in straw. I have but little more to say, sir, of his
honesty: he has everything that an honest man 250
should not have; what an honest man should have,
he has nothing.

First Lord. I begin to love him for this.

Ber. For this description of thine honesty? A pox upon
him! for me, he's more and more a cat.   255

First Sold. What say you to his expertness in war?

Par. Faith, sir, has led the drum before the English

---

255. him!] *Alexander;* him *F+*.   257. has] ha's *F;* h'as *Rowe[1];* he has *Var.* '73.

---

241. *egg . . . cloister*] Johnson paraphrases: "He will steal anything,
however trifling, from any place, however holy", but is diffident about the
correctness of the original. The anon.
conj. recorded in Thiselton—"out of a
clyster"—is plausible and very much
in Parolles' vein; however, I have not
found that eggs were common ingre-
dients, let alone extractable elements.
Certainly "eggs" is a synonym for
something worthless in this period, as
in the proverb "to take eggs for
money" (Tilley E 90) which Shakespeare uses in *Wint.,* I. ii. 161 (cf. "they
were indighted but for stealing of
Egs", *Miseries of Enforced Marriage,*
sig. F2), but why these should be in a
cloister remains unexplained.

242. *Nessus*] Only one ravishment by

Nessus is known (though it was a
famous one)—that attempted on
Deianira, wife to Hercules. But Nessus
was a centaur, and the half-bestial
forms of the centaurs (and their behaviour at the Feast of the Lapithae)
made them suitable emblems of lust.

245. *that you . . . fool*] Cf. *Wint.,* IV. iv.
587: "what a fool Honesty is". Per-
haps there is a jingle intended between
fool and the first syllable of *volubility*.

245-7. *drunkennesss . . . harm*] Sister
Miriam Joseph sees in this a reference
to the mock sorites proving that
drunkenness is blessed, used in *LLL.,*
I. i. 44-5.

246. *swine-drunk*] "Swine drunke,
heauy, lumpish and sleepie" (Nashe,
I, 207).

257-8. *led . . . tragedians*] the instru-

tragedians—to belie him I will not—and more of his
soldiership I know not, except in that country he had
the honour to be the officer at a place there called 260
Mile-end, to instruct for the doubling of files. I
would do the man what honour I can, but of this I
am not certain.

First Lord. He hath out-villain'd villainy so far that the
rarity redeems him.   265

Ber. A pox on him! He's a cat still.

First Sold. His qualities being at this poor price, I need not
to ask you if gold will corrupt him to revolt.

Par. Sir, for a cardecue he will sell the fee-simple of his
salvation, the inheritance of it, and cut th' entail 270
from all remainders, and a perpetual succession for it
perpetually.

First Sold. What's his brother, the other Captain
Dumaine?

Second Lord. Why does he ask him of me?   275

First Sold. What's he?

Par. E'en a crow a' th' same nest; not altogether so great
as the first in goodness, but greater a great deal in
evil. He excels his brother for a coward, yet his
brother is reputed one of the best that is. In a retreat 280
he outruns any lackey; marry, in coming on he has
the cramp.

ment symbolic of war (see note on
III. v. 87 above) was also more basely
used, like the 'big drum' of modern
circus advertising (and the drum of
I Pagliacci), by the processions of
strolling players, who visited not only
the provinces of England but also the
continental countries.

258. *to belie him*] for this use of the
infinitive see Abbott §357.

261. *Mile-end*] the exercise-ground
of the London citizen militia—a force
not generally respected.

doubling of files] the simplest item of
military drill, similar to "forming
fours".

269. *cardecue*] a quart d'écu was
worth about eightpence in Malone's
day. Compare with Shakespeare's

spelling the phonetic rendering of
Eliot, the contemporary teacher of
French: "kar-de-kew" (*Ortho-epia Gal-
lica* [1593], p. 58).

269–72. *sell . . . perpetually*] "An
estate in fee-simple is the most nearly
absolute and perpetual estate in land
known to the law" (Clarkson and
Warren, *The Law of Property in Shakespeare*). Dumaine will not only sell this
absolute possession but will break the
entail—the provision that it should
pass to his heirs—and not only in respect of the immediate heir but in
respect of all subsequent heirs, in per-
petuity.

281. *outruns any lackey*] The lackey or
running footman of this time ran
errands and ran before the convey-

First Sold. If your life be saved will you undertake to
    betray the Florentine?

Par. Ay, and the captain of his horse, Count Rossillion.   285

First Sold. I'll whisper with the general and know his
    pleasure.

Par. I'll no more drumming. A plague of all drums! Only
    to seem to deserve well, and to beguile the supposi-
    tion of that lascivious young boy, the count, have I   290
    run into this danger; yet who would have suspected
    an ambush where I was taken?

First Sold. There is no remedy, sir, but you must die. The
    general says you that have so traitorously discover'd
    the secrets of your army, and made such pestiferous   295
    reports of men very nobly held, can serve the world
    for no honest use; therefore you must die. Come,
    headsman, off with his head.

Par. O Lord, sir, let me live, or let me see my death!

First Sold. That shall you, and take your leave of all your   300
    friends.   [*Unmuffling him.*]
    So; look about you; know you any here?

Ber. Good morrow, noble captain.

Second Lord. God bless you, Captain Parolles.

First Lord. God save you, noble captain.   305

Second Lord. Captain, what greeting will you to my Lord
    Lafew? I am for France.

First Lord. Good captain, will you give me a copy of the
    sonnet you writ to Diana in behalf of the Count
    Rossillion. And I were not a very coward I'd compel   310
    it of you; but fare you well.   *Exeunt [Bertram and Lords].*

301. S.D. *Unmuffling him.*] *Var. '93; not in* F.   310. And] *F;* an *Capell.*
311. S.D. *Exeunt Bertram and Lords*] *Exeunt* F.

ance of his employers; the Irish
running-footman is quite a common
figure in the drama of the time, e.g. in
Dekker, *2 Honest Whore.*

   289-90. *beguile the supposition*] deceive the imagination.

   302 ff.] Cf. the parallel episode in
Jasper Mayne's *The Amorous Warre*
(1648—but probably written c. 1638),
in which Act V Scene II seems to

be based on the present scene:
   ... Mean time we leave you
   To you [*sic*] stout *Resolutions,* and
     Chronicle,
   To be set forth in *Epicke Meeter* on
     you.
Mel: Farewell brave *Champions* ...
   ... Adiew sweet *Captains;*
   We will report your Bounty to the
     Campe.

First Sold. You are undone, captain—all but your scarf;
  that has a knot on't yet.

Par. Who cannot be crush'd with a plot?

First Sold. If you could find out a country where but 315
  women were that had received so much shame you
  might begin an impudent nation. Fare ye well, sir.
  I am for France too; we shall speak of you there.

           Exeunt [Soldiers].

Par. Yet am I thankful. If my heart were great
  'Twould burst at this. Captain I'll be no more, 320
  But I will eat and drink and sleep as soft
  As captain shall. Simply the thing I am
  Shall make me live. Who knows himself a braggart,
  Let him fear this; for it will come to pass
  That every braggart shall be found an ass. 325
  Rust, sword; cool, blushes; and Parolles live
  Safest in shame; being fool'd, by fool'ry thrive.
  There's place and means for every man alive.
  I'll after them.   *Exit.*

[SCENE IV.—*Florence. The Widow's house.*]

Enter HELENA, WIDOW, *and* DIANA.

Hel. That you may well perceive I have not wrong'd you
  One of the greatest in the Christian world
  Shall be my surety; fore whose throne 'tis needful,
  Ere I can perfect mine intents, to kneel.

318.S.D. *Exeunt Soldiers.*] *Exit. F.*

Scene IV

Scene IV] *Capell; not in F.* *Florence. The Widow's house.*] *The Widow's house at*
Florence. Pope; not in F. *Florence. The Widow's house.*] *The Widow's house at*
Enter Helena] *Enter Hellen F.* 3. fore] *F2; for F.*

320. *burst*] Cf. *Lr.*, II. iv. 283–5, and
Woodstock (M.S.R.), 2567 f:
 princes have hartes like poynted
  Diamonds
 that will in sunder burst afore they
  bend.
327. *being . . . thrive*] Since I've been

made a fool of why shouldn't I live by
exhibiting my folly? Looks forward to
v. iii. 316.

Scene IV

2. *One . . . world*] glancing perhaps at
the French King's style: "most
Christian king".

Time was, I did him a desired office,   5
Dear almost as his life; which gratitude
Through flinty Tartar's bosom would peep forth
And answer thanks. I duly am inform'd
His grace is at Marcellus, to which place
We have convenient convoy. You must know   10
I am supposed dead. The army breaking,
My husband hies him home, where, heaven aiding,
And by the leave of my good lord the king,
We'll be before our welcome.

Wid.   Gentle madam,
You never had a servant to whose trust   15
Your business was more welcome.

Hel.   Nor you, mistress,
Ever a friend whose thoughts more truly labour
To recompense your love. Doubt not but heaven
Hath brought me up to be your daughter's dower,
As it hath fated her to be my motive   20
And helper to a husband. But, O strange men!
That can such sweet use make of what they hate,
When saucy trusting of the cozen'd thoughts
Defiles the pitchy night; so lust doth play
With what it loathes for that which is away.   25
But more of this hereafter. You, Diana,

9. Marcellus] *This edn; Marcellæ F; Marseilles Rowe*[3]+.   16. you] *F4;* your *F.*

6. *which gratitude*] gratitude for which.

9. *Marcellus*] Marseilles was pronounced as a trisyllable. The spelling given here may well be Shakespeare's (cf. below, IV. v. 77 and *Shr.*, II. i. 367); the -ae ending of F would be an easy misreading for -us.

19. *brought me up*] "We should now use the biblical phrase 'raised me up'" (*N.S.*); perhaps only means "raised me"="reared me".

20. *motive*] Onions glosses, "mover, prompter, instigator", but Helena prompted Diana, not vice versa. *N.S.* gives "something or somebody that causes another thing or person to move", but Diana did not *cause* Helena to move; she *allowed* her to

move, nothing more. The context demands a meaning more like "means, moving part, engine, limb", a sense not recorded outside Shakespeare, but cf. *Troil.*, IV. v. 57 and *R 2*, I. i. 193.

23. *saucy . . . thoughts*] wanton acceptance of lust's delusions. Cf. "Their saucy sweetness that do coin heaven's image / In stamps that are forbid" (*Meas.*, II. iv. 45–6).

24. *Defiles the pitchy night*] based on the proverb (taken from Ecclesiasticus, xiii, 1) that "who so toucheth pitche, shall be difiled withall" (see *Ado*, III. iii. 53). Shakespeare suggests here that even the defiling pitch of night is defiled by *saucy trusting*.

25. *for that*] taking it to be that.

Under my poor instructions yet must suffer
Something in my behalf.

Dia.   Let death and honesty
Go with your impositions, I am yours,
Upon your will to suffer.

Hel.   Yet, I pray you;   30
But with the word: "the time will bring on summer"—
When briars shall have leaves as well as thorns
And be as sweet as sharp. We must away;
Our wagon is prepar'd, and time revives us.
All's well that ends well; still the fine's the crown.   35
Whate'er the course, the end is the renown.   *Exeunt.*

[SCENE V.—*Rossillion. The Count's palace.*]

Enter CLOWN, COUNTESS, *and* LAFEW.

Laf. No, no, no, your son was misled with a snipp'd-taffeta
fellow there, whose villainous saffron would have

30–1. pray you; / But with the word: "the] *This edn;* pray you: / But with the
word the *F;* pray you, / Bear with the word: the *Hanmer;* pay you / But with the
word; the *Grant White;* pray you . . . / But with the word, that *N.S.*

Scene v

Scene v] *Capell; not in F.   Rossillion. The Count's palace.*] *Rossillion. A Room in the
Count's Palace. Capell; not in F.   Enter Clown, Countess, and Lafew.*] *Enter Clowne,
old Lady, and Lafew. F; Enter Countess, Lafeu, and Clown. Rowe*[1].

28. *death and honesty*] an honest death.
I am willing to die for you, provided
I can remain chaste.

30. *Yet*] yet further, yet awhile.

31–3. *But . . . sharp*] obscure, as
Brigstocke remarks. His suggestion
that *word* means "promise" is attractive, though *the word* for "my promise"
is curious in a passage of personal per-
suasion. I have taken *word* to have the
sense of "motto", common in Elizabethan English (see *Per.*, ii. ii. 21 and
Ham., i. v. 110) and punctuated accordingly. On the other hand the simple
sense "when the words of my letter are
delivered all will be well" is possible.

34. *revives*] present for future.

35.] Both halves of this line are proverbial. For the second half cf. "La fin
couronne les œuvres" (*2 H 6*, v. ii. 28)
and "the end crowns all" (*Troil.*, iv. v.
224).

Scene v

1. *snipp'd-taffeta*] silk slashed (to
allow another material to show
through). Parolles' flashy dress and
his insubstantiality (see above, ii. v.
15, 43 f) are both glanced at.

2. *saffron*] was used to dye both
starch (and so ruffs) and cakes. As
Warburton points out, both uses are
referred to here, the clothing reference
looking back to "snipp'd-taffeta" and
the culinary reference pointing forward to *unbak'd and doughy youth.*

made all the unbak'd and doughy youth of a nation
in his colour. Your daughter-in-law had been alive
at this hour, and your son here at home, more   5
advanc'd by the king than by that red-tail'd humble-
bee I speak of.

Count. I would I had not known him; it was the death of
the most virtuous gentlewoman that ever nature had
praise for creating. If she had partaken of my flesh   10
and cost me the dearest groans of a mother I could
not have owed her a more rooted love.

Laf. 'Twas a good lady; 'twas a good lady. We may pick
a thousand sallets ere we light on such another herb.

Clo. Indeed, sir, she was the sweet-marjoram of the sallet,   15
or, rather, the herb of grace.

Laf. They are not herbs, you knave; they are nose-herbs.

Clo. I am no great Nabuchadnezzar, sir; I have not much
skill in grass.

Laf. Whether dost thou profess thyself—a knave or a   20
fool?

Clo. A fool, sir, at a woman's service, and a knave at a
man's.

Laf. Your distinction?

Clo. I would cozen the man of his wife and do his service.   25

Laf. So you were a knave at his service indeed.

Clo. And I would give his wife my bauble, sir, to do her
service.

---

17. not herbs] *F;* not Sallet-Herbs *Rowe*[1]*;* knot-herbs *N.S.*   19. grass] *Rowe*[1]*;*
grace *F.*

6–7. *red-tail'd humble-bee*] large,
noisy, but unprofitable. Some have
seen a reference to military red, but
the epithet is used elsewhere (*MND.*,
IV. i. 11–12) without any such significance.

11. *dearest*] most dire (On.); or perhaps "heartfelt".

14. *sallets*] salads.

16. *herb of grace*] rue.

17. *not herbs … nose-herbs*] To modern
minds the antithesis between *herbs*
(salad plants) and *nose-herbs* (scented
plants) seems feeble and obscure. *N.S.*
suggestion that we should read "knot-

herbs" is attractive, but "knot-herbs"
is not a known locution, nor is it clear
that it could mean anything more
definite than "bedding plants" does
today. It seems best to leave the perfectly intelligible Folio reading.

19. *grass*] The F word "grace" had,
presumably, much the same pronunciation as *grass*, and the clown is pun-
ning on the two senses here, as above
in l. 16. See Daniel, iv, 28–37.

27. *bauble*] the Fool's truncheon,
used with obscene equivocation (as in
Rom., II. iv. 89).

28. *service*] The sexual sense of *ser-*

Laf. I will subscribe for thee; thou art both knave and
    fool.   30

Clo. At your service.

Laf. No, no, no.

Clo. Why, sir, if I cannot serve you I can serve as great a
    prince as you are.

Laf. Who's that? a Frenchman?   35

Clo. Faith, sir, 'a has an English name; but his fisnomy is
    more hotter in France than there.

Laf. What prince is that?

Clo. The black prince, sir, alias the prince of darkness,
    alias the devil.   40

Laf. Hold thee, there's my purse. I give thee not this to
    suggest thee from thy master thou talk'st of; serve
    him still.

Clo. I am a woodland fellow, sir, that always loved a great
    fire, and the master I speak of ever keeps a good fire;   45
    but sure he is the prince of the world; let his nobility
    remain in's court, I am for the house with the narrow
    gate, which I take to be too little for pomp to enter;
    some that humble themselves may, but the many
    will be too chill and tender, and they'll be for the   50
    flow'ry way that leads to the broad gate and the
    great fire.

36. name] *Rowe*[1]; maine *F;* mein *conj. Anon.*

vice (*O.E.D.* service[1] 36 [cf. 6c]) is first
quoted from 1844; but since the cog-
nate use of the verb "serve" is dated
1577—and Shakespeare shows some
awareness of this (*2 H 4*, II. iv. 48 f)—it
seems safe to suppose that the sexual
meaning of *service* is drawn on here as
in Webster, *Dutchesse of Malfy*, II. v. 15.

36. *name*] F "maine" is defended by
Thiselton on the grounds of a quibble
between *Frenchman* and *English mane.*
Against this one must set the superior
sense of *name*, and note a possible play
on *name* and *fisnamy* (a common alternative spelling to F *fisnomie*).

37. *more hotter*] (1) because the Black
Prince spent his life warring in France;
(2) owing to pox, 'the French disease'.

42. *suggest*] tempt. Cf. ". . . Pamela

(whom thy Maister most perniciously
hath suggested out of my dominion)"
(Sidney's *Arcadia*, ed. Feuillerat, I,
429).

46. *the prince of the world*] a biblical
phrase for the devil. Noble cites John,
xii, 31 and xiv, 30.

47–52. *I am . . . great fire*] Noble compares Matthew, vii, 13: "Enter yee in
at the straite gate, for wide is the gate,
and broad is the way that leadeth to
destruction, and many there be which
goe in thereat." Shakespeare's rendering of "broad . . . way" as *flow'ry way*
(repeated in the Porter's "primrose
way" in *Mac.*, II. iii. 18–19) does not
find any warrant in Scripture.

50. *chill and tender*] sensitive, easily
deterred, wedded to comfort. *chill*

Laf. Go thy ways; I begin to be aweary of thee; and I tell
thee so before, because I would not fall out with thee.
Go thy ways; let my horses be well look'd to, without   55
any tricks.

Clo. If I put any tricks upon 'em, sir, they shall be jades'
tricks, which are their own right by the law of
nature.   *Exit.*

Laf. A shrewd knave and an unhappy.   60

Count. So 'a is. My lord that's gone made himself much
sport out of him; by his authority he remains here,
which he thinks is a patent for his sauciness; and indeed he has no pace, but runs where he will.

Laf. I like him well; 'tis not amiss. And I was about to tell   65
you, since I heard of the good lady's death and that
my lord your son was upon his return home, I moved
the king my master to speak in the behalf of my
daughter; which, in the minority of them both, his
majesty out of a self-gracious remembrance did first   70
propose. His highness hath promis'd me to do it; and
to stop up the displeasure he hath conceived against
your son there is no fitter matter. How does your
ladyship like it?

Count. With very much content, my lord, and I wish it   75
happily effected.

Laf. His highness comes post from Marcellus, of as able
body as when he number'd thirty. 'A will be here tomorrow, or I am deceiv'd by him that in such intelligence hath seldom fail'd.   80

77. Marcellus] *F;* Marseilles *Pope.*

looks back, of course, to *loved a good
fire.*

56. *tricks*] the cheating tricks of
ostlers—such as greasing the horses'
teeth (see *Lr.,* II. iv. 124).

57–8. *jades' tricks*] vicious and irresponsible mischief, such as might be
expected from a "jade" or ill-broken
horse.

60. *shrewd . . . unhappy*] biting and
mischievous. For the use of *unhappy* cf.
"A knauish answer of an vnhappy
Country wench, to a foolish yong

fellow" (where the answer is only
sharp) in *Pasquils Jests* (1629), sig.
C1ᵛ. In *MND.* Puck is a "shrewd and
knavish sprite" (II. i. 33).

64. *pace*] the trained gait of a horse
(*O.E.D.* sb. II.6b), in antithesis to *runs.*
Johnson remarks that "we say of a . . .
horse who moves irregularly, that he
has *no paces*".

70. *self-gracious remembrance*] He
remembered graciously without having to be prompted. Cf. "self-unable"
above, III. i. 13.

Count. It rejoices me that I hope I shall see him ere I die.
  I have letters that my son will be here tonight. I shall
  beseech your lordship to remain with me till they
  meet together.

Laf. Madam, I was thinking with what manners I might   85
  safely be admitted.

Count. You need but plead your honourable privilege.

Laf. Lady, of that I have made a bold charter; but, I
  thank my God, it holds yet.

[*Re-*]*enter* CLOWN.

Clo. O madam, yonder's my lord your son with a patch   90
  of velvet on's face; whether there be a scar under't or
  no, the velvet knows; but 'tis a goodly patch of velvet. His left cheek is a cheek of two pile and a half,
  but his right cheek is worn bare.

Laf. A scar nobly got, or a noble scar, is a good liv'ry of   95
  honour; so belike is that.

Clo. But it is your carbonado'd face.

Laf. Let us go see your son, I pray you. I long to talk with
  the young noble soldier.

Clo. Faith, there's a dozen of 'em with delicate fine hats,   100
  and most courteous feathers which bow the head and
  nod at every man.   *Exeunt.*

89. S.D. *Re-enter*] *Enter F.*   95–6.] *As Theobald*[1]; . . . got, / . . . honor, / . . .
that. / *F* (*verse*).   98–9.] *As Theobald*[1]; . . . see / . . . talke / . . . souldier. / *F*
(*verse*).

85–6.] *N.S.* remarks that it is odd
that Lafew who "moved the king" to
make Bertram his son-in-law, should
"now hesitate to meet him". Surely
the *admitted* refers to staying at the
castle of the Countess, where *they* (i.e.
the King and Bertram) will *meet
together.*

90–1. *patch of velvet*] These were used
to cover both *a noble scar* and the car-
bonadoes (incisions) made to relieve syphilitic chancres. Cf. *Meas.*, I. ii. 31–4.

94. *is worn bare*] i.e. he wears no velvet patch on it, but only skin.

95–9.] As *N.S.* points out, the compositor prints this prose in short lines,
probably in order to be able to fill up
the first column on the Folio page, and
so start *Actus Quintus* at the head of the
second column. He is then forced to
crowd his second column in order
to complete the page of "cast-off"
copy (see Hinman in *Sh. Q.*, VI, 259–
73).

ACT V

[SCENE I.—*Marseilles.*]

Enter HELENA, WIDOW, *and* DIANA, *with two Attendants.*

Hel. But this exceeding posting day and night
    Must wear your spirits low. We cannot help it;
    But since you have made the days and nights as one
    To wear your gentle limbs in my affairs,
    Be bold you do so grow in my requital   5
    As nothing can unroot you.

Enter a Gentleman, a stranger.

               In happy time!
This man may help me to his majesty's ear,

ACT V

Scene 1

Act V Scene 1] *Rowe[1]; Actus Quintus F.*   *Marseilles.] Marseilles. A Street.*
Capell; not in F.   *Enter Helena] Enter Hellen F.*   6. S.D. *Enter a Gentleman, a*
stranger.] F3 (after time*); Enter a gentle Astringer. F; Enter a gentle Astranger. F2;*
Enter a Gentleman. Rowe[1]; Enter a gentleman Usher. conj. E. K. Chambers.

5. *bold*] confident, assured.

6. S.D. *Enter . . .*] The strongest
argument for the authenticity of F
"gentle Astringer" is the real existence
of the curious word it contains: an
"Astringer" (Austringer, Ostringer)
was a keeper of goshawks (Lat.
astur). It seems improbable that a compositor would invent anything at once
so remote and so possible. However,
the acceptance of the F reading, following *lectio difficilior*, raises more difficulties than it avoids, for the rank of
the man is never mentioned in the text
(how would it be conveyed in Shakespeare's theatre?), has no parallels and

no dramatic significance; when he
next appears he is merely (in F) "a
Gentleman" (v. iii. 128). In view of
this, the correction of the later folios
"a stranger" (though no doubt without authority, and based on F2's corruption "Astranger") seems likely to
be right. If the original S.D. read
"Enter a gentle" (i.e. a gentleman),
the further words "a stranger" might
well be of the kind common in this
play and discussed in Intro., p. xiii,
i.e. be a memorandum by the author
that the gentleman is not one of those
that have appeared already, not one of
the "French Gentlemen".

If he would spend his power. God save you, sir!

Gent. And you.

Hel. Sir, I have seen you in the court of France.   10

Gent. I have been sometimes there.

Hel. I do presume, sir, that you are not fall'n
From the report that goes upon your goodness,
And therefore, goaded with most sharp occasions
Which lay nice manners by, I put you to   15
The use of your own virtues, for the which
I shall continue thankful.

Gent. What's your will?

Hel.   That it will please you
To give this poor petition to the king,
And aid me with that store of power you have   20
To come into his presence.

Gent. The king's not here.

Hel.   Not here, sir?

Gent.   Not indeed.
He hence remov'd last night, and with more haste
Than is his use.

Wid.   Lord, how we lose our pains!

Hel. All's well that ends well yet,   25
Though time seem so adverse and means unfit.
I do beseech you, whither is he gone?

Gent. Marry, as I take it, to Rossillion;
Whither I am going.

Hel.   I do beseech you, sir,
Since you are like to see the king before me,   30
Commend the paper to his gracious hand,
Which I presume shall render you no blame,
But rather make you thank your pains for it.
I will come after you with what good speed
Our means will make us means.

Gent.   This I'll do for you.   35

Hel. And you shall find yourself to be well thank'd,
Whate'er falls more. We must to horse again.
Go, go, provide.   [*Exeunt.*]

36–8. And . . . provide.] *As Pope; prose* F.   38. S.D. *Exeunt.*] *Rowe*[1]; *not in* F.

35. *Our means . . . means*] which our resources will allow us.

[SCENE II.—*Rossillion. The Count's palace.*]

Enter CLOWN *and* PAROLLES.

Par. Good Master Lavatch, give my Lord Lafew this
    letter; I have ere now, sir, been better known to you,
    when I have held familiarity with fresher clothes;
    but I am now, sir, muddied in Fortune's mood, and
    smell somewhat strong of her strong displeasure.   5

Clo. Truly, Fortune's displeasure is but sluttish if it smell
    so strongly as thou speak'st of. I will henceforth eat
    no fish of Fortune's butt'ring. Prithee, allow the
    wind.

Par. Nay, you need not to stop your nose, sir. I spake but   10
    by a metaphor.

Clo. Indeed, sir, if your metaphor stink I will stop my
    nose, or against any man's metaphor. Prithee, get
    thee further.

Par. Pray you, sir, deliver me this paper.   15

Clo. Foh! Prithee stand away. A paper from Fortune's
    close-stool, to give to a nobleman! Look, here he
    comes himself.

Enter LAFEW.

Here is a pur of Fortune's, sir, or of Fortune's cat, but

Scene II

Scene II] *Pope; not in* F.   *Rossillion. The Count's palace.*] *Rossillion. Inner-Court of
the Palace. Capell; not in* F.   I. Master] *Neilson;* M[r] *F;* Monsieur *Var. '93.*
Lavatch] *F;* Lavache *Camb., conj. Tollet.   4.* mood] *F;* moat *Theobald*[1].
19. Here] *Theobald*[1]*; Clo.* Heere *F.*

I. *Master*] With this expansion of F
M[r]. cf. *Wiv.*, III. ii. (M[r]. Doctor, M[r].
Page etc.).

Lavatch] usually taken as equivalent
to *La vache* (there actually was a well-
known English family of this name);
the Clarkes suggest *lavage* (slop) and
Hotson *lavaccio*, the Italian form of the
same word, as alternative derivations.

4. *mood*] anger, displeasure (On.).
There is probably a jingle intended between "mud" and *mood* (Kökeritz, 80
and 242). Theobald's emendation of
mood to "moat" cannot be allowed,

since the original makes sense, but
some idea involving sewage seems
necessary to account for the stercora-
ceous imagery which follows. If
Parolles had fallen into Fortune's
moat it would be clearer (since moats
acted as sewers in early sanitation, and
"moat" can also mean "fish-pond")
why the clown replies as he does.

8. *fish of Fortune's buttering*] Possibly
this means "any fish bred in the mud
of Fortune's strong-smelling fish-
pond". Cf. Tilley F 305.

19. *pur*] the knave in the card game

not a musk-cat, that has fall'n into the unclean fish-   20
pond of her displeasure and, as he says, is muddied
withal. Pray you, sir, use the carp as you may, for
he looks like a poor, decayed, ingenious, foolish,
rascally knave. I do pity his distress in my similes of
comfort, and leave him to your lordship.   [*Exit.*]   25

Par. My lord, I am a man whom Fortune hath cruelly
scratch'd.

Laf. And what would you have me to do? 'Tis too late to
pare her nails now. Wherein have you played the
knave with Fortune that she should scratch you, who   30
of herself is a good lady and would not have knaves
thrive long under her? There's a cardecue for you.
Let the justices make you and Fortune friends; I am
for other business.

Par. I beseech your honour to hear me one single word.   35

Laf. You beg a single penny more. Come, you shall ha't;
save your word.

Par. My name, my good lord, is Parolles.

Laf. You beg more than "word" then. Cox my passion!

---

20. musk-cat] *Theobald*[1]*;* Muscat *F.*   23. ingenious] *F;* ingenuous *conj. Anon.;*
ingenerous *N.S., conj. Brigstocke.*   24. similes] *Theobald*[1]*, conj. Warburton;*
smiles *F.*   25. S.D. *Exit.*] *Exit Clown. Capell; not in F.*   32. under her] *F2;*
vnder *F.*   39. "word"] word *F;* one word *F3.*

---

of "post and pair", used here to re-
mind us of the noise of a cat (see above,
IV. iii. 229); also (as Thyssen first
pointed out (Herrig's *Archiv,* 1877),
animal excrement. See Dr Hulme in
R.E.S. VI (1955), 137–9 for a full
explication of all the possible levels of
meaning.

20. *not a musk-cat*] not scented. Cf.
"muske-cod" in *Ham.,* v. ii. 8 (Q1).

22. *carp*] (1) a fish commonly bred
in manured fishponds; (2) one who
carps, i.e. prates, chatters (*O.E.D.*
v. 4).

23. *ingenious*] cannot mean what the
word normally means; but on the
analogy of *Cym.,* I. vi. 108 where
"illustrious" must stand for "in-
lustrious" i.e. "unlustrous" we may
suppose that *ingenious* = un-genious,

i.e. without intellectual capacity.

24. *similes*] The emendation is very
probable; it assumes only a minim
error. Lavatch has said that Parolles
looks like *a poor . . . knave,* not that
he is one, and to this extent may be
said to *comfort* him.

33. *the justices*] They were, under the
Elizabethan poor law, responsible or
beggars.

39. "*word*"] with reference to the
name Parolles.

Cox my passion] One of the many
curious oaths produced by the substitution of "Cock" for "God"; i.e. =
"God's my passion" or "by the suf-
ferings of Christ". Mrs 'Espinasse
points out that the possessive in the
middle (cf. 'Od's my little life in *AYL.,*
III. v. 43) probably has its origin in

Give me your hand. How does your drum?   40
Par. O my good lord, you were the first that found me.
Laf. Was I, in sooth? And I was the first that lost thee.
Par. It lies in you, my lord, to bring me in some grace, for
    you did bring me out.
Laf. Out upon thee, knave! dost thou put upon me at   45
    once both the office of God and the devil? One
    brings thee in Grace and the other brings thee out.
                       [*Trumpets sound.*]
    The king's coming; I know by his trumpets. Sirrah,
    inquire further after me. I had talk of you last night;
    though you are a fool and a knave you shall eat. Go   50
    to; follow.
Par. I praise God for you.   [*Exeunt.*]

[SCENE III.—*The same.*]

Flourish. Enter KING, COUNTESS, LAFEW, *the two French Lords,*
with Attendants.

King. We lost a jewel of her, and our esteem
    Was made much poorer by it; but your son,
    As mad in folly, lack'd the sense to know
    Her estimation home.
Count.   'Tis past, my liege,
    And I beseech your majesty to make it   5

---

47. S.D. *Trumpets sound.*] *Sound trumpets. Theobald*[1]; *not in* F.   48. coming;]
coming, *Rowe*[1]; *comming* F.   52. S.D. *Exeunt*] *Rowe*[1]; *not in* F.

Scene III] *Pope; not in* F.   *The same.*] *The same. A Room of State in the Palace.*
Capell; not in F.   *Enter . . . Countess*] *Enter . . . old Lady* F.

phrases of the "God's my life" kind
where "God's" is short for"God save",
and was then extended to phrases
which could not have had this origin.
Cf. Jonson, *Poet*, ii. i. 108.

   41–2. *found me . . . lost thee*] See note
on ii. iii. 204–5.

Scene III
1. *of*] See i. i. 6 n.
   esteem] worth, value (like *estima-*
tion below). In losing her, one of my
jewels, my total value is reduced.
   4. *home*] fully, satisfactorily, thoroughly (On.).

Natural rebellion done i' th' blade of youth,
When oil and fire, too strong for reason's force,
O'erbears it and burns on.

King.   My honour'd lady,
I have forgiven and forgotten all,
Though my revenges were high bent upon him   10
And watch'd the time to shoot.

Laf.   This I must say—
But first I beg my pardon—the young lord
Did to his majesty, his mother and his lady
Offence of mighty note, but to himself
The greatest wrong of all. He lost a wife   15
Whose beauty did astonish the survey
Of richest eyes; whose words all ears took captive;
Whose dear perfection hearts that scorn'd to serve
Humbly call'd mistress.

King.   Praising what is lost
Makes the remembrance dear. Well, call him
     hither;   20
We are reconcil'd, and the first view shall kill
All repetition. Let him not ask our pardon;

---

6. blade] *F;* blaze *Capell, conj. Theobald.*

6. *blade*] The metaphor of *blade* (green shoot) is not congruous with that of *oil,* though it agrees with *Natural.* This mixing of metaphors, however, is common enough in Shakespeare to make the emendation to "blaze" unnecessary. For other examples of "in the blade" see *O.E.D.* Blade sb. 2.b.

10. *high bent*] The bow was strongly bent.

12. *But . . . pardon*] Why does Lafew beg pardon? Is it for appearing unexpectedly at Rossillion (see note on IV. v. 85–6 above)?

17. *richest*] most experienced. Cf. "to have seen much . . . is to have rich eyes" (*AYL.,* IV. i. 21–2).

words . . . captive] The idea of eloquent words chaining up the ears of auditors was a Renaissance commonplace, deriving ultimately, in all probability, from Lucian's description of the Gallic Hercules, and given pictorial form in Alciati's emblems.

21–2. *kill All repetition*] "check any mention of what is past" (On.). Johnson notes here: "Shakspeare is now hastening to the end of the play, finds his matter sufficient to fill up his remaining scenes, and therefore, as on such other occasions, contracts his dialogue and precipitates his action. Decency required that Bertram's double crime of cruelty and disobedience, joined likewise with some hypocrisy, should raise more resentment; and that though his mother might easily forgive him, his King should more pertinaciously vindicate his own authority and Helen's merit. Of all this Shakespeare could not be ignorant, but Shakespeare wanted to conclude his play."

The nature of his great offence is dead,
And deeper than oblivion we do bury
Th' incensing relics of it. Let him approach   25
A stranger, no offender; and inform him
So 'tis our will he should.

Gent.   I shall, my liege.   [*Exit.*]
King. What says he to your daughter? Have you spoke?
Laf. All that he is hath reference to your highness.
King. Then shall we have a match. I have letters sent me   30
That sets him high in fame.

Enter BERTRAM.

Laf.   He looks well on't.
King. I am not a day of season,
For thou may'st see a sunshine and a hail
In me at once. But to the brightest beams
Distracted clouds give way; so stand thou forth;   35
The time is fair again.

Ber.   My high-repented blames
Dear sovereign, pardon to me.
King.   All is whole.
Not one word more of the consumed time;
Let's take the instant by the forward top;

27. S.D. *Exit.*] *Exit Gentleman. Capell; not in F.*   28.] *As Theobald*[1]; . . .
daughter, / . . . spoke? / F (verse).   30–1.] *As Pope; prose F.*   31. sets] *F;*
set *Rowe*[1]+.

23. *The nature . . . dead*] i.e. is dead to
me; I have forgotten what its nature
was.

25. *relics*] memories.

29. *hath reference to*] is submitted to.
Cf. "fear nothing. / Make your full
reference freely to my lord" (*Ant.*, v.
ii, 22–3).

32. *I am . . . season*] a day here presumably means "one (single) day", so
that the phrase means: "I am consistently neither a summer's day
(smiling for your return) nor a winter's day (frowning, or weeping over
Helena's fate)."

34–5. *But to . . . way*] Tilley (C 442)
notes a connection with the proverb

"After black clouds clear weather".

35. *give*] may be indicative, but
reads better as an imperative.

39. *the forward top*] the lock of hair
which Occasion (= Opportunity) has,
in the emblematic representations of
her, at the front of her head. Cf. *Disticha Catonis* (II, xxvi): "Fronte capil-
lata, post est occasio calva"; and

Her lockes, that loathly were and
    hoarie gray,
Grew all afore, and loosely hong
    vnrold,
But all behind was bald, and worne
    away,
That none thereof could euer
    taken hold. (*Faerie Queene*, II. iv. 4)

For we are old, and on our quick'st decrees   40
Th'inaudible and noiseless foot of time
Steals ere we can effect them. You remember
The daughter of this lord?
Ber. Admiringly, my liege. At first
I stuck my choice upon her, ere my heart   45
Durst make too bold a herald of my tongue;
Where, the impression of mine eye infixing,
Contempt his scornful perspective did lend me,
Which warp'd the line of every other favour,
Scorn'd a fair colour or express'd it stol'n,   50
Extended or contracted all proportions
To a most hideous object. Thence it came
That she whom all men prais'd, and whom myself
Since I have lost, have lov'd, was in mine eye
The dust that did offend it.
King.   Well excus'd.   55
That thou didst love her, strikes some scores away
From the great compt; but love that comes too late,
Like a remorseful pardon slowly carried,
To the great sender turns a sour offence,

---

44. Admiringly, my liege.] *Rowe*[1]; Admiringly my Liege, *F.*   58-9. carried,
... sender] *Theobald*[1]; carried ... sender, *F.*

45-9. *ere my heart ... favour*] It seems
possible to read this passage in two
ways; we may suppose that it refers to
Helena, in which case 45-6 will mean
"before I said too rashly what I felt";
and 49, "which twisted her features
away from any appearance other than
contemptible"; on the other hand we
may take it to refer to Maudlin, in
which case 45-6 will mean "before I
dared say that I had chosen her" (*too
bold* being stretched to mean "bold
enough") and 49, "which made every
face other than Maudlin's seem
hideous". In either case the best antecedent for *Where* will be the *heart*, into
which the eye, in a well-established
Alexandrian, Medieval, and Petrar-
chan convention, conveys its impression (cf. *Sonn.*, XXIV); *infixing* presumably has a reflexive sense, "im-
pressing itself".

48. *perspective*] "an optical instrument ... for producing some special or
fantastic effect" (*O.E.D.*)—accented
on the first syllable.

52-5. *Thence . . . offend it*] Tilley
(W 924) compares the proverb: "the
worth of a thing is best known by the
want."

55. *The dust*] The image is particularly apt, for the dust not only offended
Bertram, but bleared his vision.

57. *the great compt*] *compt* is "account"; *the great compt* suggests the
final (divine) reckoning, as in *Oth.*, V.
ii. 276, but may mean nothing more
than "your long account".

58-60. *Like . . . gone*] The simile presents a situation parallel to that in *R 3*,
II. i. 79-140.

59. *turns a sour offence*] The slowness
of the transport has made it go bad,
turn sour on him.

Crying, "That's good that's gone". Our rash faults   60
Make trivial price of serious things we have,
Not knowing them until we know their grave.
Oft our displeasures, to ourselves unjust,
Destroy our friends and after weep their dust;
Our own love waking cries to see what's done,   65
While shameful hate sleeps out the afternoon.
Be this sweet Helen's knell, and now forget her.
Send forth your amorous token for fair Maudlin.
The main consents are had, and here we'll stay
To see our widower's second marriage-day.   70
Count. Which better than the first, O dear heaven, bless!
Or, ere they meet, in me, O nature, cesse!
Laf. Come on, my son, in whom my house's name
Must be digested; give a favour from you
To sparkle in the spirits of my daughter,   75
That she may quickly come.   *[Bertram gives a ring.]*
                    By my old beard
And ev'ry hair that's on't, Helen that's dead
Was a sweet creature; such a ring as this,
The last that e'er I took her leave at court,
I saw upon her finger.
Ber.   Hers it was not.   80

66. shameful hate] *F*; shame full late *Globe, conj. W. G. Clark.*   71. *Count.*
Which] *Theobald¹*; Which *F.*   72. meet,] *Rowe¹*; meete *F.*   76. S.D.
Bertram gives a ring.] *Hanmer; not in F.*   79. that e'er I] *F*; that e'er she *Rowe¹*;
time e'er she *Hanmer.*

61–2. *have . . . grave*] *N.S.* finds a
"soft rhyme" between these two words
(p. 109); but to Elizabethan ears the
rhyme may have been perfect. For the
sense, cf. *Ado*, IV. i. 217 ff.

65–6. *Our own . . . afternoon*] Love
sleeps while hate does its work, and
then, when it wakes and sees what hate
has done, it cries; but the object of love
is destroyed and hate can slumber
soundly, to our shame.

69. *main consents*] We have already
heard approval of the union from
Lafew, the Countess, the King, Bertram and (by report) Maudlin.

71–2.] Though these lines are
assigned to the King in F they are

more appropriate in the mouth of the
Countess.

72. *cesse*] a form of "cease" "not
generally current in Shakespeare's
time" (On.), used presumably to
procure a rhyme.

74. *digested*] Commentators gloss
"amalgamated", but "swallowed-up"
would be better, since the wife's name
disappears.

79. *The last . . . leave*] *last* must stand
for "last time"; *took her leave* must =
"took leave of her". When Lafew
took his leave of Helena she would
offer him her hand to kiss; this would
be the obvious time to observe the
ring.

King. Now pray you let me see it; for mine eye,
　　While I was speaking, oft was fasten'd to't.
　　This ring was mine, and when I gave it Helen
　　I bade her, if her fortunes ever stood
　　Necessitied to help, that by this token   85
　　I would relieve her. Had you that craft to reave her
　　Of what should stead her most?
Ber.　　　　　　　　　　My gracious sovereign,
　　Howe'er it pleases you to take it so,
　　The ring was never hers.
Count.　　　　　　　Son, on my life,
　　I have seen her wear it, and she reckon'd it   90
　　At her life's rate.
Laf.　　　　　I am sure I saw her wear it.
Ber. You are deceiv'd, my lord; she never saw it.
　　In Florence was it from a casement thrown me,
　　Wrapp'd in a paper which contain'd the name
　　Of her that threw it. Noble she was, and thought   95
　　I stood ingag'd; but when I had subscrib'd
　　To mine own fortune, and inform'd her fully
　　I could not answer in that course of honour
　　As she had made the overture, she ceas'd
　　In heavy satisfaction, and would never   100
　　Receive the ring again.
King.　　　　　　Plutus himself,

96. ingag'd] *F;* engag'd *Rowe[1];* ungag'd *Theobald[1].*

83–6. *when I . . . relieve her*] Some have
seen in this a reflection of the story
that Essex, on the eve of his execution,
sent to Queen Elizabeth a ring which
she had given him for use in an
emergency, and that the token was
intercepted by the Countess of Not-
tingham or Sir Robert Cecil. See
Webster, *The Devils Law-Case,* III. iii.
303 ff and Lucas' note thereon. As
Lowes MS. and H. F. Brooks point
out, the story is rejected by modern
historians.

84–5. *I bade her . . . that*] Brigstocke
remarks that this is an elliptical
construction. "To make it quite
clear, understand 'I bade her . . .

(remember) that by this token . . .' "

85. *Necessitied to*] in need of.

87. *stead*] benefit.

96. *ingag'd*] may mean (1) not gaged
(pledged) to another woman; (2) en-
gaged (to her)—because he had received her ring. Thiselton points out
that *ingag'd, subscrib'd, course of honour*
are all taken from the technical
language of the duel.

96–7. *subscrib'd To*] acknowledged,
given an account of.

100. *heavy satisfaction*] convinced but
sad.

101. *Plutus*] The god of riches is here
represented as an alchemist who
knows *the tinct and multiplying medicine*

That knows the tinct and multiplying med'cine,
Hath not in nature's mystery more science
Than I have in this ring. 'Twas mine, 'twas Helen's,
Whoever gave it you; then if you know   105
That you are well acquainted with yourself,
Confess 'twas hers, and by what rough enforcement
You got it from her. She call'd the saints to surety
That she would never put it from her finger
Unless she gave it to yourself in bed,   110
Where you have never come, or sent it us
Upon her great disaster.

Ber.   She never saw it.

King. Thou speak'st it falsely, as I love mine honour,
And mak'st conjectural fears to come into me
Which I would fain shut out. If it should prove   115
That thou art so inhuman—'twill not prove so,
And yet I know not; thou didst hate her deadly,
And she is dead; which nothing but to close
Her eyes myself could win me to believe,
More than to see this ring. Take him away.   120
My fore-past proofs, howe'er the matter fall,
Shall tax my fears of little vanity,
Having vainly fear'd too little. Away with him.
We'll sift this matter further.

Ber.   If you shall prove
This ring was ever hers, you shall as easy   125
Prove that I husbanded her bed in Florence,
Where yet she never was.   [*Exit, guarded.*]

King. I am wrapp'd in dismal thinkings.

Enter [the] Gentleman [stranger].

115. out.] out; *F4*; out, F.   127. S.D. *Exit, guarded.*] *Rowe*[1]*; not in* F.
128. S.D. *Enter the Gentleman stranger.] Collier*[3]*; Enter a Gentleman. F (after 127).*

i.e. the Elixir by which base metal
could be turned into gold, and gold
multiplied indefinitely. Cf. *Ant.*, I. v.
36–7.

103. *nature's mystery*] how to turn
base metals into gold.

105–6. *then . . . yourself*] presumably
= if you know what's good for you,
though *self* in the sense of "personal

welfare" is first quoted in *O.E.D.*
(C.5.) from 1680.

115–20.] The disjointed syntax
serves well to express the King's wild
and whirling thoughts.

121–3. *My fore-past . . . too little*]
"*The proofs which I have already had* are
sufficient to show that my *fears* were
not *vain* and irrational. I have rather

Gent.   Gracious sovereign,
   Whether I have been to blame or no, I know not:
   Here's a petition from a Florentine   130
   Who hath for four or five removes come short
   To tender it herself. I undertook it,
   Vanquish'd thereto by the fair grace and speech
   Of the poor suppliant, who, by this, I know,
   Is here attending; her business looks in her   135
   With an importing visage, and she told me,
   In a sweet verbal brief, it did concern
   Your highness with herself.

King. [*Reads the letter*] *Upon his many protestations to marry*
me when his wife was dead, I blush to say it, he won me. 140
Now is the Count Rossillion a widower; his vows are for-
feited to me and my honour's paid to him. He stole from
Florence, taking no leave, and I follow him to his country for
justice. Grant it me, O king! In you it best lies; otherwise a
seducer flourishes, and a poor maid is undone.   145

                DIANA CAPILET.

Laf. I will buy me a son-in-law in a fair, and toll for this.
   I'll none of him.
King. The heavens have thought well on thee, Lafew,
   To bring forth this discov'ry. Seek these suitors.   150
   Go speedily, and bring again the count.
                    [*Exeunt Attendants.*]

---

139. S.D. *King. Reads the letter*] *A Letter. F.*   151. S.D. *Exeunt Attendants.*] *Exeunt*
some Attendants. Capell; not in F.

been hitherto more easy than I ought, and have *unreasonably* had *too little fear*" (Johnson).

131. *for four . . . short*] has failed to catch up with the King at halting-places, for on each occasion when she arrived she found that the court had already *removed* on the next stage of its journey. The phrase "these arrant removes" is used of the stages of James' Progress in a letter of 1603 (quoted in Chambers, *Elizabethan Stage*, I, 122).

136. *importing*] "full of import or significance" or perhaps "urgent".

137. *verbal brief*] a summary delivered by word of mouth.

147. *in a fair*] The chance of buying stolen goods in a fair was exceptionally high. Even so the transaction would be preferable to this one.

toll for this] enter Bertram as for sale in the "toll-book" or entry-register of a market. Notice the string of commercial images: *forfeited, paid, stole, buy, fair, toll,* applied to the marriage arrangements.

150. *suitors*] petitioners—Diana and her mother—though it is not clear how the King knows of more than one.

I am afear'd the life of Helen, lady,
Was foully snatch'd.
Count.   Now justice on the doers!

[Re-]enter BERTRAM *[guarded]*.

King. I wonder, sir, since wives are monsters to you,
And that you fly them as you swear them lordship,   155
Yet you desire to marry.

Enter WIDOW *and* DIANA.

What woman's that?
Dia. I am, my lord, a wretched Florentine,
Derived from the ancient Capilet;
My suit, as I do understand, you know,
And therefore know how far I may be pitied.   160
Wid. I am her mother, sir, whose age and honour
Both suffer under this complaint we bring,
And both shall cease, without your remedy.
King. Come hither, count; do you know these women?
Ber. My lord, I neither can nor will deny   165
But that I know them. Do they charge me further?
Dia. Why do you look so strange upon your wife?
Ber. She's none of mine, my lord.
Dia.   If you shall marry
You give away this hand and that is mine,

153. S.D.] *Capell; Enter Bertram. F (after 151)*.   154. sir, since] *Tyrwhitt;* sir, sir,
F.   156. S.D.] *Rowe*[1] *(after* that*) ; Enter Widdow, Diana, and Parrolles.F (after* that).

154. *sir, since*] Dyce's emendation
"sir, sith" for F "sir, sir" has been
accepted by modern editors, but
Tyrwhitt's "sir, since" has as much
plausibility and uses the commoner word. The compositor presumably started to set the "si-" of "since"
(or "sith") but his eye caught the
"si-" of "sir", and he set that word
again.

155. *as . . . lordship*] as soon as you
promise them marriage.

156. S.D.] Folio S.D. "*Enter Widdow, Diana, and Parolles*" cannot be
right as the text stands; but Diana

states below that she has already seen
Parolles; the introduction of the
wronged maid by the cashiered captain is one of those moments which
could be effective on the stage; its
retention in a text which also contains
the entry for Parolles at l. 229 below is
presumably part of the heritage of
Shakespeare's "foul papers".

163. *both shall cease*] My age shall
cease, for the sorrow will kill me, and
my honour shall cease, if Bertram does
not marry my daughter.

169. *this hand*] Bertram's hand. Cf.
Meas., v. i. 207f.

You give away heaven's vows and those are mine,   170
You give away myself which is known mine;
For I by vow am so embodied yours
That she which marries you must marry me—
Either both or none.

Laf. Your reputation comes too short for my daughter;   175
you are no husband for her.

Ber. My lord, this is a fond and desp'rate creature
Whom sometime I have laugh'd with. Let your highness
Lay a more noble thought upon mine honour
Than for to think that I would sink it here.   180

King. Sir, for my thoughts, you have them ill to friend
Till your deeds gain them; fairer prove your honour
Than in my thought it lies!

Dia.   Good my lord,
Ask him upon his oath if he does think
He had not my virginity.   185

King. What say'st thou to her?

Ber.   She's impudent, my lord,
And was a common gamester to the camp.

Dia. He does me wrong, my lord; if I were so
He might have bought me at a common price.
Do not believe him. O behold this ring   190
Whose high respect and rich validity
Did lack a parallel; yet for all that
He gave it to a commoner a' th' camp—
If I be one.

Count.   He blushes and 'tis hit.

---

182. them; fairer] *Theobald*[2]*;* them fairer: *F.*   194. hit] *F;* his *Pope;* it *Capell+.*

170–4.] Cf. Marriage Service: "He that loveth his wife loveth himself: for no man ever yet hated his own flesh."

182. *them; fairer*] This version (Theobald's) has been universally accepted but perhaps we ought to follow F more closely and read: ". . . them fairer. Prove your honour; / Then . . ." ("then" and "than" were interchangeable Elizabethan spellings).

191. *high . . . validity*] the ring was both honourable and valuable.

194. *'tis hit*] probably *O.E.D.* "hit" vb. II.11: "to light upon, get at, reach, find"; but may represent the old emphatic form of "it", in which case the modernization to "it" in most texts is justified. I take it to be more dramatic if the Countess's exclamation is a praise of Diana's forensic marksmanship rather than a gasp of recognition. Cf. Marston, *The Fawne,* II. i. 502: "You both admire, yes, say is't not hit?"

Of six preceding ancestors, that gem   195
Conferr'd by testament to th' sequent issue,
Hath it been owed and worn. This is his wife:
That ring's a thousand proofs.
King.   Methought you said
You saw one here in court could witness it.
Dia. I did, my lord, but loath am to produce   200
So bad an instrument; his name's Parolles.
Laf. I saw the man today, if man he be.
King. Find him and bring him hither.   [*Exit an Attendant.*]
Ber.   What of him?
He's quoted for a most perfidious slave
With all the spots a' th' world tax'd and debosh'd,   205
Whose nature sickens but to speak a truth.
Am I or that or this for what he'll utter,
That will speak anything?
King.   She hath that ring of yours.
Ber. I think she has. Certain it is I lik'd her
And boarded her i' th' wanton way of youth.   210
She knew her distance and did angle for me,
Madding my eagerness with her restraint,
As all impediments in fancy's course
Are motives of more fancy; and in fine
Her inf'nite cunning with her modern grace   215

203. S.D. *Exit an Attendant*] *Dyce*[1]*; not in F.*   206. sickens ... truth.] sickens ...
truth; *Hanmer;* sickens: ... truth, *F.*   215. inf'nite cunning] infinite cunning
Singer[2], *conj. W. S. Walker;* insuite comming *F;* in suit coming *Hanmer.*

196. *sequent issue*] next heir.

197. *owed*] owned.

198–9. *Methought . . . witness it*]
Diana has not said this in the play, but
Shakespeare, very properly, never
hesitates to foreshorten his dramas in
this way.

204. *quoted*] set down as (On.).

205. *tax'd and debosh'd*] censured for
being debauched.

207. *Am I . . . utter*] "Can the evidence of such a rascal decide my
character?" (Case *apud* Brigstocke).

210. *boarded*] accosted.

211. *distance*] *N.S.* takes this to be a
metaphor from fencing: "the interval
to be kept between the combatants"

but the reference is rather to her power
to "draw him on".

214. *fancy*] amorous imagination.

215. *inf'nite . . . grace*] Walker's
emendation (deriving its strength
from the virtual identity of "insuite"
and "infnite" in Elizabethan writing
—and even typography—and the
commonness of the spelling "con-
ning"—misprinted "Comming" in
QF of *Troil.*, III. ii. 129) restores to the
line its clever forensic antithesis. It
was not so much Diana's *grace*
(attractiveness) that won him, for that
is merely *modern* (commonplace), but
her *inf'nite cunning*—and that seems to
be subduing the King too. It is just

Subdu'd me to her rate; she got the ring,
And I had that which any inferior might
At market-price have bought.

Dia.   I must be patient.
You that have turn'd off a first so noble wife
May justly diet me. I pray you yet—   220
Since you lack virtue I will lose a husband—
Send for your ring, I will return it home,
And give me mine again.

Ber.   I have it not.

King. What ring was yours, I pray you?

Dia.   Sir, much like
The same upon your finger.   225

King. Know you this ring? This ring was his of late.

Dia. And this was it I gave him, being abed.

King. The story then goes false you threw it him
Out of a casement?

Dia.   I have spoke the truth.

Enter PAROLLES.

Ber. My lord, I do confess the ring was hers.   230

King. You boggle shrewdly; every feather starts you.
Is this the man you speak of?

Dia.   Ay, my lord.

King. Tell me, sirrah—but tell me true I charge you,
Not fearing the displeasure of your master,
Which on your just proceeding I'll keep off—   235
By him and by this woman here what know
    you?

224–5. Sir ... finger] *As Capell; one line F.*

possible, however, that Thiselton is right and that "insuite" is intended as an anglicization of Lat. *insuetus* (unusual)—which would preserve the antithesis with *modern*.

216. *rate*] the price she demanded.

220. *diet*] restrain from full enjoyment, as above, IV. iii. 28.

231. *You boggle shrewdly*] You are sharp to take fright (like a horse).

every...you] Cf. *Ven.*, 302: "Anon he starts at stirring of a feather". The phrase must be heavily ironic here; Bertram's confession under the weight of so much evidence cannot be said literally to be shying away from every feather. In *feather* we may see a reference to Parolles' (now bedraggled) finery.

236. *By him*] about, concerning him. See Abbott §145.

Par. So please your majesty, my master hath been an honourable gentleman. Tricks he hath had in him, which gentlemen have.

King. Come, come, to th' purpose. Did he love this woman?

Par. Faith, sir, he did love her; but how?   241

King. How, I pray you?

Par. He did love her, sir, as a gentleman loves a woman.

King. How is that?

Par. He lov'd her, sir, and lov'd her not.   245

King. As thou art a knave and no knave. What an equivocal companion is this!

Par. I am a poor man, and at your majesty's command.

Laf. He's a good drum, my lord, but a naughty orator.

Dia. Do you know he promis'd me marriage?   250

Par. Faith, I know more than I'll speak.

King. But wilt thou not speak all thou know'st?

Par. Yes, so please your majesty. I did go between them as I said; but more than that, he loved her, for indeed he was mad for her and talk'd of Satan and of Limbo 255 and of furies and I know not what; yet I was in that credit with them at that time that I knew of their going to bed and of other motions, as promising her marriage and things which would derive me ill will to speak of; therefore I will not speak what I know.   260

---

243. gentleman] Gent. *F*.   254. that,] *F3;* that *F*.

---

237. *master*] Notice that the word which Parolles so objected to in II. iii is now accepted without demur.

237 ff.] The continual equivocation in Parolles' answers is caused, presumably, by his desire to offend neither Bertram nor the King.

238. *honourable*] a final indication of the fatal ambiguity of this word. See Intro., p. xliii.

243. *as a . . . woman*] as one of noble birth loves one of mean birth.

245. *He lov'd . . . not*] loved her carnally, but not with intent to marry her.

247. *companion*] used disparagingly.

249. *a good . . . orator*] The connection between *drum* and *orator* remains mysterious. There is, of course, a glance at Parolles' exploit to recover a drum and at his "Jack Drum" nickname, but Shakespeare normally provides a greater coherence between his terms than this provides. There is an antithesis between *good* and *naughty* (no good), but this is as much as can be certain. It seems possible that Lafew is paraphrasing l. 248 with the sense "what he really means is that he's easy to get a noise (i.e. reply) out of (like a drum or a drummer), but no good at making out a case or defending anyone". Cf. *John,* v. ii. 166 f:

Indeed, your drums being beaten, will cry out;

And so shall you, being beaten.

258. *motions*] proposals, offers (On.).

King. Thou hast spoken all already, unless thou canst say
    they are married; but thou art too fine in thy evi-
    dence; therefore, stand aside.
    This ring you say was yours?
Dia.   Ay, my good lord.
King. Where did you buy it? Or who gave it you?   265
Dia. It was not given me, nor I did not buy it.
King. Who lent it you?
Dia.   It was not lent me neither.
King. Where did you find it then?
Dia.   I found it not.
King. If it were yours by none of all these ways
    How could you give it him?
Dia.   I never gave it him.   270
Laf. This woman's an easy glove, my lord; she goes off
    and on at pleasure.
King. This ring was mine; I gave it his first wife.
Dia. It might be yours or hers for ought I know.
King. Take her away. I do not like her now.   275
    To prison with her. And away with him.
    Unless thou tell'st me where thou hadst this ring
    Thou diest within this hour.
Dia.   I'll never tell you.
King. Take her away.
Dia.   I'll put in bail, my liege.
King. I think thee now some common customer.   280
Dia. By Jove, if ever I knew man 'twas you.
King. Wherefore hast thou accus'd him all this while?
Dia. Because he's guilty and he is not guilty.
    He knows I am no maid, and he'll swear to't;
    I'll swear I am a maid and he knows not.   285
    Great king, I am no strumpet; by my life
    I am either maid or else this old man's wife.
King. She does abuse our ears. To prison with her.

---

262. *fine*] fine-spun, subtle.

264–98.] Johnson remarks that "the
dialogue is too long, since the audience
already knew the whole transaction;
nor is there any reason for puzzling the
King and playing with his passions;
but it was much easier than to make a

pathetical interview between Helen
and her husband, her mother, and the
King". Cf. Intro., pp. liii ff.

280. *customer*] prostitute. Cf. *Oth.*,
IV. i. 119.

284–7.] Cf. the similarly-placed
conundrum in *Meas.*, v. i. 171–87.

Dia. Good mother, fetch my bail. Stay, royal sir;

[Exit Widow.]

    The jeweller that owes the ring is sent for   290
    And he shall surety me. But for this lord
    Who hath abus'd me as he knows himself—
    Though yet he never harm'd me—here I quit him.
    He knows himself my bed he hath defil'd;
    And at that time he got his wife with child.   295
    Dead though she be she feels her young one kick.
    So there's my riddle: one that's dead is quick,
    And now behold the meaning.

        [Re-]enter WIDOW *[with]* HELENA.

King.   Is there no exorcist
    Beguiles the truer office of mine eyes?
    Is't real that I see?
Hel.   No, my good lord;   300
    'Tis but the shadow of a wife you see;
    The name and not the thing.
Ber.   Both, both. O pardon!
Hel. O my good lord, when I was like this maid
    I found you wondrous kind. There is your ring,
    And, look you, here's your letter. This it says: 305
    When from my finger you can get this ring
    And is by me with child, &c. This is done;
    Will you be mine now you are doubly won?
Ber. If she, my liege, can make me know this clearly
    I'll love her dearly, ever, ever dearly.   310
Hel. If it appear not plain and prove untrue
    Deadly divorce step between me and you!
    O my dear mother, do I see you living?
Laf. Mine eyes smell onions; I shall weep anon.
    [To Parolles] Good Tom Drum, lend me a handkercher.

289. S.D. *Exit Widow*] *Pope; not in* F.   298 S.D.] *Enter Hellen and Widdow.* F.
307. *is*] F; *are Rowe*[1]+.   310. dearly, ever] F; dearly ever *conj. Fripp.*   315.
S.D. *To Parolles*] *Rowe*[1]; *not in* F.

    293. *quit*] acquit.
    298. *exorcist*] now confined to one
who lays spirits, but used by Elizabethans also of one who raised them.

    299. *truer office*] i.e. natural sight.
    301. *shadow*] playing on two senses
of the word: (1) ghost (cf. modern
"shade"); (2) imitation, counterpart.

So, I thank thee. Wait on me home, I'll make sport   316
with thee. Let thy curtsies alone, they are scurvy
ones.

King. Let us from point to point this story know
To make the even truth in pleasure flow.   320
[*To Diana*] If thou beest yet a fresh uncropped flower
Choose thou thy husband and I'll pay thy dower;
For I can guess that by thy honest aid
Thou kept'st a wife herself, thyself a maid.
Of that and all the progress more and less   325
Resolvedly more leisure shall express.
All yet seems well, and if it end so meet,
The bitter past, more welcome is the sweet.

Flourish.

[EPILOGUE]

The king's a beggar, now the play is done;
All is well ended if this suit be won,
That you express content; which we will pay
With strife to please you, day exceeding day.
Ours be your patience then and yours our parts;   5
Your gentle hands lend us and take our hearts.

Exeunt omnes.

317. curtsies] *F;* Courtesies *Rowe*[1].   321. S.D. *To Diana*] *Rowe*[1]; *not in F.*   Epi-
logue] *Rowe*[1]; *not in F.*

320. *even*] exact, precise (On.).
326. *Resolvedly*] "so that doubt and
uncertainty are removed" (On.).

Epilogue
1. The king's a beggar] "though
these lines are sufficiently intelligible in
their obvious sense, yet perhaps there
is some allusion to the old tale of The
King and the Beggar, which was the
subject of a ballad" (Malone). Cf.
LLL., I. ii. 105–6.

4. strife to please you] H. F. Brooks
compares *Tw. N.*, v. i. 394: "we'll
strive to please you every day."
5. Ours . . . parts] We will listen
patiently to the audience's applause,
as you have listened patiently to our
performance; you will be the actors
then, for your applause is the only
action at the end of the play.
6.] (1) you clap and we shall be
grateful; (2) you present the action
and we'll give the response.

APPENDIX

'GILETTA OF NARBONA", THE THIRTY-EIGHTH NOVEL OF WILLIAM PAINTER'S *THE PALACE OF PLEASURE*

¶*Giletta*[1] *a Phisitions doughter of Narbon, healed the French King of a Fistula, for reward whereof she demaunded Beltramo Counte of Rossiglione to husband. The Counte being maried against his will, for despite fled to Florence, and loved another. Giletta his wife, by pollicie founde meanes to lye with her husbande, in place of his lover, and was begotten with childe of two sonnes: which knowen to her husband, he received her againe, and afterwards he lived in great honour and felicitie.*

In Fraunce there was a gentleman called *Isnardo*, the Counte of *Rossiglione*, who because he was sickely and diseased, kepte alwayes in his house a Phisition, named maister *Gerardo of Narbona*. This Counte had one onely sonne called *Beltramo*, a very yonge childe, amiable and fayre. With whom there was nourished and brought uppe, many other children of his age, amonges whom one of the doughters of the said Phisition, named *Giletta*, who fervently fill in love with *Beltramo*, more then was meete for a maiden of her age. This *Beltramo* when his father was deade, and left under the royall custody of the king, was sente to Paris, for whose departure, the maiden was very pensife. A litle while after, her father being likewise deade, shee was desirous to go to Paris, onelye to see the yonge Counte, if for that purpose she could get any good occasion. But being diligently loked unto by her kinsfolke (because she was riche

1. I have reprinted here the version of the tale contained in the third (and final) edition of Painter's *The Palace of Pleasure*, vol. I (1575) rather than that in the first edition (1566), for the following reasons: (1) the third edition is nearer in time to Shakespeare's own day and is therefore, if anything, more likely to have been the edition he read; (2) the first edition has often been reprinted with *All's Well* (e.g. in Arden and N.S.), while the third edition has not; (3) the third edition is considerably revised and may be considered the definitive version; the revisions, however, do not take it any nearer Boccaccio (or le Maçon) and Shakespeare is nowhere close enough to Painter for the changes to have any bearing on his text.

and fatherlesse) she could see no convenient waye, for her intended journey: and being now mariageable, the love she bare to the Counte, was never out of her remembraunce, and refused manye husbandes, with whom her kinsfolke would have matched her, without making them privie, to the cause of her refusall. Now it chaunced that she burned more in love with *Beltramo*, then ever shee did before, because she hearde tell, that hee was growen to the state of a goodly yong gentleman. She heard by report, that the French king had a swelling upon his breast, which by reason of ill cure, was growen to be a Fistula, which did put him to marveilous paine and griefe, and that there was no Phisition to be found (although many were proved) that could heale it, but rather did impaire the griefe & made it worse and worse. Wherfore the king, like one in dispaire, would take no more counsell or helpe. Wherof the yong mayden was wonderfull glad, thinckinge to have by this meanes, not onely a lawfull occasion to go to Paris: but if the disease were such (as she supposed) easelye to bringe to passe, that shee mighte have the Counte *Beltramo* to her husbande. Whereuppon with such knowledge, as she had learned at her fathers hands before time, shee made a pouder of certaine herbes, which she thought meete for that disease, and rode to Paris. And the first thing she went about when she came thither, was to see the Counte *Beltramo*. And then she repayred to the king, praying his grace to vouchsafe to shew her his griefe. The king perceyving her to be a fayre yonge maiden and a comelie, would not hide it, but opened the same unto her. So soone as shee saw it, shee put him in comforte, that shee was able to heale him, saying. 'Sir, if it maye please your grace, I truste in God, without anye great paine unto your highnesse, within eighte dayes, to make you whole of this disease.' The king hearing her say so, began to mocke her, saying. How is it possible for thee, beinge a yong woman to do that which the beste renowmed Phisitions in the world can not? Hee thancked her, for her good will, and made her a direct aunsweare, that hee was determined no more, to followe the counsaile of any Phisition. Whereunto the maiden aunsweared: 'Sir, you dispise my knowledge because I am yonge and a woman, but I assure you, that I do not minister Phisicke by profession, but by the aide and helpe of God: and with the cunninge of maister *Gerardo of Narbona*, who was my father, and a Phisition of great fame, so longe as he lived.' The king hearing those words, sayd to himselfe. 'This woman peradventure, is sente unto me of God, and therefore, why should I disdaine to prove her cunninge? for so muche as she promiseth to heale me within a litle space, without any offence or griefe unto mee.' And being determined to prove her, he said. 'Damosel, if thou doest not heale me, but make me to breake my determination, what wilt thou shal folow therof.' 'Sir' said the maiden: 'Let me be kept in what guard and keeping you list: and if I do not heale you within these eight dayes, let me be burnt: but if I do heale your grace, what recompence shall I have then?' To whom the kinge aunswered. 'Because thou art a maiden and unmaried, if thou heale me according to thy promise, I wil bestow thee uppon some gentleman, that shalbe of right good worship and estimation.' To whom she aunsweared: 'Sir I am very well content, that you bestow me in mariage: but I beseech your grace let me have such a husband, as I my selfe shall demaund: without presumption to any of your children, or other of your bloud.' Which request the king incontinently graunted. The yong maiden began to minister her Phisicke, and in short space before her appointed time, she had throughly cured the king. And when the king perceived himselfe whole, said unto her. 'Thou hast well deserved a husbande (*Giletta*) even such a one as thy selfe shalt chose.' I have then my Lord (quoth she) deserved the Countie *Beltramo* of *Rossiglione*, whom I have loved from my youth. The king was very loth to graunt him unto her: but for that he had made a promise, which he was loth to breake, he caused him to be called forth, and said unto him: 'Sir Countie, knowing full well that you are a gentleman of great honour, oure pleasure is, that you returne home to your owne house, to order your estate, according to your degree: & that you take with you a Damosell, which I have appointed to be your wife.' To whom the Countie gave his humble thanks, & demaunded what she was? 'It is she (quoth the king) that with her medecines hath healed me.' The Counte knew her wel, & had already seen her, although she was faire, yet knowing her not to be of a stocke, convenable to his nobility, skornefully said unto the king, Will you then (sir) give me a Phisition to wife? It is not the pleasure of God that ever I should in that wise bestow my selfe. To whom the king said: 'Wilt thou then, that wee should breake our faith, which wee to recover health, have given to the damosell, who for a reward asked thee to husband?' 'Sir (quoth *Beltramo*) you may take from me all that I have, and give my person to whom you please because I am your subject: but I assure you, I shal never be contented with that mariage.' 'Wel, you shall have her (said the king) for the maiden is faire and wise, and loveth you most intirely: thinking verely you shal leade a more joyful life with her, then with a Lady of a greater house.' The Countie therewithal held his peace: & the kinge made great preparation for the mariage. And when the appointed day was come, the Counte in the presence of the king (although it were against his wil) maried the maiden, who loved him better then her owne selfe. Which done the Counte determining before, what he would do, praied license to retourne to his countrye to consummat the mariage. And when he was on horsebacke hee went not thither, but toke his journey into *Tuscane*, where understanding that the *Florentines* and *Senois* were at warres, he determined to take the *Florentines* parte, and was willingly received, and honourablie intertaigned and was made captaine of a certaine nomber of men, continuing in their service a long time. The new maried gentlewoman, scarce contented with his unkindnes, hopinge by her well doinge to cause him to retourne into his countrye, went to *Rossiglione*, where she was received of all his subjects for their Lady. And perceyving that through the Countes absence, all thinges were spoiled and out of order: shee like a sage Ladye, with greate dilligence and care, disposed his thinges in order againe, whereof the subjectes rejoysed very much, bearing to her their harty love & affection, greatly blaming the Counte, because he coulde not content himselfe with her. This notable gentlewoman, having restored all the countrie againe to their auncient liberties, sent word to the Counte her husband, by two knights, to signifie unto him, that if it were for her sake, that hee had abandoned his countrie, uppon retourne of aunsweare, she to do him pleasure, would departe from thence. To whom he chorlishly replyed. 'Let her do what she liste. For I do purpose to dwell with her, when she shall have this ring (meaning a ring which he wore) upon her finger, and a sonne in her armes begotten by mee.' He greatly loved that ring, and kepte it very carefully, and never toke it from his finger, for a certaine vertue that he knew it had. The knights hearinge the harde condition, of two thinges impossible: and seinge that by them he could not be removed from his determination, retourned againe to the Lady, tellinge her his aunsweare: who very sorowfull, after shee had a good while bethoughte her, purposed to finde meanes, to attaine the two thinges, that thereby she might recover her husbande. And havinge advised her selfe what to doe, shee assembled the noblest and chiefest of her Countrie, declaring unto them in lamentable wyse, what shee had alreadye done, to winne the love of the Counte, shewinge them also what folowed thereof. And in the ende saide unto theim, that shee was lothe the Counte for her sake, should dwell in perpetuall exile: therefore shee determined, to spende the reste of her time in Pilgrimages and devotion, for preservation of her Soule, prayinge theim to take the charge and governemente of the Countrie, and that they would let the Counte understande,

that shee had forsaken his house, and was removed farre from
thence: with purpose never to returne to *Rossiglione* againe. Many
teares were shed by the people, as she was speaking those wordes, &
divers supplications were made unto him to alter his opinion, but
all in vaine. Wherefore commending them all unto God, she toke
her way, with her maide, and one of her kinsemen, in the habite of
a pilgrime, well furnished with silver and precious Jewels: telling
no man whither shee wente, and never rested, till shee came to
Florence: where arrivinge by Fortune, at a poore widowes house,
shee contented her selfe, with the state of a poore pilgrime, desirous
to heare newes of her Lord, whom by fortune she sawe the next day,
passing by the house (where she lay) on horsebacke with his company. And althoughe shee knewe him well enoughe, yet shee
demaunded of the good wife of the house what hee was: who auns-
swered that hee was a straunge gentleman, called the Counte
Beltramo of *Rossiglione*, a curteous knight, and wel beloved in the
City, and that he was marvelouslye in love with a neighbour of
hers, that was a gentlewoman, verye poore and of small substance,
neverthelesse of right honest life & good report, and by reason of
her poverty, was yet unmaried, & dwelte with her mother, that
was a wise and honest Ladye. The Countesse well noting these
wordes, and by litle & litle debating every particular point thereof,
comprehending the effecte of those newes, concluded what to do,
and when she had well understanded, which was the house, and the
name of the Ladye, and of her doughter, that was beloved of the
Counte: uppon a day repaired to the house secretely, in the habite
of a pilgrime, where finding the mother and doughter, in poore
estate amonges their familie, after she had saluted them, told the
mother, that shee had to saye unto her. The gentlewoman rysing
up, curteously intertayned her, and being entred alone in a chamber, they sate downe, and the Countesse began to speake unto her
in this wise. 'Madame, me thincke that ye be one, upon whom
Fortune doth frowne, so wel as upon me: but if you please, you may
both comfort me & your selfe.' The Lady answered, that there was
nothing in the world, wherof she was more desirous, then of honest
comfort. The Countesse proceeding in her talke, said unto her.
'I have neede now of your fidelitie and truste, whereuppon if I do
staye, and you deceive mee, you shall both undoe me, and your
selfe.' Tell me then what it is hardlie (said the gentlewoman:) for
you shall never bee deceived of mee. Then the Countesse beganne
to recite her her whole estate of love: tellinge her what she was, and
what had chaunced to that present daye, in such perfite order as
the gentlewoman beleevinge her, because shee had partly heard

report before, began to have compassion uppon her, and after that
the Countesse had rehearsed the whole circumstaunce, she continued her purpose, saying. 'Now you have heard amonges other
my troubles, what two things they bee, which behoveth mee to
have, if I doe recover my husband, which I know none can helpe
me to obtaine, but onelye you, if it be true that I heare, which is,
that the Counte my husband, is farre in love with your doughter.'
To whom the gentlewoman sayd. 'Madame, if the Counte love my
doughter, I knowe not, albeit the likelyhoode is greate: but what
am I able to doe, in that which you desire?' 'Madame, aunsweared
the Countesse, I will tell you: but first I will declare what I meane
to doe for you, if my purpose be brought to effecte, I see your faire
doughter of good age, readie to marie, but as I understande the
cause, why shee is unmaried, is the lacke of substance to bestowe
her. Wherfore I purpose, for recompence of the pleasure, which
you shall doe for mee, to give so much readie money to marie her
honourablie, as you shall thincke sufficient.' The Countesse offer
was very well liked of the Ladie, because she was poore: yet having
a noble hart, she said unto her. 'Madame, tell me wherein I may do
you service: and if it be a thinge honest, I will gladlye performe it,
and the same being brought to passe, do as it shall please you.'
Then said the Countesse, 'I thincke it requisite, that by some one
whom you truste, you give knowledge to the Counte my husband,
that your doughter is, and shalbe at his commaundement. And
to the intent she may be well assured, that hee loveth her in deede
above anye other, she must pray him to sende her a ring that hee
weareth uppon his finger, which ring as she knoweth, he loveth
very dearely. And when he sendeth the ring, you shal give it unto
me, and afterwards sende him woorde, that your doughter is readie
to accomplishe his pleasure, and then you shall cause him secretelye
to come hither, & place me by him (in steede of your doughter)
peradventure God will give me the grace, that I may be with child,
and so having this ring on my finger, and the childe in mine armes
begotten by him, I maye recover him, and by your meanes continue with him, as a wife ought to do with her husbande.' This
thinge seemed difficulte unto the gentlewoman: fearing that there
woulde folowe reproche unto her doughter. Notwithstandinge,
considering what an honest part it were, to be a meane, that the
good Ladie might recover her husbande, and that shee mighte doe
it for a good purpose, havinge affiaunce in her honest affection, not
onely promised the Countesse, to bring this to passe: but in fewe
dayes with greate subtiltie, folowing the order wherein she was
instructed, she had gotten the ringe, although it was with the

Countes ill will, and toke order that the Countesse in steede of her doughter did lye with him. And at the first meeting, so effectuously desired by the Counte: God so disposed the matter that the Countesse was begotten with child, of two goodly sonnes, and her delivery chaunced at the due time. Whereuppon the gentlewoman, not onelye contented the Countesse at that time, with the companye of her husbande, but at manye other times so secretly, as it was never knowen: the Counte not thinkinge that he had lien with his wife, but with her whom he loved. To whom at his uprising in the morning, he used many curteous and amiable woords, and gave divers faire and precious Jewels, which the Countesse kept most carefully: and when she perceived herselfe with child, she determined no more to trouble the gentlewoman, but said unto her. Madame, thanckes be to God and you, I have the thing that I desire, & even so it is time, to recompence your desert, that afterwards I may depart. The gentlewoman said unto her, that if she had done anye pleasure agreeable to her minde, she was right glad thereof, which she did, not for hope of reward: but because it appertayned to her by well doing so to doe. Whereunto the Countesse said, 'Your sayinge pleaseth me well, and for my part, I doe not purpose to give unto you, the thing you shal demaunde in reward, but for consideration of your well doing, which dutie forceth me to do.' The gentlewoman then constrained with necessity, demaunded of her with great bashfulnesse, an hundred poundes to marie her daughter. The Countesse perceivinge the shamefastenesse of the gentlewoman, and her curteous demaunde, gave her five hundred poundes, and so many faire and costly Jewels, as almost amounted to like valour. For which the gentlewoman more then contented, gave most harty thankes to the Countesse, who departed from the gentlewoman, & retourned to her lodging. The gentlewoman to take occasion from the Counte, of anye farther repaire, or sendinge to her house, toke her doughter with her, and went into the country to her frends. The Counte *Beltramo*, within fewe dayes after, being revoked home to his owne house by his subjectes, (hearinge that the Countesse was departed from thence) retourned. The Countesse knowinge that her husbande was goone from *Florence* and retourned home, was verye gladde, continuing in *Florence* till the time of her childbedde, being brought a bedde of twoo sonnes, whiche were very like unto their father, and caused them carefully to be noursed and brought up, and when she sawe time, she toke her journey (unknowen to anie) and arrived at *Monpellier*, and resting her selfe there for certayne dayes, hearing newes of the Counte, and where he was, and that upon the daye of Al Sainctes, he purposed to make a great feaste, & assembly of Ladies & Knightes, in her pilgrimes weede she repaired thither. And knowing that they were all assembled, at the palace of the Counte, readie to sitte downe at the table, shee passed through the people, without chaunge of apparell, with her twoo sonnes in her armes. And when shee was come up into the hall, even to the place where the Counte sat, falling downe prostrate at his feete, weeping saying unto hym: 'My Lorde, I am thy poore infortunate wyfe, who to thintent thou mightest retourne and dwel in thine owne house, have bene a great whyle begging aboute the worlde. Therefore I nowe beseche thee, for the honoure of God, that thou wilt observe the conditions, which the twoo (knightes that I sent unto thee) did commaunde me to doe: for beholde, here in myne armes, not onely one sonne begotten by thee, but twayne, and likewyse thy Ryng. It is nowe time then (if thou kepe promise) that I should be received as thy wyfe.' The Counte hearing this, was greatly astonned, and knewe the Ryng, and the children also, they were so like hym. But tell me (quod he) howe is this come to passe? The Countesse to the great admiration of the Counte, and of all those that were in presence, rehersed unto them in order all that, whiche had bene done, and the whole discourse thereof. For which cause the Counte knowing the thinges she had spoken, to be true (and perceiving her constant minde, and good witte, and the twoo faire young boyes to kepe his promise made, and to please his subjectes, & the Ladies that made sute unto him, to accept her from that tyme foorth, as his lawefull wyfe, and to honour her) abjected his obstinate rigour: causing her to rise up, and imbraced and kissed her, acknowledging her againe for his lawefull wyfe. And after he had apparelled her, according to her estate, to the great pleasure and contentation of those that were there, & of al his other frendes not onely that daye, but many others, he kept great chere, and from that time forth, hee loved and honoured her, as his dere spouse and wyfe.